Sous Vide
Basics

Sous Vide Basics

100+
Recipes
for
Perfect
Results

Jay Nutt & Jennifer MacKenzie

Robert ROSE

For complete cataloguing information, see page 186.

Disclaimer
The recipes in this book have been carefully tested by our kitchen and our tasters. To the best of our knowledge, they are safe and nutritious for ordinary use and users. For those people with food or other allergies, or who have special food requirements or health issues, please read the suggested contents of each recipe carefully and determine whether or not they may create a problem for you. All recipes are used at the risk of the consumer. Consumers should always consult their sous vide manufacturer's manual for recommended procedures and cooking times.

We cannot be responsible for any hazards, loss or damage that may occur as a result of any recipe use.

For those with special needs, allergies, requirements or health problems, in the event of any doubt, please contact your medical adviser prior to the use of any recipe.

Design and production: Kevin Cockburn/PageWave Graphics Inc.
Layout: Alicia McCarthy/PageWave Graphics Inc.
Editor: Sue Sumeraj
Proofreader: Kelly Jones
Indexer: Gillian Watts
Photographer: Matt Johannsson/Reflector Inc.
Food stylist: Michael Elliott
Prop stylist: Charlene Erricson

Cover image: Argentinian Flank Steak with Chimichurri (page 84)

The publisher gratefully acknowledges the financial support of our publishing program by the Government of Canada through the Canada Book Fund.

Canadä

Published by Robert Rose Inc.
120 Eglinton Avenue East, Suite 800, Toronto, Ontario, Canada M4P 1E2
Tel: (416) 322-6552 Fax: (416) 322-6936
www.robertrose.ca

Printed and bound in China

2 3 4 5 6 7 8 9 LEO 25 24 23 22 21

Contents

Introduction

AS A COUPLE who also happen to be a long-time chef (Jay) and a professional home economist and food writer (Jennifer), we often receive questions from our friends and guests along the lines of "How do you cook steaks/chops/fish like [insert the name of your favorite chef/author/restaurant]?" We usually gently suggest that it takes practice to learn how to handle the variables of focus, controlling heat and monitoring time. These variables can be affected by something as simple as a distracting phone call, a grease flare on a barbecue or an extra minute looking for that ingredient or item you swore was just right there.

But if somebody were to ask us that question now, we'd immediately declare "Sous vide!" For many foods, sous vide cooking is the answer, allowing home cooks to achieve restaurant-quality results with little effort and eliminating much of the guesswork of cooking.

Sous vide translates from French as "under vacuum." Food is placed raw into food-safe plastic bags or pouches, or glass jars or containers — sometimes with flavoring agents, spices or marinades — then vacuum-sealed to remove excess air and cooked in a heat-controlled water bath, generally at lower temperatures and for longer times than cooking methods that use traditional heat (oven, stovetop, grills and even slow cookers). The results? Food is cooked evenly, meats remain juicy, and tough cuts become tender but still retain some pink and loads of flavor.

Cooking sous vide gives you exacting control over heat, as most home sous vide devices now allow you to set the precise desired temperature to within half a degree. Home ovens, stovetops and barbecues are all susceptible to factors like seasonal weather conditions, room temperature, surges in electrical current or gas flow, and opening and closing of lids and oven doors.

Sous vide creates a controlled cooking environment with fewer outside factors.

It's also a very forgiving technique that allows you to leave food cooking for minutes or even hours longer, without the risk of it becoming overcooked — which can happen very quickly with other cooking methods. Certain foods, such as grains, rice and some meats, *can* get overcooked with sous vide if you leave them too long, but you're not going to ruin dinner should you take a phone call or forget to put a pot of water on to boil for the pasta.

Like braising, sous vide is ideal for tough foods that need a long cooking time to become tender. But sous vide's advantage over braising is that you don't need to add liquid to help tenderize tough meats, so the food retains its natural, true flavor rather than tasting like the sauce it is cooked in. The same goes for poaching. Tender foods, such as fish and asparagus, that are often poached in liquid (water with aromatics or broth) become perfectly cooked, tender and moist when cooked sous vide, yet they don't lose any flavor to the liquid, since they are essentially poached in their own juices.

One of our most surprising discoveries while creating these recipes was the effects of sous vide cooking on chicken. All too often, chicken becomes dry when you've cooked it long enough for food safety. Or you struggle to get the thigh cooked through without overcooking the breast. Or the results are just plain rubbery. With sous vide, chicken is flavorful, evenly cooked and so juicy. It is literally falling-off-the-bone tender — not something we commonly associate with chicken!

Sous vide requires your full attention only at the beginning and end of the process; other than keeping an eye on the water level, it is mainly hands-off during the cooking time. It gives you confidence that the food is properly cooked (no more guesswork or poking juicy steaks with forks) and the freedom to focus on planning and preparing the rest of the meal — or to do something else entirely with your time. It helps guarantee even doneness throughout the dish, and the food tends to be more flavorful, as no juices are lost to evaporation. Many dishes require only a couple minutes of "finishing" in a hot pan, in the broiler or on your barbecue grill.

We've discovered many uses for the sous vide, well beyond steak, and it's not just for hard-core food science enthusiasts anymore. The convenience of the smaller appliances, especially those you can use in any heatproof vessel that holds water, makes it a great technique to add to your cooking repertoire. You can cook sous vide at home for everyday meals, in your RV, on a boat or at a cottage — anywhere there is water and electricity, really — and you'll definitely want to use it to simplify your meal prep and dazzle your guests when entertaining.

Do read all of the how-tos and whys and get comfortable with The Basics (see page 19) by cooking a steak, a fish fillet or a simple piece of chicken. Before long, you'll be creating perfectly cooked sous vide meals that just might have your family and friends calling you Chef.

Advantages of Sous Vide Cooking

Besides being able to guarantee a steak cooked to a perfect medium-rare or a piece of chicken that remains moist and juicy, cooking sous vide has many other benefits:

- There are fewer variables due to weather and climate. The water temperature will be the same regardless of the temperature in the room, and humidity in the air won't affect the cooking.

- A lower-temperature water bath doesn't heat up the kitchen as much as a hot oven or simmering pot on the stove, so sous vide is ideal for cooking in hot weather.

- Aromas from pungent foods, such as fish, onions and cabbage, won't permeate the air when these foods are cooked sous vide. This is a huge benefit when you're cooking overnight (as you'll appreciate if you've ever used a slow cooker overnight and woken to the smell of chili).

- When cooking for a crowd, you can precook numerous steaks, pieces of chicken, racks of ribs, cobs of corn, etc., well ahead, then just warm them up and brown them before serving, rather than cooking from raw while your guests are waiting.

- You can cook steaks to different doneness temperatures in the sous vide ahead of time so everyone can have theirs just how they like it, and you won't have to juggle and time multiple pieces of meat on the grill.

- Cheesecake and egg-based custards, such as crème caramel and crustless quiche, tend to crack or curdle when there are temperature fluctuations in the oven (thus they benefit from a water bath in the oven, which can be cumbersome). With sous vide, they cook slowly and evenly in the water bath, resulting in evenly cooked, creamy results.

Sous Vide Fundamentals

WHILE SOUS VIDE cooking at home is a relatively recent development, the science has been around for quite some time. Sous vide works by using a device that controls both the temperature of the water (with a thermostat-controlled heater) and the movement of the water (with a mechanical agitator or carefully placed heating elements that create currents). It cooks the food gently all the way through at the exact same temperature as the water in the cooking vessel. Most food won't overcook, because it never gets hotter than the temperature of the water bath.

Although sous vide technology was originally created in the 1960s as a tool for laboratory research, it wasn't long before it was being used for food preparation in hospitals and factories. And by the mid-1970s, French chefs were using it to prepare foie gras, as the longer cooking times at lower temperatures meant that this decadent dish wasn't losing as much of its desirable fat content to frying pans and terrines.

Over the ensuing years, sous vide cooking was gradually adopted by chefs in high-end restaurants as a way to prepare perfectly cooked meats, fish, desserts and vegetables. But until recently, sous vide equipment was expensive, bulky and sometimes hard to operate, characteristics that made it unsuitable for home kitchens.

That has all changed. Now that smaller, more affordable technology is widely available, home cooks can finally duplicate the results of professional chefs, with unprecedented ease and efficiency.

Food Safety

When you first see the temperatures recommended for sous vide cooking, you might be a bit alarmed, as they are much lower than the temperatures used in traditional cooking techniques and even lower than the internal doneness temperatures of food cooked by other methods. We've had it drilled into our food-safety-conscious heads that poultry must be cooked to 165°F (74°C), so how is 148°F (64°C) safe?

The role of heat in cooking is to destroy any harmful microorganisms that may be present in the food so it is safe for us to eat and won't make us sick. Sous vide cooking accomplishes this with lower heat for a longer time. The food is brought to the set temperature by the circulating heated water until the temperature throughout the food is the same as that of the water, and then held at that temperature long enough to destroy the microorganisms. That's why a steak that would be cooked in 10 minutes on a smoking-hot grill takes 1½ hours at 130°F (54.5°C) with sous vide.

The science of sous vide — how those temperatures and times are determined — is quite technical, but if you'd like to read more about it, see the appendix (page 185); otherwise, you can rest assured that your food will be safe if you follow the recommended cooking temperatures and times in these recipes. We do recommend reading the rest of the food safety information in the appendix, even if you want to gloss over the science bits.

TOOLS OF THE TRADE

Along with the essential sous vide equipment and the typical cooking tools (measuring cups and spoons, cutting boards, knives and bowls, etc.), we strongly recommend some additional items that will help you achieve success in sous vide cooking, and suggest a few others that may come in handy.

Essential Equipment

There are several types of sous vide devices available on the market. The two most common are water bath sous vide cookers and immersion circulators. If using an immersion circulator, you'll also need a sturdy container for your water bath.

Water Bath Sous Vide Cookers

Water bath sous vide cookers are self-contained devices, similar to a slow cooker, with an insulated cooking tank and built-in heater. They typically have lids to keep in the steam. The water is circulated by careful placement of the heating elements along the bottom of the tank to create convection currents. Water bath cookers range from the size of a bread machine to that of a picnic cooler, which means you must take into consideration both storage space and ease of setup when choosing one.

Immersion Circulators

Immersion circulators look similar to a handheld immersion blender, with the heating element and agitator designed as a wand that clamps to the side of a container. The electronic controls are on top of the wand and are generally very simple to operate. There's an electrical cord to plug in, a wheel or buttons to set the temperature and an on/off switch. Some of them even have Bluetooth capability so they can be controlled from your smartphone.

Because of their small size and adaptability to any container with minimum depth and volume requirements, immersion circulators are easily transportable. They are easy to clean and require minimal storage space. They are also considerably more affordable than most water bath sous vide cookers. We tested the recipes using the Anova Precision Cooker and the more expensive PolyScience Immersion Circulator and found they both worked consistently well and there were no appreciable differences in results between the two.

For your water bath, you can attach your immersion circulator to any container that has a wide base sturdy enough that the circulator can be clipped to the side without tipping the container, that is deep and wide enough to allow the water to flow freely around the bag(s) of food by at least 1 inch (2.5 cm), that is deep enough to hold more than the minimum water level required by the circulator and the food, and that has no cracks or leaks. Options include a stockpot, a deep roasting pan, a large canning pot, a heat-resistant polycarbonate container or even the stoneware insert from a slow cooker. We had good success using a medium pot for single and small portions of food, a stockpot for most 2- to 4-portion recipes and a large, deep oval roasting pan (with a custom-size rack for the bottom) for roasts, ribs, casserole dishes and desserts in jars.

Do check your circulator's manual to make sure that the amount of water your sous vide container requires isn't more than the maximum amount the appliance will heat.

Recommended Equipment

- **Wire cooling racks:** We set our water bath container on a wire cooling rack to protect the countertop from the heat. When we're cooking food in jars or a casserole dish, we place a rack in the water bath to prevent the jars or dish from clunking on the bottom of the container. We also use wire racks for cooling hot cooked foods.

DIY Cooler Hack

A food cooler makes a terrific large insulated water bath for sous vide cooking large pieces of meat (such as brisket) or multiple portions for a feast. Use a large cooler with a removable lid. You may want to go online and view one of the many pictorial or video demos, but here's the basic gist of how to convert from cooler to cooker:

1. Fit an electric drill with a hole saw bit the same diameter as your immersion circulator's wand.

2. Drill a hole near one short end of the cooler lid. The circulator should fit through the hole with the heating element below the lid and the controls above the lid.

3. Use sandpaper, if necessary, to carefully shave the hole so that the circulator fits snugly.

4. Fill the cooler with water, ensuring that the water level will be between the minimum and maximum markings when the circulator is in place. Place the lid on the cooler and insert the circulator through the hole. Preheat the water bath.

5. After adding the food, replace the lid snugly to insulate the water bath.

We recommend placing the cooler on a towel, and make sure to use it on a waterproof and heatproof surface just in case any water leaks or drips when you're transferring food in and out.

- **Resealable freezer bags:** Use brand-name, high-quality freezer bags (not storage bags) to ensure that you're using food-safe plastic, that you are getting the best vacuum seal and that the bag will stand up to the heat. Thinner, inferior-quality bags tend to spring leaks, tear easily and don't seal as tight. All sous vide recipes are cooked below 200°F (100°C), so you don't need to worry about the heavy-duty plastic of freezer bags breaking down. You'll want to have medium, large and extra-large resealable freezer bags on hand to prepare the recipes in this book.

- **Metal or heatproof clips:** These can be as simple as stationery clips (the black or colored clips designed for thick stacks of paper) or a heavy-duty chip clip. Use them to clip resealable bags to the side of your sous vide container to prevent the seal portion of the bag from sinking into the water.

- **Cooking timers:** Digital cooking timers are definitely good to have on hand so you can time cooking accurately; two or three are useful if you're cooking multiple recipes in the sous vide at once. For long cooking times, you can use the timer or the alarm function on your cellphone. It's easy to lose track of what time you put the food in the sous vide bath, and minimum cooking times are critical for food safety, so don't rely on a guess or estimate.

- **Silicone oven mitts:** Waterproof or water-resistant silicone or silicone-coated oven mitts will protect your hands from the hot water when you're handling wet bags and jars.

- **Silicone-coated tongs:** These are handy for pulling bags out of the water, placing a rack in the water bath and removing the rack. Metal tongs without silicone ends may tear freezer bags, so avoid using those.

- **Large slotted spoon:** This will come in handy for lifting eggs in the shell in and out of the water bath and for lifting cooked food out of sauces.

- **Large rimmed baking sheets:** Many of the recipes call for broiling food after sous vide cooking, and a rimmed baking sheet will help prevent any juices from running off.
- **Heavy cast-iron skillet:** When searing food after sous vide cooking, it's important to use a heavy pan that will get very hot and provide a good sear without further cooking the inside of the food (negating your perfectly cooked steak!). Thinner pans don't hold the heat as well and aren't as good for searing.
- **Digital thermometer:** Use a thermometer to test the temperature of your water bath periodically (to make sure the thermostat is working properly) and to check internal temperatures of food, if desired. You can also check the water temperature when you're topping up your sous vide bath to make sure you don't cool it down too much.

Optional but Helpful Equipment

- **Vacuum sealer with pouches:** A vacuum sealer is a handy gadget to quickly remove air and create a tightly sealed pouch for sous vide cooking. A vacuum sealer works well for foods without a lot of added moisture. The pouches come as individual bags and in rolls, so you can customize the size to the food you're cooking.
- **Canning jar lifter:** These specialized silicone-coated tongs have a broad, curved end to grasp jars and lower and lift them from the water bath. They are sold where home canning supplies are stocked, such as hardware stores, housewares stores, well-stocked supermarkets and online.
- **Barbecue grill and/or grill pan:** As an alternative to broiling or pan-searing, a barbecue grill or grill pan will add that desired sear, browning and attractive marks on sous vide cooked meats.
- **Immersion blender, food processor and/or blender:** These appliances are used in several recipes for puréeing marinades, sauces and so on.
- **Sous vide rack:** This rack with a horizontal base and vertical bars to hold bags or pouches of food in your sous vide bath is handy when you are cooking multiple portions of food, to keep them spaced apart.

BASIC TECHNIQUES

Now that you have your equipment ready to go, you're ready to start sous vide cooking. Here's a basic how-to guide for cooking food in freezer bags or vacuum-seal pouches. See page 14 for details on sous vide cooking in mason jars and page 15 for instructions on cooking in casserole dishes. If you're using a water bath sous vide cooker, start with step 3 and follow the manufacturer's directions for filling and preheating the water bath.

1. Place the sous vide container on a wire rack. (Or, if you have a gas stovetop, you can use the burner grate, as long as the grate is cool and the adjacent burners are not going to be used.) Be sure to position the container near an electrical outlet.
2. Clip the immersion circulator to the side of the sous vide container, securing it with the clamp.
3. Fill the sous vide container with water, making sure the water level is above the minimum level mark on the immersion circulator and well below the maximum mark, leaving room in the container for the food to be added.
4. Set the temperature on your sous vide appliance, cover the container (see page 16) and preheat the water bath while you prepare your recipe (or while foods marinate). We suggest starting the

bath about 30 minutes before you plan to cook, to allow enough time for it to come up to temperature. Most appliances will beep to alert you that the target temperature has been reached.

5. Place the food to be cooked in the freezer bag or pouch. Arrange the food in a single layer, as directed, and/or space foods apart. The thickness of food extends the time required for the heat to penetrate it, so arranging the food properly is important.

6. Remove the air from the freezer bag and seal the bag, creating as tight a vacuum seal as possible. If you're using a vacuum sealer and pouch, the seal will be created by the vacuum sealer after it sucks out the air.

7. Immerse the sealed bag in the water bath. The water level should be above the food in the bag, but if using a resealable bag, you don't want the seal to go underwater. Clip the seal portion of the bag to the side of the container to secure it. Alternatively, you can suspend a wooden spoon, chopstick or other long, thin stick across the top of the container and clip the bag to the handle (this is helpful when you're cooking more than one bag). If the food is floating, use a large, heavy spoon, plate, pot lid or other heatproof utensil to weigh the bag down and keep the food submerged.

8. Cover the container, if desired (see page 16), and set a timer for the recommended cooking time.

9. Let the sous vide do the work. For long cooking times, check periodically to make sure the water level remains above the food. If you need to add water, heat it on the stovetop or in the microwave to approximately the same temperature as your sous vide bath to avoid cooling it down too much (or heating it too much) with the added water.

10. Once the food is cooked, use silicone-coated tongs, a slotted spoon or silicone oven mitts to remove the bag from the water bath. Turn off the appliance. Follow the recipe directions for resting and browning. (Browning steps are included for most meat and poultry. This not only adds desired color and flavor, but also helps to ensure that foods are properly cooked. We recommend you do not skip this step if it's included in the recipe.)

Efficiency Tips

- To speed up heating of the water, especially when you're cooking at higher temperatures, heat the water on the stovetop in a pot, then pour it into your sous vide container once it's heated.

- For foods cooked for a long time (more than 6 hours) and if the room is especially cool, wrap the outside of the sous vide container in a towel, keeping it away from the sous vide appliance, to add insulation and reduce heat loss.

- Plan ahead by choosing more than one recipe that cooks at the same temperature and cook items together. As long as there is enough room in the container, you can cook foods that don't even go together, as the flavors and aromas won't transfer — even if there are onions in one bag and dessert in another.

- If you've used your sous vide to cook dinner, don't let the hot water go to waste. Prep a recipe that cooks overnight to go into the water bath after you've taken your dinner out.

Advantages of Freezer Bags

There are definite advantages to using resealable freezer bags rather than vacuum-seal pouches.

- When you're not sure whether your food may need more cooking time and you need to check for doneness, you can open and reseal a freezer bag — no need to start over with a new one.
- You can remove a portion of the cooked food right away and refrigerate leftovers in the same bag you cooked in.
- You can often reuse freezer bags. Be sure to wash them thoroughly and let them air-dry before you put them away. Check carefully to make sure there are no holes and the seal still zips tight. To do this, add some water, seal the bag and gently squeeze to make sure the air and water don't spurt out. If there are any holes, discard the bag or reserve it for non-food uses.

Using a Vacuum Sealer

A vacuum sealer works very well for foods without added liquid, but moist vegetables and foods with marinade, sauce, oil or butter can prevent the sealer from working. A general rule of thumb for using a vacuum sealer is a maximum of about 2 tbsp (30 mL) liquid using the moist setting; more than that risks the liquid getting sucked into the machine, preventing a tight vacuum seal. Some machines may be able to handle more liquid than others, so check the manufacturer's instructions for your machine.

If you plan to make food ahead to freeze, the vacuum-seal pouches do help keep foods better, as they stay vacuum-sealed and prevent freezer burn.

Follow the directions for your vacuum sealer, making sure your pouch is the right size for the food you're cooking. You don't want the food to be too crowded, so that it overlaps or bends or folds in the pouch.

Vacuum Sealing without a Vacuum Sealer

A vacuum sealer is not essential and, for saucy foods, doesn't work. All you really need to create a vacuum-sealed packet of food is a heavy-duty resealable freezer bag and one of two low-tech techniques — the water displacement method or the straw method.

Water Displacement Method

The water displacement method is versatile and works well for most recipes. There are many videos demonstrating this technique online, which you may find helpful. But here are the basic steps:

1. Fill a sink or a large bowl with water. The temperature of the water should be cool, so that you can comfortably immerse your hands in it.
2. Lay the freezer bag on the counter for dry foods, or set the bag upright in a bowl for wet mixtures. Add food to the bag. For most meats and larger chunks of vegetables, arrange the pieces in a single layer, as directed, or in as even a layer as possible for smaller pieces. For wet foods, you can press them into an even layer as you remove the air.
3. Squeeze out as much air from the bag as possible with your hands and pinch the seal closed, starting at one side and going almost all the way across, leaving about 1 inch (2.5 cm) open.

4. Holding the bag at the top, where the seal is, immerse the bag in the sink or bowl of water, keeping it fairly horizontal if you've arranged pieces in a single layer, or vertical if there is only one piece that won't fall out of arrangement. Immerse the bag to just below the seal, pressing as necessary to keep the food submerged and help push out the air. As you immerse the bag, the pressure from the water will press out the air. You should see the bag suctioned around the food, with few or no air pockets. Quickly press the remaining portion of the seal closed.

Straw Method

For foods with no food safety issues when raw, such as vegetables, fruit and grains, the old-fashioned method of using a straw to suck out the air works extremely well. This is a technique that is often used for freezing fruits and vegetables.

1. Fill the freezer bag with food and squeeze or press out as much air as you can with your hands, pressing the food into a single layer as you remove the air.
2. Seal the bag to about $\frac{1}{2}$ inch (1 cm) from one end of the zipper, then insert a straw into the opening, with the end of the straw about $\frac{3}{4}$ inch (2 cm) into the bag.
3. Pinch the seal on either side of the straw with your fingers to hold the straw in place and prevent air from squeezing in beside the straw, then suck out air through the straw. If you need to pause for a breath, squeeze the straw closed with two fingers while you breathe (keeping the seal around the straw pinched as well), to prevent the air from flowing back in. Once you're ready to suck again, place your mouth around the straw and suck while you move your pinched fingers off the straw and back to the seal beside the straw.
4. Once you've sucked out as much air as possible and you see the bag suctioned around the food, quickly pull the straw

out with your mouth while pinching the open portion of the zipper tightly closed.

Removing Air Pockets

Sometimes as food cooks — typically vegetables and fruits — air will be released, causing an air pocket to form in the bag. This will cause the bag to float, and the food won't cook as evenly. If this happens, wearing water-resistant silicone mitts and using a spoon to help press the bag down into the water, unseal about 1 inch (2.5 cm) of the bag and press out the air as described in the instructions for the water displacement method, then reseal the bag and continue cooking.

If a vacuum-seal pouch gets air pockets, you can't open it and reseal, so the best tactic is to weigh down the bag and keep it immersed as best as possible.

Sous Vide Cooking in Mason Jars

Mason jars, also known as canning jars, are a convenient vessel for making individual desserts, egg dishes and grains with sous vide cooking. Use only jars that are designed for home canning, not jars from commercially prepared foods (such as pickle jars or commercial jam jars), as they are not designed to be reused and may not stand up to sous vide cooking. Use the two-piece metal lids designed for the canning jars to ensure a tight seal, to allow air to escape and to stand up to the heat. The plastic storage caps for canning jars are not designed to be heated.

Be sure your canning jars are in perfect condition, with no cracks, chips or fractures. If they have weak spots, the likelihood of breakage is high, and you'll not only lose your food but also make a mess of your water bath.

We found 8-oz (250 mL) wide-mouth jars (also called half-pint wide-mouth jars) the most versatile for egg dishes and individual desserts, and pint (16 oz/500 mL) jars with a wide or standard mouth best for grains. There are a couple of recipes where the small 4-oz (125 mL) jars are handy.

You'll need to place a rack in the bottom of your sous vide container to rest the jars on. This will prevent the glass from bouncing on the bottom of the container as the water circulates, and will allow the water to flow all the way around the jars, for even heat distribution. Some options are a wire cooling rack that fits flat in the bottom of the container; a canning rack; a few metal rings from the jar lids, tied together with twist ties or string; or even a scrunched tea towel that you can nest the jars in.

The glass of the canning jars must be warmed before they are added to the sous vide bath. A cold jar filled with cold food immersed in a hot water bath is a recipe for breakage. We include instructions in each recipe to warm the glass with hot tap water — do not skip this step! (Ask us how we know . . . egg drop soup, anyone?) Work quickly when adding the food to the warmed jars and getting the jars into the bath; you don't want to let the food cool the jars down.

A canning jar lifter (see page 11) is very handy to have for sous vide cooking with jars. It allows you to grip the jar around the neck and lower it into the water bath, then reach in and lift it out again. If you don't have a jar lifter, a waterproof silicone oven mitt with a textured grip is a good option for placing the jars in the water and pulling them out.

1. Fill the jars with hot tap water and let stand for 5 to 10 minutes to warm the glass.

2. Dump out the water and fill the jars with food as instructed in the recipe. When stirring food in canning jars, use a silicone spatula or wooden utensil to avoid stressing the glass and causing cracks or fractures.

3. Working quickly, wipe the rims of the jars to remove any spilled food and place the lid disc on the jar. Screw on the metal band just until fingertip-tight. If it's too tight, air won't be able to escape the jar, preventing a vacuum seal, and the jars are more likely to float.

4. Place a rack in the water bath (preheated as instructed in steps 1 to 4 on pages 11 to 12), then immerse the jars in the water, dipping them in and out of the water a couple of times as you go to further temper the glass, until they are resting on the rack. The water level should be at least $\frac{1}{2}$ inch (1 cm) above the top of the jars.

5. To weigh down jars that are floating, invert a plate or metal lid on top of the jars, gently pressing down to help them sink (use tongs or protect your hand with a silicone oven mitt for this), then place a pint (500 mL) jar filled with hot water, a heavy bowl or another heatproof container on top of the plate or lid to keep the jars submerged.

Sous Vide Cooking in a Casserole Dish

You can cook sous vide using a casserole dish, baking dish, bowl or baking pan, as long as it is heat-safe and you can fit it into a freezer bag and your sous vide container.

1. Fill the dish, bowl or pan with the food. Cover the top with parchment paper and foil, or with plastic wrap (we recommend different coverings for different recipes, but you can use what you prefer; the goal is to cover the dish tightly, to prevent food from leaking out into the bag).

2. Place the dish in the freezer bag, then remove excess air and seal the bag with

the water displacement method or the straw method (see pages 13 to 14).

3. Place a rack in the water bath (preheated as instructed in steps 1 to 4 on page 11 to 12). Perching the dish on a slotted spoon and lowering it down, or protecting your hands with silicone oven mitts, immerse the bag containing the dish and lower the dish gently onto the rack.

4. To weigh down a dish that is floating, invert a plate or metal lid on top of the dish, gently pressing down to help it sink (use tongs or protect your hand with a silicone oven mitt for this), then place a pint (500 mL) jar filled with hot water, a heavy bowl or another heatproof container on top of the plate or lid to keep the dish submerged.

Covering the Sous Vide Container

The sous vide appliance thermostat kicks in and turns off to regulate the water temperature and keep it at your target. To reduce evaporation and increase heat efficiency (the less often the appliance has to heat the water, the less power it uses), we recommend covering the sous vide container for all recipes cooked at 170°F (77°C) and above, and for anything cooked for 4 hours or more. You may also want to cover the container if the ambient temperature of the room is cool, regardless of the cooking temperature or time.

With regards to evaporation, you need to make sure the water stays above the minimum level required by your appliance and above the food. The longer the cooking time, the more the water evaporates and the more you have to top up the water level. Covering will reduce the need to babysit.

Sous vide cooking is not affected by whether the container is covered or not. If you don't cover, the recipes will still work, but you'll be using more power and possibly more water.

Using an immersion circulator that clips onto the side of the container does make it a little trickier to cover the sous vide container, but we have a few suggestions for overcoming that problem:

Foil
Use a sheet of foil large enough to cover the container with 2 to 3 inches (5 to 7.5 cm) of overhang on all sides around the container. Place the foil on top and pinch it around the sous vide appliance and the rim of the container, leaving a small vent at the side opposite the appliance to let a little steam escape (this prevents water from dripping out from under the foil down the sides of the container). When lifting the foil, carefully lift from the edges so you don't rip it. It can be reused many times, as long as it's not torn.

Foil-Covered Rack
Use a wire cooling rack that fits across the top of your container, perches on the rim and covers most of the container, leaving room for the sous vide appliance. Wrap the rack in foil to make it a solid lid. Place the rack on top of the container, leaving a small opening at the side opposite the appliance to let a little steam escape (this prevents water from dripping out from under the covering down the sides of the container).

A foil-covered rack works well when you're cooking foods that you want to check often, as you can lift and replace the "lid" many times without damaging it. You can also reuse this lid for many cooking sessions.

Plastic Wrap
Stretch one large piece of plastic wrap (or more pieces, as necessary) across the container, leaving about 3 inches (7.5 cm) of overhang down the sides. Wrap the plastic tightly around the body of the sous vide appliance, pinching to seal so steam doesn't escape to the appliance. Press to seal around the rim of the container, leaving a small vent at the side opposite the appliance to let a little steam escape (this prevents water from dripping out from under the plastic down the sides of the container).

Plastic wrap creates the tightest seal of these options, which is particularly useful for long cooking times where you want to leave the container unattended, so you don't have to replenish the water as often. The heated plastic wrap does tend to shrink, wrinkle and stick to itself as soon as you lift it off, so it can't be reused. You'll most likely need to start with new sheets of plastic wrap if you have to remove the cover during cooking for any reason.

How Do I Know When the Food Is Done?

We have included descriptions for doneness in recipes where there may be a variable amount of time required, such as for vegetables. Some potatoes, for example, soften more quickly than others and may need more cooking time. When checking for doneness, if you need to continue cooking, remove the air and reseal the bag before returning it to the water bath. It is warm on the fingers at this stage, and it is helpful to have flexible, water-resistant hand protection, such as silicone oven mitts, so you can use the hot water bath to displace the air from the bag. Alternatively,

have a bowl or sink of room-temperature water at the ready to use for the water displacement method (see page 13). Don't use cold water at this stage, as you don't want to cool the food off and slow down the cooking process.

For tough meats, we suggest poking them with a fork to determine if they are tender after the recommended cooking time. (This is the same way you tell with traditional cooking techniques.) Sous vide cooking breaks down the connective tissue of tough meats after a length of time at the right temperature, so it's easy to determine when that goal has been achieved.

For other foods cooked sous vide, it's much trickier to determine doneness. Take a piece of steak, for example, for which we offer a finite cooking time and don't include a doneness test. The goal of sous vide cooking for tender cuts is to get the food to a consistent temperature throughout for the minimum length of time for food safety. You can check the internal temperature of the steak with a digital thermometer, as you would with other cooking methods, and the center of the steak should be at the target temperature (the same temperature you've set for your water bath), but you also need to be sure that the steak has been

Sous Vide Ingredients and Seasonings

Use the highest-quality and freshest ingredients available when cooking sous vide. The food cooks in its own juices, so you want to make sure those juices have the best possible flavor.

When seasoning with salt, it's better to use a little less than you would to season foods cooked by traditional methods, especially with meats, poultry and fish. With the longer cooking times, salt in high concentration can infuse into the meat and cause a spongy, ham-like texture. You can season to taste with salt after cooking.

You'll see garlic powder used frequently in our recipes, particularly when a marinade or seasoning is added raw to the bag. Raw garlic can become strong and bitter when cooked sous vide; garlic powder helps avoid this. Cooking garlic with some of the other seasoning elements also reduces the bitterness, but even then, we tend to use less garlic than we would in traditional cooking. Be sure not to use garlic salt; pure, high-quality garlic powder is what you want here.

at that temperature for the right length of time. That's difficult to do without checking it multiple times, and that's tedious: you'd need to open and reseal the bag, and put lots of holes in your steak. Plus, all those checks would extend the cooking time in the long run, because you'd keep cooling the steak down while checking it. So our best advice is to simply use the timing guidelines we've given in our recipes.

The great thing about sous vide cooking is that, for tender cuts of meat, it takes hours more cooking to ruin the food, so if you're not sure it's cooked through, it's best to err on the side of caution and let the food cook longer. It won't get overcooked. We have added notes in places where longer cooking does affect the texture adversely, but for the most part, 30 to 60 minutes longer won't hurt.

The Health Benefits of Sous Vide Cooking

In addition to providing flavorful and enjoyable food, sous vide cooking also offers several advantages when it comes to putting healthy food on your plate.

- Sous vide generally requires less oil or fat to cook with. The natural juice and moisture of the food is retained in the cooking process.

- Vitamins, essential fatty acids and antioxidants are not dissolved away by steam or boiling water. The cooked food retains a higher level of water-soluble nutrients.

- Meat that is cooked sous vide and then finished on a grill or in a pan to achieve the final browning spends less time exposed to high heat or open flame.

- The slow, gentle cooking process makes for more easily digested food.

- Sous vide requires mindfulness. If you're taking the time to prepare your meals, you're more likely to choose good ingredients.

- Any time you cook from scratch, you control what goes into your food, and you know exactly what you're eating — which is bound to be more nutritious than packaged who-knows-what out of a box.

The Basics

Tender Beef Steaks

This recipe works for any tender beef cut, also called grilling steaks, including strip loin, rib steak, rib eye, T-bone, porterhouse, tenderloin medallions and top sirloin. Bone-in and boneless steaks cook in the same temperature water bath for the same time; it's the thickness of the steak that determines the cooking time. These are the cooking temperatures we found resulted in the doneness specified when the steaks were seared after sous vide cooking, though you may wish to experiment with different temperatures (but no lower than 120°F/49°C), according to your tastes.

Sous vide time: $1\frac{1}{2}$ hours

Tips

Use the size of bag or pouch appropriate to the size of steak you're cooking. Be sure the steak fits in the bag without bending or folding. If cooking more than 1 steak, choose a bag that fits the steaks in a single layer, allowing space between each, for the most even cooking.

If you want to marinate your steak, place steak and marinade in freezer bag. Turn bag and gently massage steak to evenly coat with marinade. Remove excess air and seal bag. Refrigerate for at least 2 hours or up to 1 day. The longer you let the steak marinate, the more the flavors will infuse into the meat.

- **Preheat water bath to 130°F (54.5°C) for medium-rare (see variation)**
- **Medium or large resealable freezer bag or vacuum-seal pouch**
- **Barbecue grill, grill pan or cast-iron skillet**

> Boneless or bone-in beef grilling steak(s), about $\frac{3}{4}$ inch (2 cm) thick
> Salt and freshly ground black pepper
> Vegetable oil or cooking spray

1. Season steak(s) on both sides with salt and pepper.
2. Place steak(s) in freezer bag or pouch. If cooking more than 1 steak per bag, space them apart. Remove excess air and seal bag using the water displacement method (see page 13) or seal pouch using vacuum sealer.
3. Cook steak(s) in preheated water bath for $1\frac{1}{2}$ hours (or, for convenience, up to $2\frac{1}{2}$ hours).
4. Remove bag from water bath and let rest for 10 minutes.

To Finish on the Barbecue

5. Meanwhile, preheat barbecue grill to medium-high.
6. Remove steak from bag, discarding liquid, and transfer to a plate. Pat dry and season on both sides with salt and pepper.
7. Oil grill and place steak on grill. Grill, turning once, for 1 to 2 minutes per side or until sizzling and marked.

Tips

To cook steak ahead, cook as directed through step 3, then immerse bag in ice water to chill. Refrigerate in the sealed bag for up to 3 days or freeze for up to 2 months. Thaw in the refrigerator overnight, if frozen. In a water bath preheated to the same temperature you originally cooked at, reheat in the sealed bag for 30 minutes, then proceed with step 4.

These times and temperatures do not apply to mechanically tenderized steaks, which we recommend avoiding for sous vide cooking.

To Finish in a Grill Pan or Cast-Iron Skillet

5. Meanwhile, preheat pan over medium-high heat until hot and almost smoking (turn on your hood vent or open the windows).

6. Remove steak from bag, discarding liquid, and transfer to a plate. Pat dry and season on both sides with salt and pepper.

7. Lightly oil pan and sear steak, turning once, for 1 to 2 minutes per side or until sizzling and grill-marked or browned.

Variations

If you prefer a rare steak, preheat water bath to 120°F (49°C); for medium, preheat to 139°F (59°C); and for medium-well, preheat to 149°F (65°C). We don't recommend cooking tender cuts well-done. Steaks cooked rare will not be pasteurized; if food safety is a concern, and especially for those with compromised immune systems, cook meat to at least medium-rare.

For steaks 1 to $1\frac{1}{2}$ inches (2.5 to 4 cm) thick, increase the cooking time to $2\frac{1}{2}$ hours.

Tough Beef Steaks and Roasts

This recipe works for any tougher beef cut, also called marinating or simmering steaks, such as round, flank and short ribs, as well as stewing beef and larger cuts such as tri-tip and brisket. These are the cooking temperatures we found resulted in the doneness specified when the steaks were seared after sous vide cooking.

Sous vide time:
4 to 6 hours

Tips

Use the size of bag or pouch appropriate to the size of steak or roast you're cooking. Be sure the beef fits in the bag without bending or folding. If cooking more than 1 steak or roast, choose a bag that fits them in a single layer, allowing space between each, for the most even cooking.

If you want to marinate your steak or roast, place it and marinade in freezer bag. Turn bag and gently massage beef to evenly coat with marinade. Remove excess air and seal bag. Refrigerate for at least 2 hours or up to 1 day. The longer you let the beef marinate, the more the flavors will infuse into the meat.

Tough cuts with cooking times of 12 to 48 hours (see box) can, for convenience, cook for up to 6 hours longer; longer than that tends to have an adverse effect on the texture of the meat, as the fibers break down and the meat becomes mushy.

- **Preheat water bath to 130°F (54.5°C) for medium-rare (see variation)**
- **Medium or large resealable freezer bag or vacuum-seal pouch**
- **Barbecue grill, grill pan, cast-iron skillet or broiler**

Boneless or bone-in beef marinating or simmering steak(s), about ¾ inch (2 cm) thick
Salt and freshly ground black pepper
Vegetable oil or cooking spray (optional)

1. Season steak(s) on both sides with salt and pepper.
2. Place steak(s) in freezer bag or pouch. If cooking more than 1 steak per bag, space them apart. Remove excess air and seal bag using the water displacement method (see page 13) or seal pouch using vacuum sealer.
3. Cook steak(s) in preheated water bath, covered, for 4 to 6 hours (or, for convenience, up to 8 hours), replenishing water as necessary to keep meat immersed.
4. Remove bag from water bath and let rest for 10 minutes.

To Finish on the Barbecue
5. Meanwhile, preheat barbecue grill to medium-high.
6. Remove steak from bag, discarding liquid, and transfer to a plate. Pat dry and season on both sides with salt and pepper.
7. Oil grill and place steak on grill. Grill, turning once, for 1 to 2 minutes per side or until sizzling and marked.

To Finish in a Grill Pan or Cast-Iron Skillet
5. Meanwhile, preheat pan over medium-high heat until hot and almost smoking (turn on your hood vent or open the windows).
6. Remove steak from bag, discarding liquid, and transfer to a plate. Pat dry and season on both sides with salt and pepper.
7. Lightly oil pan and sear steak, turning once, for 1 to 2 minutes per side or until sizzling and grill-marked or browned.

Tips

Broiling works best for flank steak, stewing beef cubes and short ribs. We do not recommend it for thinner steaks and roasts.

To cook steak ahead, cook as directed through step 3, then immerse bag in ice water to chill. Refrigerate in the sealed bag for up to 3 days or freeze for up to 2 months. Thaw in the refrigerator overnight, if frozen. In a water bath preheated to the same temperature you originally cooked at, reheat in the sealed bag for 30 minutes, then proceed with step 4.

Variation

If you prefer a medium steak, preheat water bath to 139°F (59°C); for medium-well, preheat to 149°F (65°C). We don't recommend cooking tough cuts rare or well.

To Finish under the Broiler (see tip)

5. Meanwhile, preheat broiler with rack 6 or 8 inches (15 or 20 cm) from heat, depending on thickness of meat.
6. Remove steak from bag, discarding liquid, and transfer to a plate. Pat dry and season on both sides with salt and pepper.
7. Place steak on a wire rack set over a foil-lined rimmed baking sheet, or on a broiler pan. Broil for 3 to 4 minutes per side or until sizzling.

Other Cuts

- **Tri-tip:** Cook, covered, for 6 hours, replenishing water as necessary.
- **Stewing beef cubes:** Cut beef into 1- to $1\frac{1}{2}$-inch (2.5 to 4 cm) cubes. Cook, covered, for 12 hours, replenishing water as necessary. Skip the searing steps and add to a simmering sauce for 5 minutes, or thread onto skewers to make grilling or broiling easier. To broil skewers, preheat broiler with rack 6 inches (15 cm) from heat. Place skewers on a wire rack set over a foil-lined rimmed baking sheet, or on a broiler pan. Broil for 3 to 4 minutes per side or until sizzling.
- **Thick-sliced blade or chuck roast:** Choose a roast that is $1\frac{1}{2}$ to 2 inches (4 to 5 cm) thick. Cook, covered, for 12 hours, replenishing water as necessary.
- **Short ribs:** For either boneless or bone-in ribs, cook, covered, for 24 hours, replenishing water as necessary. These may be too fall-apart tender to sear on a barbecue grill or pan; the broiler is easiest. To broil short ribs, preheat broiler with rack 8 inches (20 cm) from heat. Place ribs on a wire rack set over a foil-lined rimmed baking sheet, or on a broiler pan. Broil for 3 to 4 minutes per side or until sizzling.
- **Eye-of-round roast:** Choose a roast about 3 to $3\frac{1}{2}$ inches (7.5 to 8 cm) in diameter. Cook, covered, for 36 hours, replenishing water as necessary. When searing at the end, turn to brown all sides.
- **Brisket:** Choose a brisket about 3 inches (7.5 cm) thick. Cook, covered, for 36 to 48 hours, replenishing water as necessary.

Tender Pork Cuts

This recipe works for any tender cut of pork: loin chops or tenderloin. Bone-in and boneless chops cook in the same temperature water bath for the same time; it's the thickness of the chop that determines the cooking time. Leaving pork in the water bath longer than the maximum recommended time tends to have an adverse effect on the texture of the meat, as the fibers break down and the meat becomes mushy.

Sous vide time:
$1^1/_2$ hours

Tips

Use the size of bag or pouch appropriate to the size of the meat pieces you're cooking. Be sure the piece(s) fit in the bag without bending or folding (thus the recommendation to cut tenderloin in half crosswise). If cooking more than 1 piece, choose a bag that fits the pieces in a single layer, allowing space between each, for the most even cooking.

If you want to marinate your pork, place pork and marinade in freezer bag. Turn bag and gently massage pork to evenly coat with marinade. Remove excess air and seal bag. Refrigerate for at least 2 hours or up to 1 day. The longer you let the pork marinate, the more the flavors will infuse into the meat.

- **Preheat water bath to 140°F (60°C) for medium (see variation)**
- **Medium or large resealable freezer bag or vacuum-seal pouch**
- **Barbecue grill, grill pan or cast-iron skillet**

> Boneless or bone-in pork grilling chop(s), about $3/_4$ inch (2 cm) thick, or pork tenderloin, cut in half crosswise
>
> Salt and freshly ground black pepper
>
> Vegetable oil or cooking spray

1. Season pork on both or all sides with salt and pepper.
2. Place pork in freezer bag or pouch. If cooking more than 1 piece per bag, space them apart. Remove excess air and seal bag using the water displacement method (see page 13) or seal pouch using vacuum sealer.
3. Cook pork in preheated water bath for $1^1/_2$ hours (or, for convenience, up to $2^1/_2$ hours).
4. Remove bag from water bath and let rest for 10 minutes.

To Finish on the Barbecue

5. Meanwhile, preheat barbecue grill to medium-high.
6. Remove pork from bag, discarding liquid, and transfer to a plate. Pat dry and season on both sides or all over with salt and pepper.
7. Oil grill and place pork on grill. Grill, turning once or to brown all sides, for 1 to 2 minutes per side or until sizzling and marked.

Tip

To cook pork ahead, cook as directed through step 3, then immerse bag in ice water to chill. Refrigerate in the sealed bag for up to 3 days or freeze for up to 2 months. Thaw in the refrigerator overnight, if frozen. In a water bath preheated to the same temperature you originally cooked at, reheat in the sealed bag for 30 minutes, then proceed with step 4.

To Finish in a Grill Pan or Cast-Iron Skillet

5. Meanwhile, preheat pan over medium-high heat until hot and almost smoking (turn on your hood vent or open the windows).

6. Remove pork from bag, discarding liquid, and transfer to a plate. Pat dry and season on both sides or all over with salt and pepper.

7. Lightly oil pan and sear pork, turning once or to brown all sides, for 1 to 2 minutes per side or until sizzling and grill-marked or browned.

Variations

If you prefer a medium-rare chop or tenderloin, preheat water bath to 130°F (54.5°C); for medium-well, preheat to 149°F (65°C). We don't recommend cooking tender cuts well-done.

For chops or tenderloins 1 to $1\frac{1}{2}$ inches (2.5 to 4 cm) thick, increase the cooking time to $2\frac{1}{2}$ hours.

Larger and Less Tender Pork Cuts

These cuts are just as easy with sous vide as cooking a pork chop, and the meat will be moist and tender throughout. Ribs become tender and stay moist, yet still keep a nice meaty texture. Use these instructions for loin roasts, shoulder roasts and back or side ribs.

Tips

Use the size of bag or pouch appropriate to the size of the meat pieces you're cooking. Be sure the piece(s) fit in the bag without bending or folding. If cooking more than 1 piece, choose a bag that fits the pieces in a single layer, allowing space between each, for the most even cooking.

If you want to marinate your pork, place pork and marinade in freezer bag. Turn bag and gently massage pork to evenly coat with marinade. Remove excess air and seal bag. Refrigerate for at least 2 hours or up to 1 day. The longer you let the pork marinate, the more the flavors will infuse into the meat.

- **Preheat water bath to 140°F (60°C) for medium (see variation)**
- **Medium or large resealable freezer bag or vacuum-seal pouch**
- **Barbecue grill, grill pan or cast-iron skillet**

> Boneless pork single loin roast, tied (about 3½ inches/8.5 cm in diameter)
> Salt and freshly ground black pepper
> Vegetable oil or cooking spray

1. Season pork on all sides with salt and pepper.
2. Place pork in freezer bag or pouch. If cooking more than 1 piece per bag, space them apart. Remove excess air and seal bag using the water displacement method (see page 13) or seal pouch using vacuum sealer.
3. Cook pork in preheated water bath for 3 hours (or, for convenience, up to 4 hours).
4. Remove bag from water bath and let rest for 10 minutes.

To Finish on the Barbecue

5. Meanwhile, preheat barbecue grill to medium-high.
6. Remove pork from bag, discarding liquid, and transfer to a plate. Pat dry and season all over with salt and pepper.
7. Oil grill and place pork on grill. Grill, turning to brown all sides, for 1 to 2 minutes per side or until sizzling and marked.

To Finish in a Grill Pan or Cast-Iron Skillet

5. Meanwhile, preheat pan over medium-high heat until hot and almost smoking (turn on your hood vent or open the windows).
6. Remove pork from bag, discarding liquid, and transfer to a plate. Pat dry and season all over with salt and pepper.
7. Lightly oil pan and sear pork, turning to brown all sides, for 1 to 2 minutes per side or until sizzling and grill-marked or browned.

Tips

Longer-cooking pork cuts (see box) can, for convenience, cook for up to 4 hours longer; longer than that tends to have an adverse effect on the texture of the meat, as the fibers break down and the meat becomes mushy.

To cook pork ahead, cook as directed through step 3, then immerse bag in ice water to chill. Refrigerate in the sealed bag for up to 3 days or freeze for up to 2 months. Thaw in the refrigerator overnight, if frozen. In a water bath preheated to the same temperature you originally cooked at, reheat in the sealed bag for 1 hour, then proceed with step 4.

Other Cuts

- **Shoulder blade (butt) roast:** Choose a boneless or bone-in roast about 4 to 5 inches (10 to 12.5 cm) thick. Increase the water bath temperature to 160°F (71°C) and cook, covered, for 14 to 18 hours, replenishing water as necessary. The pork should be tender; if it isn't, return bag to water bath and cook, checking for doneness every 30 minutes. This roast will be very tender and, if cooked in a sauce (as for pulled pork), does not need browning at the end, so you can skip those steps if you prefer. If browning, turn carefully, using two sets of tongs, so the roast doesn't fall apart.
- **Back or side ribs:** Increase the water bath temperature to 144°F (62°C) and cook, covered, for 12 to 15 hours, replenishing water as necessary. The ribs should be fork-tender; if they aren't, return bag to water bath and cook, checking for doneness every 30 minutes. Ribs can be browned before or after cooking. See Retro Sweet-and-Sour Spareribs (page 110) for instructions on browning before cooking.

Basic Chicken

Whether you want to batch-cook plain boneless skinless chicken to use in recipes, or simply have a succulent piece of bone-in, skin-on chicken, the sous vide cooks the chicken evenly and keeps it moist and flavorful. Air-chilled chicken is a must when cooking sous vide to make sure you get a rich chicken flavor rather than a watery one.

Sous vide time: 3 hours

Tips

If you want to marinate your chicken, place chicken and marinade in freezer bag. Turn bag and gently massage chicken to evenly coat with marinade. Remove excess air and seal bag. Refrigerate for at least 2 hours or up to 8 hours. The longer you let the chicken marinate, the more the flavors will infuse into the meat.

For flattened whole chickens and bone-in chicken leg quarters, we find broiling the easiest way to brown the chicken; it is so tender, it tends to fall apart on the grill or in a pan.

Be gentle when transferring cooked larger pieces and whole flattened chicken to a plate or baking sheet: it is fall-off-the-bone tender. Reduce splashing of the hot liquid by keeping the bag in the sink and sliding the chicken onto the plate or baking sheet.

- **Preheat water bath to 140°F (60°C)**
- **Large resealable freezer bag**
- **Barbecue grill, grill pan or cast-iron skillet**

Boneless skinless chicken breasts (each about 6 oz/175 g and up to 1½ inches/4 cm thick)

Salt and freshly ground black pepper

Vegetable oil or cooking spray

1. Season chicken on both sides with salt and pepper.
2. Place chicken in freezer bag or pouch. If cooking more than 1 piece per bag, space them apart. Remove excess air and seal bag using the water displacement method (see page 13) or seal pouch using vacuum sealer.
3. Cook chicken in preheated water bath for 3 hours (or, for convenience, up to 4 hours).
4. Remove bag from water bath and let rest for 10 minutes.

To Finish on the Barbecue

5. Meanwhile, preheat barbecue grill to medium-high.
6. Remove chicken from bag, discarding liquid, and transfer to a plate. Pat dry and season on both sides with salt and pepper.
7. Oil grill and place chicken on grill. Grill, turning once, for 1 to 2 minutes per side or until sizzling and marked.

To Finish in a Grill Pan or Cast-Iron Skillet

5. Meanwhile, preheat pan over medium-high heat until hot and almost smoking (turn on your hood vent or open the windows).
6. Remove chicken from bag, discarding liquid, and transfer to a plate. Pat dry and season on both sides with salt and pepper.
7. Lightly oil pan and sear chicken, turning once, for 1 to 2 minutes per side or until sizzling and grill-marked or browned.

Tip

To make chilled chicken ahead for use in salad or sandwiches, prepare through step 3, then immerse bag in ice water to chill. Refrigerate in the sealed bag for up to 3 days. Skip the finishing steps and remove the skin (if necessary) before serving cold.

Variation

If using skin-on chicken, another finishing option is under the broiler. Preheat broiler with rack 4 to 8 inches (10 to 20 cm) from heat, depending on the thickness of the chicken. Remove chicken from bag, discarding liquid, and place, skin side up, on a rimmed baking sheet lined with foil. Season to taste with salt and pepper. Broil chicken for 5 to 7 minutes or until skin is golden brown and crispy.

Other Cuts

- **Boneless skinless chicken thighs:** Flatten thighs before placing them in the bag. Increase the water bath temperature to 148°F (64°C) and cook for 3 hours.
- **Bone-in chicken breasts or thighs:** Choose skin-on or skinless breasts or thighs up to 2 inches (5 cm) thick. Increase the water bath temperature to 148°F (64°C) and cook for 3½ hours.
- **Bone-in chicken leg quarters:** Choose skin-on or skinless chicken leg quarters. Increase the water bath temperature to 148°F (64°C) and cook, covered, for 4 hours.
- **Flattened whole chicken:** When flattening the chicken or asking the butcher to do so, make sure it is no more than 3 inches (7.5 cm) at the thickest part. Increase the water bath temperature to 148°F (64°C) and cook, covered, for 4 hours. Be gentle when removing a flattened chicken, as it will want to fall apart (see tip, page 28). We don't recommend cooking a whole chicken without flattening it.

Basic Burgers

We love burgers and eat them regularly all year round, even grilling them in the depths of our Canadian winters — in depths of snow on the deck. We always have homemade patties in the freezer, ready to cook up on the barbecue grill, and we never really thought you could improve on a fresh-cooked homemade burger patty. We were pleasantly surprised to discover that the sous vide actually does improve a burger! Patties cooked sous vide stay super-moist and tender, and then a quick grill gives them enough traditional flavor to satisfy that barbecue hankering. They're a boon to entertaining, as there's no need to worry that the burgers won't cook through or that you'll be fighting flare-ups on the grill after you get sidetracked pouring drinks.

**MAKES
4 BURGERS**

Sous vide time:
2 hours

Tips

Ground meat that is about 85% to 90% lean is best for these burgers. There is enough fat to keep them moist and tender, but not so much that they fall apart or become greasy.

This recipe will work with other ground meats, such as lamb, bison, venison or pork. Ground poultry tends to be very wet and doesn't hold well as patties.

To make burgers ahead, prepare through step 5, then immerse bag in ice water to chill. Refrigerate in the sealed bag for up to 3 days or freeze for up to 6 months. Reheat in a 165°F (74°C) water bath for 30 minutes (or 1 hour if frozen), until warmed through, then proceed with step 6.

- Baking sheet, lined with plastic wrap
- Large resealable freezer bag or vacuum-seal pouch
- Barbecue grill, grill pan or cast-iron pan

1	large egg	1
½ tsp	salt	2 mL
½ tsp	freshly ground black pepper	2 mL
1¼ lbs	ground beef (see tips)	625 g
⅓ cup	quick-cooking rolled oats	75 mL
	Vegetable oil or cooking spray	

1. In a large bowl, using a fork, whisk together egg, salt and pepper. Add beef and oats, mixing with the fork just until evenly blended (do not overwork). Divide into 4 equal portions and shape each portion into a ¾-inch (2 cm) thick patty.
2. Place patties on prepared baking sheet, spacing them apart. Freeze for 15 to 30 minutes or until firm but not solid.
3. Meanwhile, preheat water bath to 140°F (60°C).
4. Place patties in freezer bag or pouch, spacing them apart. Remove excess air and seal bag using the water displacement method (see page 13) or seal pouch using vacuum sealer.
5. Cook in preheated water bath for 2 hours. Remove bag from water bath and let rest for 5 minutes.

To Finish on the Barbecue

6. Meanwhile, preheat barbecue grill to medium-high.
7. Remove burger patties from bag, discarding liquid, and transfer to a plate. Pat dry and season on both sides with salt and pepper.
8. Oil grill and place burgers on grill. Grill, turning once, for 1 to 2 minutes per side or until sizzling and marked.

Tips

The burgers can be frozen solid in step 2, then placed in the freezer bag or pouch, sealed and stored in the freezer for up to 2 months. Cook from frozen, increasing the cooking time in step 5 to 3 hours. You may want to freeze patties in smaller batches in medium freezer bags so you can cook 1 or 2 at a time.

This is a recipe where a vacuum sealer does make removing the air and sealing the food easier, especially if you want to freeze the patties ahead of cooking. Make sure the patties are firm before placing them in the pouches, and use the delicate setting if you have one.

To Finish in a Grill Pan or Cast-Iron Skillet

6. Meanwhile, preheat pan over medium-high heat until hot and almost smoking (turn on your hood vent or open the windows).

7. Remove burger patties from bag, discarding liquid, and transfer to a plate. Pat dry and season on both sides with salt and pepper.

8. Lightly oil pan and sear burgers, turning once, for 1 to 2 minutes per side or until sizzling and grill-marked or browned.

Serving Suggestions

- Serve on buns with traditional burger toppings such as ketchup, mustard, relish, barbecue sauce, mayonnaise, lettuce, pickles, sliced tomatoes or sliced avocado.
- Other fancy topping options are Caramelized Onions (page 58), Spicy Mayo (page 62), Mushrooms in Brown Butter and Thyme (page 82, made with sliced mushrooms), Cherry Chipotle Barbecue Sauce (page 106), Sweet Peppers and Onions (page 180) or Cranberry Chutney (page 182).

Fish and Seafood

Delicate fish works extremely well with sous vide cooking and keeps a true, natural flavor. A bonus when cooking fish sous vide is that the aromas stay in the bag rather than spreading through your house, so you don't have that fishy smell lingering days later. We've provided instructions for salmon as the main recipe here, and it's a good one to start with. But you can use the same basic technique for any fish, though we recommend different times and temperatures depending on their thickness and fragility (see box).

Sous vide time: 45 minutes

Tips

If you prefer a little browning color, transfer cooked salmon, skin side down, to a foil-lined rimmed baking sheet and pat dry. Preheat broiler with rack 4 inches (10 cm) from heat and broil salmon for 2 to 3 minutes or just until light golden.

When cooking shrimp, arrange them so they are somewhat straight and lined up in the freezer bag to help them cook up in a nice, uniform shape.

Any time you are purchasing fish and seafood, check for sustainable choices at seafoodwatch.org or oceanwise.ca, or ask at your grocery store or fishmonger for the best options.

- **Preheat water bath to 130°F (54.5°C)**
- **Medium resealable freezer bag**

Center-cut skin-on or skinless salmon fillet portions (each about 6 oz/175 g and 1 inch/2.5 cm thick)

Salt and freshly ground black pepper

1. Rinse salmon and pat dry. Season flesh side with salt and pepper. Place fish pieces in freezer bag, spacing them slightly apart. Remove excess air and seal bag using the water displacement method (see page 13).

2. Cook in preheated water bath for 45 minutes. Remove bag from water bath.

3. Remove salmon from bag, discarding any liquid. Serve hot.

Other Fish and Seafood

- **Other firm, meaty-textured fish:** For fish such as swordfish or mahi-mahi, choose steaks about 1 inch (2.5 cm) thick. Cook at the same temperature and for the same time as salmon.

- **Thin, more delicate fish:** For fish such as trout, sole or haddock, choose fillets about $1/2$ inch (1 cm) thick. Reduce the water bath temperature to 120°F (49°C) and cook for 30 minutes. Finish under the broiler (see tip).

- **Tuna:** Choose steaks about 1 inch (2.5 cm) thick. Reduce the water bath temperature to 129°F (54°C). For rare, cook for 10 minutes; for medium, cook for 20 minutes; for well-done, with no pink, cook for 30 minutes.

- **Shrimp:** Choose large or jumbo shrimp, either peeled and deveined or unpeeled (though shells can puncture bags). Increase the water bath temperature to 140°F (60°C) and cook for 15 minutes. To serve hot, remove from bag, discarding liquid; to serve cold, first immerse the bag in ice water until chilled.

Other Fish and Seafood

- **Sea scallops:** Scallops should be out of the shell. Increase the water bath temperature to 140°F (60°C). For scallops up to ¾ inch (2 cm) thick, cook for 15 minutes. For scallops 1 to 1½ inches (2.5 to 4 cm) thick, cook for 30 minutes. To serve hot, remove from bag, discarding liquid; to serve cold, first immerse the bag in ice water until chilled. We do not recommend cooking tiny bay scallops sous vide.

- **Chunks of fish:** Cut fish into chunks of about ¾ inch (2 cm). Increase the water bath temperature to 140°F (60°C) and cook for 15 minutes.

- **Fish or seafood to be added to a soup or a sauce:** Reduce the water bath temperature to 120°F (49°C) and cook for 30 minutes. Add cooked fish or seafood, with liquid from bag as desired, to simmering soup, sauce or stew and simmer for 1 to 2 minutes, until hot.

Basic Eggs

The texture of sous vide eggs poached in their shells is different from traditional poaching in water, as the yolk and the two types of egg white (did you know there were two?) — the thin white and the thick white — firm up at different rates, so you get softer whites than with traditional poaching. And if you cook them until they hold their shape, the yolks are on the verge of gooey. But many people rave about the quality and experience of sous vide eggs poached in their shell, and it is a handy way to poach several eggs at a time, so if you're feeding a crowd, you can put poached eggs on the menu without putting the cook "in the weeds," as we say in the restaurant biz. We like the medium-soft set best, but some people love the soft eggs. We recommend experimenting with cooking eggs for different amounts of time (when you don't have a houseful waiting for breakfast) to determine what set you like best.

> **Sous vide time:**
> **15 to 17 minutes**

Tips

These poached eggs will not be pasteurized, so if the food safety of undercooked eggs is a concern for you, pasteurize the eggs first (see variation), plunge them into cold water until they are at room temperature, then proceed with the poaching instructions.

Let eggs warm to room temperature for about 30 minutes before cooking, or place them in a container, cover with warm (not hot) tap water and let stand for 5 to 10 minutes. If the eggs are too cold when you put them in the water bath, they tend to crack and you end up with egg-drop soup.

- **Preheat water bath to 164°F (73°C)**

> Large eggs, at room temperature
> Salt and freshly ground black pepper

1. Using a slotted spoon, slowly and carefully lower eggs, one or two at a time, into preheated water bath. Cook for 15 minutes for softly set poached eggs or 17 minutes for medium-soft eggs.
2. Using the slotted spoon, lift eggs from water bath and place on a tea towel on the counter. Let cool for 1 minute.
3. Working with one egg at a time, tap the side of the egg on the counter and carefully crack it into a bowl. Season to taste with salt and pepper. Serve immediately.

Eggs Benedict

Make the Hollandaise Sauce (page 177), placing the jar in the preheated water bath for 6 minutes. Add the eggs to the water bath and cook for 17 minutes longer. Meanwhile, fry or broil slices of ham or peameal bacon and toast split English muffins (one half per egg). Lightly spread muffins with butter, place on serving plates and top with ham. Crack poached eggs, one at a time, into a small bowl, then carefully tip on top of ham. Spoon warm Hollandaise over eggs. Season with salt and pepper. Serve immediately. *Variations:* Replace the ham with wilted spinach, Perfect Poached Asparagus (page 148) or slices of smoked salmon.

Tips

We found it tricky to cook eggs to a texture more than medium-soft with this method. If you prefer a firmer yolk, you can cook for 19 minutes, but the yolk does tend to become jellylike rather than a traditional cooked texture.

When cooking or pasteurizing eggs sous vide, make sure there is plenty of water surrounding the eggs (at least 1 inch/2.5 cm above the eggs) and do not overcrowd the container; to cook evenly, the eggs should swirl freely in the water to allow maximum water and heat circulation.

Variations

Poached Eggs-in-a-Jar: Since it's impossible to see the doneness of eggs poached in the shell, you can poach them in jars instead. Warm 4-oz (125 mL) canning jars with hot tap water. Crack 1 egg into each jar and cover with a two-piece metal lid. Place a wire rack in the sous vide container and place jars on the rack, weighing them down as necessary (see step 5, page 15). Cook for 21 minutes for softly set eggs or 23 minutes for medium-soft eggs. Lift a jar out of the water and gently shake it to see if the egg is set enough; if it isn't, return jar to the water bath and continue cooking, checking every 2 minutes, until eggs are the desired doneness.

Hard-Cooked Eggs: Preheat water bath to 200°F (100°C). Add room-temperature eggs to the water bath as directed and cook for 2 minutes. Reduce the appliance temperature to 180°F (82°C) and gradually pour in cold water, in a thin stream, just until the water temperature drops to 180°F (82°C). Cook eggs for 15 minutes. Lift from water bath and immediately transfer to a bowl of cold water; let stand, refreshing water as necessary to keep cold, until eggs are cold to the touch. Peel and serve immediately, or return to egg carton (marked that they are hard-cooked) and refrigerate for up to 5 days.

Pasteurized Raw Eggs: For eggs to be used in salad dressing, mayonnaise or any other recipe that calls for raw eggs, follow the instructions for poaching eggs, but reduce the water bath temperature to 131°F (55°C) and cook (though technically they will only heat, not cook) for 2 hours. Lift from water bath and immediately transfer to a bowl of cold water; let stand, refreshing water as necessary to keep cold, until eggs are cold to the touch. Use immediately or return to egg carton (marked that they are pasteurized) and refrigerate for up to 2 weeks, or the "best before" date marked on the carton.

Basic Grains

Cooking grains in jars in the water bath is a hands-off, set-it-and-forget-it method that is handy when your stove is occupied by other dishes. And if you're running your sous vide for other recipes at the same temperature, you can pop in a jar of grains alongside, to accompany your meal. The basic instructions work for rice, barley, wheat berries and quinoa (okay, quinoa is a seed, but we eat it like a grain); follow the method for white rice, with the adjustments outlined in the box.

**MAKES ABOUT
1¾ CUPS
(425 ML)**

**Sous vide time:
45 minutes**

Tips

To drain off excess liquid using the lid as a strainer, wear water-resistant silicone-coated oven mitts and slide the lid on top of the jar until there is a small opening that water can drain through but the grains cannot. Hold the lid against the jar and tip the jar over the sink, letting the water drain out. Avoid dumping tender grains, such as rice, quinoa or barley, into a metal sieve to drain, as that can cause mushy grains; a sieve does work fine for wheat berries. Most colander holes are too large, and the grains will fall through.

Cooked grains can be cooled in a cold water bath (not ice water, or the jar may break) until cold, then covered and refrigerated in the jar for up to 3 days.

- Preheat water bath to 180°F (82°C)
- Pint (500 mL) canning jar, with two-piece lid
- Wire rack

½ cup	long-grain parboiled (Converted) white rice	125 mL
¼ tsp	salt	1 mL
1 cup	water	250 mL

1. Fill jar with hot tap water and let the glass warm for 5 to 10 minutes.

2. Empty water from jar and add rice, salt and water. Wipe rim of jar and place lid disc on jar, then screw on band just until fingertip-tight.

3. Place wire rack in preheated water bath and place jar on rack. Cook, covered, for 45 minutes. The rice should be tender, and most, but not all, of the water should be absorbed; if the rice isn't done, replace lid, return jar to water bath and cook, checking for doneness every 10 minutes. Remove jar from water bath and let stand for 5 minutes.

4. Open jar and drain off any excess liquid using the lid as a strainer (see tip). Using a chopstick or narrow silicone spatula in the jar, or pouring the rice out into a warmed serving bowl and using a fork, fluff the rice.

Other Grains

- **Long-grain brown rice:** Increase the water to 1¼ cups (300 mL) and cook for 45 minutes.
- **Basmati rice:** Rinse and drain rice in a sieve before adding it to the jar. Cook for 40 minutes.
- **Barley:** Rinse and drain pot or pearl barley in a sieve before adding it to the jar. Increase the water to 1¼ cups (300 mL) and cook for 1½ hours.
- **Quinoa:** Rinse and drain quinoa in a sieve before adding it to the jar. Cook for 45 minutes.
- **Wheat berries:** Increase the water to 1½ cups (375 mL) and cook, covered, for 4 hours, replenishing water as necessary.

Breakfasts

Maple Mustard Breakfast Sausage

When frying sausages, it's tricky to get them cooked through without being tough on the outside (plus you have a messy pan to deal with after breakfast). Thanks to sous vide cooking, that's no longer a problem. The sausages stay moist, with a pleasantly firm texture inside, and you need only a quick sear on the stovetop to give them the desired browned color and flavor. A glaze of maple and mustard adds a finishing touch.

MAKES 4 TO 6 SERVINGS

Sous vide time: 45 minutes

Tips

The sausages can be held in the water bath for up to 3 hours for convenience; beyond that, they tend to take on a spongy texture.

You can multiply this recipe two or three times, using separate freezer bags for each pound (500 g) of sausages. For big batches, you may want to broil the sausages on a foil-lined baking sheet instead of browning them in a skillet; simply serve the glaze drizzled over top instead of combining it with the sausages.

To make ahead, prepare through step 2, then immerse bag in ice water to chill. Refrigerate in the sealed bag for up to 2 days or freeze for up to 3 months. Thaw in the refrigerator overnight, if frozen. When ready to serve, reheat in a 140°F (60°C) water bath for 30 minutes, then proceed with step 3.

- **Preheat water bath to 160°F (71°C)**
- **Medium resealable freezer bag**

1 lb	breakfast sausages (about $3/4$ inch/ 2 cm thick)	500 g
2 tbsp	pure maple syrup	30 mL
1 tbsp	Dijon mustard	15 mL
	Freshly ground black pepper	

1. Arrange sausages in a single layer in freezer bag. Remove excess air and seal bag.

2. Cook in preheated water bath for 45 minutes. Remove bag from water bath and let rest for 5 minutes.

3. Remove sausages from bag, discarding any liquid, and transfer to a plate. Pat sausages dry.

4. In a small bowl, combine maple syrup and mustard.

5. Heat a large skillet over medium-high heat. Working in batches to avoid crowding pan, add sausages and sear, turning often, for 2 minutes or until browned on all sides. Return to the plate and repeat with the remaining sausages.

6. Return all sausages to the skillet and remove from heat. Add syrup mixture and season to taste with pepper, stirring to coat sausages.

Tomato Cheddar Crustless Quiche

While we were writing this book, a major coffee chain launched a product line for their breakfast menu — sous vide eggs (with some sort of catchy name). Upon investigation, they are pretty much the same as what we've called crustless quiche: a savory, eggy custard (just the quiche filling, without the crust). We make them in jars instead of plastic packaging, and I would bet they are less expensive to make than to buy, and super-easy. You can customize the flavor and have your own takeout breakfast ready anytime.

MAKES 4 SERVINGS

Sous vide time: 1¼ hours

Tip

To make ahead, let quiches cool slightly, then refrigerate for up to 3 days. Serve cold or reheat, uncovered, in the microwave on Medium (50%) for 1 to 2 minutes.

Variations

You can make smaller versions, using eight 4-oz (125 mL) canning jars; just be sure you have room in your sous vide container to cook the jars in a single layer (stacking can cause cracking). Reduce the cooking time to 1 hour.

Change up the cheese to any firm cheese and/or add 1 tbsp (15 mL) finely chopped ham or crumbled cooked bacon along with the cheese.

For a Mexican twist, replace the basil with chopped fresh cilantro and add 1 tbsp (15 mL) minced seeded jalapeño pepper with the tomatoes. Substitute Monterey Jack or pepper Jack cheese for the Cheddar.

- **Preheat water bath to 170°F (77°C)**
- **4 wide-mouth 8-oz (250 mL) canning jars, with two-piece lids**
- **Wire rack**

8	large eggs	8
1 tbsp	chopped fresh basil (or ½ tsp/2 mL dried)	15 mL
¼ tsp	freshly ground black pepper	1 mL
Pinch	salt	Pinch
½ cup	half-and-half (10%) cream or milk	125 mL
¾ cup	shredded sharp (old) Cheddar cheese	175 mL
½ cup	chopped seeded tomato	125 mL

1. Pour hot tap water into the canning jars to warm the glass; set aside.

2. In a large liquid measuring cup or bowl, whisk together eggs, basil, pepper and salt until blended. Whisk in cream.

3. Empty water from jars and, working quickly, pour in egg mixture, dividing equally. Add cheese and tomato, dividing equally. Wipe rims of jars and place lid discs on jars, then screw on bands just until fingertip-tight.

4. Place wire rack in preheated water bath and place jars on rack; if the jars float, weigh them down (see tip, page 40). Cook for 1¼ hours. To check for doneness, remove lid and insert the tip of a knife into the center of a custard; it should come out clean. If it doesn't, return jars to water bath and cook, checking for doneness every 15 minutes.

5. To serve, remove lids and pat surface of quiche dry with a paper towel. Serve in the jars or run a knife around the edge of each quiche and invert onto serving plates.

Serving Suggestions

- To mimic a crust, use the lid of the jar as a template to cut circles of sliced bread. Lightly toast and butter the bread (or toast English muffin halves), then invert the quiche on top to serve.
- For a very decadent dish, spoon warm Hollandaise Sauce (page 177) on top of the quiche in the jar or turned out onto a circle of toast.

Spinach and Swiss Crustless Quiche

Sometimes, you just don't mess with the classics. Okay, so cooking quiche filling without a crust, in a jar, using sous vide, isn't classic, but eggs seasoned with the combination of spinach, Swiss cheese and garlic certainly is, and it remains delicious! This technique produces a tender custard texture in delightful individual servings — for guests or just for yourself.

**MAKES
4 SERVINGS**

Sous vide time:
1¼ hours

Tips

Warming the jars and working quickly so they don't cool too much before going into the water bath are important steps to prevent temperature shock. If the glass is cold as it is immersed into the hot water, it can crack — and make a mess in your sous vide bath.

If you'd like to turn the quiches out of the jars to serve, line the bottoms of the jars with a circle of moistened parchment paper after dumping out the water and before adding the egg mixture.

Use an inverted plate to weigh down the jars in the water bath, adding a jar full of water on top of the plate, if necessary, to keep the jars submerged.

- **Preheat water bath to 170°F (77°C)**
- **4 wide-mouth 8-oz (250 mL) canning jars, with two-piece lids**
- **Wire rack**

1 tbsp	olive oil	15 mL
1	small clove garlic, minced	1
¼ tsp	freshly ground black pepper	1 mL
Pinch	salt	Pinch
2 cups	packed baby spinach, chopped	500 mL
8	large eggs	8
½ cup	half-and-half (10%) cream or milk	125 mL
1 tsp	Dijon mustard	5 mL
½ cup	shredded Swiss cheese	125 mL

1. Pour hot tap water into the canning jars to warm the glass; set aside.

2. In a small skillet, heat oil over medium heat. Add garlic, pepper and salt; cook, stirring, for 1 minute or until fragrant. Add spinach and cook, stirring, for about 3 minutes or until wilted. Remove from heat and let cool. Drain off any accumulated liquid.

3. In a large liquid measuring cup or bowl, whisk eggs until blended. Whisk in cream and mustard. Stir in spinach and cheese.

4. Empty water from jars and pour in egg mixture, dividing equally. Wipe rims of jars and place lid discs on jars, then screw on bands just until fingertip-tight.

Tip

To make ahead, let quiches cool slightly, then refrigerate for up to 3 days. Serve cold or reheat, uncovered, in the microwave on Medium (50%) for 1 to 2 minutes.

Variations

You can make smaller versions, using eight 4-oz (125 mL) canning jars; just be sure you have room in your sous vide container to cook the jars in a single layer (stacking can cause cracking). Reduce the cooking time to 1 hour.

Add 2 tbsp (30 mL) minced smoked salmon with the cheese in step 3.

5. Place wire rack in preheated water bath and place jars on rack; if the jars float, weigh them down (see tip, page 40). Cook for $1\frac{1}{4}$ hours. To check for doneness, remove lid and insert the tip of a knife into the center of a custard; it should come out clean. If it doesn't, return jars to water bath and cook, checking for doneness every 15 minutes.

6. To serve, remove lids and pat surface of quiche dry with a paper towel. Serve in the jars or run a knife around the edge of each quiche and invert onto serving plates.

Serving Suggestions

- Serve this quiche, turned out of jars, on top of a green salad with sliced tomatoes and bell peppers and dressed with a vinaigrette or Caesar salad dressing.

- To mimic a crust, use the lid of the jar as a template to cut circles of sliced bread. Lightly toast and butter the bread (or toast English muffin halves), then invert the quiche on top to serve.

- For a very decadent dish, spoon warm Hollandaise Sauce (page 177) on top of the quiche in the jar or turned out onto a circle of toast.

Broccoli and Cheddar Strata

There's a reason you often see broccoli and Cheddar as a pairing — the flavors work great together, and you can often convince those who think they don't like broccoli to eat it when it's coated in cheese! This recipe won't require any convincing or bribes after the first bite. It's great for breakfast or lunch, served with a salad, and the leftovers even make a tasty portable, cold snack on the go.

> **MAKES
> 4 SERVINGS**
>
> Sous vide time:
> 1½ hours

Tips

For the best texture in this strata, buy a sturdy, dense whole wheat loaf from the bakery rather than a package of sliced bread; the sliced bread is too fluffy and will make for a soft, mushy texture.

If your baking dish is floating in the water bath, weigh it down with an inverted plate, adding a jar of hot water on top of the plate, if necessary, for extra weight.

We tested this in a casserole dish about 8 inches (20 cm) square by 2½ inches (6 cm) deep. If you're using a smaller, deeper dish, increase the cooking time to 2 hours.

Extra strata can be cooled, covered and refrigerated for up to 3 days to serve cold.

Variation

Replace the broccoli with chopped asparagus or cauliflower florets and/ or add ½ cup (125 mL) diced red or orange bell pepper with the broccoli in step 4.

- **Preheat water bath to 175°F (79°C)**
- **8-cup (2 L) shallow casserole or baking dish, buttered**
- **Extra-large resealable freezer bag**
- **Wire rack**

3 cups	broccoli florets	750 mL
4	slices whole wheat bread (½ inch/ 1 cm thick)	4
4	large eggs	4
¼ tsp	salt	1 mL
¼ tsp	freshly ground black pepper	1 mL
1 cup	milk	250 mL
1 tbsp	honey mustard or Dijon mustard	15 mL
1 cup	shredded sharp (old) Cheddar cheese	250 mL

1. In a saucepan of boiling water over high heat, blanch broccoli for about 2 minutes or until bright green. Drain and rinse under cold water to chill. Drain well.

2. Cut bread into quarters on the diagonal to make triangles.

3. In a large liquid measuring cup or bowl, whisk eggs, salt and pepper until blended. Whisk in milk and mustard.

4. Layer half the bread in prepared baking dish, overlapping slightly. Sprinkle with half the broccoli and half the cheese. Repeat with the remaining bread and broccoli. Press down with a spatula to compact slightly. Slowly pour in egg mixture, coating bread evenly. Press down again. Sprinkle with the remaining cheese.

5. Cut a square of parchment paper to fit just inside top of dish and place directly on the surface. Cover dish with foil, sealing tightly over the top. Place dish in freezer bag, remove excess air and seal bag.

6. Place wire rack in preheated water bath and place dish on rack; weigh down, if necessary. Cook for 1½ hours. To check for doneness, remove foil and parchment and insert the tip of a knife into the center of the strata; it should come out clean. If it doesn't, replace covers, return bag to water bath and cook, checking for doneness every 15 minutes.

7. If desired, preheat broiler with rack 8 inches (20 cm) from heat. Remove dish from bag, uncover and broil for 3 to 5 minutes or until top is browned.

8. To serve, cut into squares or wedges.

Bacon and Gouda Breakfast Strata

Turn leftover baguette into a decadent breakfast or brunch that is sure to please your guests. Let it cook in the water bath while you prepare the rest of the meal and, if you like, broil it for a few minutes to golden perfection. Fresh melon slices or tomatoes make complementary, colorful accompaniments.

MAKES 4 TO 6 SERVINGS

Sous vide time: 2 hours

Tips

You want the baguette to be at least a day old, or even 2 or 3 days old, so it's dry enough to soak in the egg mixture. But make sure it's not stale-tasting, as that will ruin the flavor of the dish.

When cooking sous vide in a casserole or baking dish, make sure it fits easily into your water bath with at least 1 inch (2.5 cm) around the outside of the dish to allow the water to circulate and cook evenly.

Variations

Instead of Gouda, use a pungent washed-rind cheese, such as Oka, or try Jarlsberg or Swiss.

For a Tex-Mex version, add 2 tbsp (30 mL) chopped fresh cilantro and 1 tsp (5 mL) chili powder with the spices, and use pepper Jack cheese instead of Gouda. Serve with salsa on the side.

- **Preheat water bath to 175°F (79°C)**
- **6-cup (1.5 L) casserole dish, buttered**
- **Extra-large resealable freezer bag**
- **Wire rack**

5	large eggs	5
½ tsp	sweet paprika	2 mL
¼ tsp	salt	1 mL
¼ tsp	freshly ground black pepper	1 mL
1 cup	milk	250 mL
1 tbsp	grainy or Dijon mustard	15 mL
8 oz	day-old baguette, cut into ¾-inch (2 cm) thick slices	250 g
3	slices bacon, cooked crisp and crumbled	3
1 cup	shredded Gouda cheese	250 mL

1. In a large liquid measuring cup or bowl, whisk eggs, paprika, salt and pepper until blended. Whisk in milk and mustard.

2. Layer half the bread in prepared baking dish, overlapping slightly. Sprinkle with half the bacon and half the cheese. Repeat with the remaining bread. Press down with a spatula to compact slightly. Slowly pour in egg mixture, coating bread evenly. Press down again. Sprinkle with the remaining bacon and cheese.

3. Cut a square of parchment paper to fit just inside top of dish and place directly on the surface. Cover dish with foil, sealing tightly over the top. Place dish in freezer bag, remove excess air and seal bag.

4. Place wire rack in preheated water bath and place dish on rack; weigh down, if necessary. Cook for 2 hours. To check for doneness, remove foil and parchment and insert the tip of a knife into the center of the strata; it should come out clean. If it doesn't, replace covers, return bag to water bath and cook, checking for doneness every 15 minutes.

5. If desired, preheat broiler with rack 8 inches (20 cm) from heat. Remove dish from bag, uncover and broil for 3 to 5 minutes or until golden brown.

6. To serve, cut into squares or wedges.

Smoked Salmon Strata

A strata is one of the easiest dishes to make for breakfast or brunch entertaining, as it doesn't require any fussing over the stovetop and you get to sit down and enjoy the meal too. This one also seems fancy with the smoked salmon, but a small amount goes a long way. Serve a lightly dressed salad or sliced tomatoes on the side.

**MAKES
4 SERVINGS**

Sous vide time:
2 hours

Tips

You want the bun or baguette to be at least a day old, or even 2 or 3 days old, so it's dry enough to soak in the egg mixture. But make sure it's not stale-tasting, as that will ruin the flavor of the dish.

If you're not a fan of goat cheese, you can substitute an equal amount of cream cheese.

When shopping for smoked salmon, we found small packages that range in size from 2 to 3 oz (60 to 90 g); any of these will work.

Some store-bought smoked salmon already has herbs (often dill) added. If yours is plain, consider adding $\frac{1}{4}$ tsp (1 mL) dried dillweed or tarragon, or add $\frac{1}{2}$ tsp (2 mL) grainy Dijon mustard to the egg mixture.

When cooking sous vide in a casserole or baking dish, make sure it fits easily into your water bath with at least 1 inch (2.5 cm) around the outside of the dish to allow the water to circulate and cook evenly.

- **Preheat water bath to 175°F (79°C)**
- **4- to 6-cup (1 to 1.5 L) shallow casserole or baking dish, buttered**
- **Extra-large resealable freezer bag**
- **Wire rack**

3 oz	soft goat cheese	90 g
3	large eggs	3
1 cup	milk	250 mL
$\frac{1}{4}$ tsp	freshly ground black pepper	1 mL
6 oz	day-old ciabatta bun or baguette, cut into $\frac{1}{4}$-inch (0.5 cm) thick slices	175 g
2 oz	thinly sliced smoked salmon (see tips)	60 g

1. Place goat cheese in a microwave-safe bowl and gently warm in the microwave on Medium-Low (30%) in 30-second intervals just until easy to stir but not hot or fluid.

2. In a large liquid measuring cup or bowl, whisk eggs, milk and pepper until blended. Whisk in goat cheese until nearly smooth, resembling liquidy cottage cheese.

3. Layer one-third of the bread in prepared baking dish, overlapping slightly if necessary. Arrange half the smoked salmon on top. Repeat with a layer of bread and the remaining salmon. Arrange the remaining bread on top, overlapping slightly. Press down with a spatula to compact slightly. Slowly pour in egg mixture, coating bread evenly, gently pressing with a spatula to help the liquid soak in completely.

4. Cut a square of parchment paper to fit just inside top of dish and place directly on the surface. Cover dish with foil, sealing tightly over the top. Place dish in freezer bag, remove excess air and seal bag.

5. Place wire rack in preheated water bath and place dish on rack; weigh down, if necessary. Cook for 2 hours. To check for doneness, remove foil and parchment and insert the tip of a knife into the center of the strata; it should come out clean. If it doesn't, replace covers, return bag to water bath and cook, checking for doneness every 15 minutes.

6. If desired, preheat broiler with rack 6 inches (15 cm) from heat. Remove dish from bag, uncover and broil for 3 to 5 minutes or until golden brown.

7. To serve, cut into squares or wedges.

Overnight Porridge

I love porridge. Plain, with added fruit, leftover — absolutely any way you serve it — and I could eat it every day. Even though I work from home, I don't always have time to cook steel-cut oats in the morning, so this overnight version is the perfect solution. With just a few minutes of effort the night before, you've got warm oatmeal ready when you wake up. I prefer the texture of this sous vide version, with grains that keep their shape and are toothsome yet tender, over the overnight slow cooker versions, which tends to be on the mushy side. ~ *Jennifer*

MAKES 4 SERVINGS

Sous vide time: 8 to 12 hours

Tips

Be sure to buy regular steel-cut oats, not quick-cooking steel-cut oats, as the quick-cooking oats will turn out very mushy with this method.

I usually like to cook my oats in milk, but the long time in the water bath causes curdling (that is how you make yogurt, after all!), so it's best to stick with water and just add a drizzle of milk on each serving, if you like.

The range in cooking time is for convenience. The oats should be nice and tender after 8 hours, but will still be good if you let them cook for up to 12 hours; beyond that, they do get a bit mushy.

Oatmeal can be cooled and refrigerated in the sealed bag or another airtight container for up to 5 days. Reheat in a saucepan over medium heat, stirring often, or reheat individual servings in the microwave on Medium-High (70%) for 1 to 3 minutes, until steaming.

- Preheat water bath to 155°F (68°C)
- Large resealable freezer bag

1 cup	steel-cut oats	250 mL
1/2 tsp	ground cinnamon	2 mL
1/4 tsp	salt	1 mL
3 cups	water	750 mL
	Additional ground cinnamon	

1. In freezer bag, combine oats, cinnamon and salt. Pour in water and gently shake bag to moisten oats evenly. Remove excess air and seal bag.

2. Cook in preheated water bath, covered, for 8 to 12 hours (see tip). Remove bag from water bath.

3. Stir oatmeal and spoon into warmed bowls. For piping hot oatmeal, heat individual servings in the microwave on High for 30 to 60 seconds. Add more cinnamon and any desired toppings (see serving suggestions).

Serving Suggestions

- Top with chopped apples or pears, sliced bananas, fresh or thawed frozen berries, or warm Stewed Breakfast Fruits (page 46).

- For added protein, sprinkle with chopped toasted nuts, hemp seeds, ground flax seeds (flaxseed meal), sunflower seeds or green pumpkin seeds and/or a spoonful of nut or seed butter.

- To add some sweetness, drizzle with pure maple syrup, liquid honey or agave syrup, or sprinkle with brown sugar. A few drops of vanilla extract adds a sweet taste without any sugar.

Stewed Breakfast Fruits

Dried fruits plumped up and aromatic with cinnamon, vanilla and citrus are the perfect accompaniment to Overnight Porridge (page 45), with the bonus that you can cook them together in the water bath. Stewed fruits are also delicious as a topping for cake, waffles or ice cream, or as a simple dessert on their own.

MAKES 4 TO 6 SERVINGS

Sous vide time: 4 to 12 hours

Tips

You can use any combination of dried fruit pieces totaling about 1½ cups (375 mL), including prunes, dates, pears, pineapple, mango and even coconut. Keep in mind that dark fruits like prunes and dates will tint the compote brown, making it quite dark, but it will still be tasty.

To peel a strip of zest, use a sharp vegetable peeler (we prefer the Y-shaped peelers) and peel off just the colored part of the peel, avoiding the white pith, which is bitter.

The compote will be ready after 4 hours in the water bath, but if you want to cook it overnight with oatmeal or other foods at the same temperature, it's fine to leave it in for as long as 12 hours.

The compote can be cooled and refrigerated in the sealed bag or another airtight container for up to 2 weeks. Serve cold, or warm individual servings in the microwave on Medium-High (70%) for about 1 minute.

- **Preheat water bath to 155°F (68°C)**
- **Medium resealable freezer bag**

1 cup	dried berries (cranberries, cherries, blueberries, strawberry slices), raisins and/or chopped dried apricots	250 mL
½ cup	dried apple slices	125 mL
1	3- by ½-inch (7.5 by 1 cm) strip orange or lemon zest	1
Pinch	ground cinnamon	Pinch
Pinch	vanilla bean powder (or ¼ tsp/ 1 mL vanilla extract)	Pinch
¾ cup	water	175 mL
1 tbsp	liquid honey or pure maple syrup	15 mL

1. In freezer bag, combine berries, apple slices, orange zest, cinnamon and vanilla bean powder. Add water and honey; swish bag gently to evenly moisten fruit. Remove excess air and seal bag.

2. Cook in preheated water bath, covered, for 4 to 12 hours (see tip). Remove bag from water bath.

3. Stir fruit, discard orange zest and serve warm, or let cool and refrigerate for at least 2 hours to serve cold.

Appetizers

Chilled Salmon Fillet with Chili Lime Mayonnaise and Onion Marmalade

One of my earliest memories of fresh fish is chilled salmon with mayonnaise served on Canada's West Coast by my great-aunt Jo. This modern take adds a little more heat to the mayo, as well as a vibrant, tangy, savory marmalade, but the simplicity and delicacy of the dish remains the same. ~ *Jay*

MAKES 8 SERVINGS

Sous vide time: 45 minutes

Tips

The center-cut portion of salmon works best for sous vide cooking, as it is typically an even thickness that will cook evenly; the tail end, which starts thicker and gets very thin, won't have the same cooked texture throughout.

Keeping the skin on the salmon helps keep it from falling apart when you remove it from the bag.

The marmalade and mayonnaise benefit from being made ahead to let the flavors meld, making this a perfect dish for entertaining. Make the marmalade at least a few days ahead and the mayonnaise the day ahead. The salmon can be cooked a day ahead, too, or a few hours before you plan to serve it.

- **Preheat water bath to 130°F (54.5°C)**
- **Medium resealable freezer bag**

1 lb	skin-on center-cut salmon fillet	500 g
	Salt and freshly ground black pepper	

Red Onion Marmalade

½	red onion, thinly sliced	½
2 tbsp	granulated sugar	30 mL
¼ cup	red wine vinegar	60 mL

Chili Lime Mayonnaise

1 cup	mayonnaise	250 mL
2 tsp	Sriracha	10 mL
½ tsp	grated lime zest	2 mL
1 tsp	freshly squeezed lime juice	5 mL

1. Rinse salmon and pat dry. Season flesh side with salt and pepper. Place salmon in freezer bag. Remove excess air and seal.

2. Cook in preheated water bath for 45 minutes.

3. Remove bag from water bath and immerse in ice water to cool completely. Place sealed bag in the refrigerator for at least 2 hours, until salmon is chilled, or for up to 1 day.

4. *Marmalade:* Meanwhile, in a small saucepan, combine onion, sugar and vinegar. Bring to a gentle boil over medium-high heat, stirring to dissolve sugar. Reduce heat and simmer, stirring often, for 5 to 10 minutes or until liquid reduces to a jammy consistency and onion is tender. Transfer to a bowl or container and let cool. Cover and refrigerate for at least 1 hour or up to 1 week.

Variation

For a milder-flavored mayo, replace the Sriracha and lime with 1 tbsp (15 mL) basil pesto or 1 tbsp (15 mL) chopped fresh tarragon.

5. *Mayonnaise:* In a small bowl, whisk together mayonnaise, Sriracha, lime zest and lime juice. Cover and refrigerate until serving, for up to 1 day.

6. Remove salmon from bag, discarding liquid, and transfer to a plate or cutting board. Pat dry and transfer to a serving platter with the skin side down. Serve chili lime mayonnaise and marmalade in small side bowls alongside.

Serving Suggestions

- Serve with warm slices of fresh baguette or your favorite crackers for diners to top with salmon, mayonnaise and onion marmalade. Slices of cucumber, cut on the diagonal to make long oval slices, are also a good base in place of bread or crackers.

- Create a salad with this salmon by tossing torn romaine lettuce with some of the mayonnaise, then top with chilled salmon, onion marmalade and a dollop of mayonnaise.

Lettuce Wraps with Shrimp in Spicy Peanut Sauce

We love any excuse to make, and eat, Thai-style peanut sauce. These tender, plump shrimp cooked in and drizzled with peanut sauce and wrapped in fresh lettuce will obliterate any thoughts of serving a plain old shrimp ring as an appetizer at all future parties. In fact, your guests might start insisting that these gems appear on the menu. They also make for a great dinner salad on a hot summer night.

MAKES 8 SERVINGS

Sous vide time:
15 minutes

Tips

When measuring a portion of a can of coconut milk, open the can and whisk the milk well to combine the solid and liquid layers that tend to separate, then measure the amount for your recipe. Extra coconut milk can be refrigerated in a jar or other airtight container for up to 3 days or frozen for up to 3 months.

Arranging the shrimp so they are somewhat straight and lined up in the freezer bag helps them cook up in a nice shape that sits well on the lettuce leaf.

You can easily double this recipe, using 2 medium freezer bags for the shrimp (it's tricky to arrange a larger amount of shrimp in a large bag).

- **Preheat water bath to 140°F (60°C)**
- **Medium resealable freezer bag**

1	small clove garlic, minced	1
1 tsp	minced gingerroot	5 mL
⅓ cup	well-stirred coconut milk (see tip)	75 mL
2 tsp	reduced-sodium soy sauce	10 mL
3 tbsp	smooth peanut butter, divided	45 mL
1½ tsp	Sriracha or other Asian hot sauce, divided	7 mL
1 tbsp	freshly squeezed lime juice	15 mL
24	large (31/40 count) shrimp, thawed, peeled and deveined (about 12 oz/375 g)	24
24	small butter or Boston lettuce leaves (or 12 larger leaves, torn in half)	24
	Chopped fresh Thai basil or cilantro (optional)	

1. In a small saucepan, combine garlic, ginger, coconut milk and soy sauce. Bring to a boil over medium heat, stirring. Reduce heat and boil for 1 minute or until garlic is softened. Remove from heat and whisk in half the peanut butter and 1 tsp (5 mL) Sriracha until blended and smooth. Transfer 2 tbsp (30 mL) of the sauce to a medium bowl.

2. Whisk lime juice and the remaining peanut butter into the saucepan until blended. Transfer to a small bowl and set aside.

3. Stir the remaining Sriracha into the 2 tbsp (30 mL) reserved sauce. Pat shrimp dry and add to sauce, tossing to evenly coat.

To make ahead, prepare
through step 5, then
immerse bag in ice water
to chill. Refrigerate in
the sealed bag for up
to 2 days, storing the
peanut sauce separately
in an airtight container.
Proceed with step 6,
serving the shrimp
cold; reheat the peanut
sauce over low heat in
a saucepan, stirring,
or in the microwave
on Medium (50%) in
30-second intervals, just
until semifluid.

4. Transfer shrimp to freezer bag and add any remaining sauce from the medium bowl. Arrange shrimp in a single layer, straightening and lining them up against each other as best as possible. Remove excess air and seal bag.

5. Cook in preheated water bath for 15 minutes. Remove bag from water bath and let rest for 3 minutes.

6. Arrange lettuce leaves on serving plates or a platter. Remove shrimp from bag, discarding liquid, and arrange 1 shrimp on each lettuce leaf. Using a spoon, drizzle the reserved peanut sauce on top. Garnish with basil, if desired. Serve immediately.

Thai Shrimp Peanut Salad

To make this into a main course salad for 4 people, add more lettuce leaves to create a bed of lettuce on each serving plate. Julienne half an English cucumber, 1 large carrot and 1 red bell pepper and arrange on top of lettuce with the shrimp, then drizzle with peanut sauce. Garnish with chopped Thai basil, bean sprouts and chopped roasted peanuts, if desired.

Smoky Turkey Drumsticks

When we go to Disney World, the vacation isn't complete until we indulge in smoked turkey drumsticks. With the discovery that our sous vide can help us make these sweet and smoky turkey legs at home, we don't have to wait for a vacation to enjoy them. They're a terrific treat for summer barbecues and tailgate parties. They do take a bit of planning, and a couple of days to make (mostly hands-off), but they're worth it. The brine helps keep the meat juicy, the sous vide cooks the meat up nice and tender, and a quick sear on the barbecue crisps up the skin.

**MAKES
2 SERVINGS**

Sous vide time:
24 hours

Tips

For the best flavor when making brine, always use a pure salt with no additives such as iodine. Additives can add a metallic or medicinal taste. If using a coarse salt, you may need to let the brine stand for a bit, to help the salt dissolve, before adding the turkey.

Liquid smoke is available in well-stocked grocery stores, often shelved with barbecue sauces. It is potent, so we use only a touch to give a smoky flavor.

- **Large resealable freezer bag (see tip)**
- **Barbecue grill**

Brine

¼ cup	kosher or other pure salt	60 mL
4 cups	water	1 L
2 tbsp	pure maple syrup or packed brown sugar	30 mL
2	turkey drumsticks	2
	Salt	
	Vegetable oil or cooking spray	

Sauce

1 tbsp	packed brown sugar	15 mL
¼ tsp	ground ginger	1 mL
¼ tsp	chili powder	1 mL
¼ tsp	ground cumin	1 mL
¼ tsp	dried oregano	1 mL
¼ tsp	freshly ground black pepper	1 mL
1 tbsp	apple cider vinegar	15 mL
1 tbsp	olive oil	15 mL
¼ tsp	liquid smoke	1 mL

1. *Brine:* In freezer bag, combine salt, water and maple syrup, shaking bag to dissolve salt.
2. Add turkey drumsticks to brine and squeeze out most of the air, so brine surrounds turkey. Seal bag. Place bag in a bowl and refrigerate overnight or up to 12 hours.
3. Preheat water bath to 145°F (63°C).
4. Remove drumsticks from brine, discarding brine, and transfer to a plate. Pat dry. Rinse freezer bag.

Tips

You should be able to use the same freezer bag to brine the turkey and to cook it sous vide. After dumping out the brine, rinse the bag well to remove any excess salt and check carefully that there are no holes and the seal still zips tight. To do this, add some water, seal the bag and gently squeeze to make sure the air and water don't spurt out. If there are any holes, use a new bag to cook the turkey.

You can double, triple or even quadruple this recipe for more turkey drumsticks. Cook 2 per large bag and ensure that the sous vide container is large enough to accommodate the bags with good circulation.

5. *Sauce:* In a large bowl, combine brown sugar, ginger, chili powder, cumin, oregano, pepper, vinegar, oil and liquid smoke, stirring until sugar is dissolved. Add drumsticks, turning to evenly coat with sauce.

6. Transfer drumsticks to freezer bag and add any remaining sauce. Remove excess air and seal bag.

7. Cook in preheated water bath, covered, for 24 hours, replenishing water as necessary to keep meat immersed. Remove bag from water bath and let rest for 10 minutes.

8. Preheat barbecue grill to medium.

9. Remove drumsticks from bag, discarding liquid, and transfer to a clean plate. Gently pat dry (don't remove all of the seasoning, just the excess liquid) and season lightly with salt.

10. Oil grill and place drumsticks on grill. Grill, turning about 3 times, for 2 to 3 minutes per side or until skin is crispy and golden brown. Serve hot.

Variations

To broil instead of grilling, preheat broiler with rack 8 inches (20 cm) from heat. Place drumsticks on a foil-lined baking sheet and broil, turning about 3 times and rotating baking sheet as necessary, for 2 to 3 minutes per side or until skin is crispy and golden brown.

Baste the grilled turkey drumsticks with your favorite barbecue sauce or glaze right before serving.

Pork Tenderloin Souvlaki Skewers

These appetizer skewers are smaller versions of the traditional souvlaki marinated in oil and lemon and cooked on the grill. Sous vide keeps the meat juicy and the skewers require just a short time on the grill to finish cooking.

Sous vide time:
1½ hours

Tips

For extra zing, cut a lemon in half and grill it with the skewers. Squeeze fresh juice over the skewers before serving.

To make ahead, prepare through step 3, then immerse bag in ice water to chill. Refrigerate in the sealed bag for up to 3 days. Reheat in a 140°F (60°C) water bath for 15 minutes, then proceed with step 4.

Variation

For 4 entrée servings, use only 4 skewers, with more meat on each one.

- **Preheat water bath to 140°F (60°C)**
- **Eight 6-inch (15 cm) bamboo skewers**
- **Large resealable freezer bag**
- **Barbecue grill**

½ tsp	dried oregano	2 mL
¼ tsp	salt	1 mL
¼ tsp	freshly ground black pepper	1 mL
2 tbsp	olive oil	30 mL
2 tbsp	freshly squeezed lemon juice	30 mL
1	pork tenderloin (about 1 lb/500 g), trimmed and cut into 24 chunks	1
	Vegetable oil or cooking spray	

1. In a shallow bowl, combine oregano, salt, pepper, oil and lemon juice. Add pork chunks and toss to coat completely.
2. Thread 3 pork chunks onto each skewer. Place skewers in freezer bag, spacing them apart (be careful not to poke the bag with the skewers), and add any remaining oil mixture. Remove excess air and seal bag.
3. Cook in preheated water bath for 1½ hours. Remove bag from water bath and let rest for 10 minutes.
4. Meanwhile, preheat barbecue grill to medium-high.
5. Remove skewers from bag, discarding liquid, and transfer to a plate. Gently pat dry (don't remove all of the seasoning, just the excess liquid).
6. Oil grill and place skewers on grill. Grill, turning two or three times, for about 2 minutes per side or until sizzling and marked. Transfer skewers to a platter and serve hot.

Serving Suggestion

- After grilling, you can also turn these into an excellent wrap by removing the skewers and placing the meat in a warmed pita with tomatoes, cucumbers and yogurt.

Maple Whiskey Glazed Chicken Wings

A perfect snack for poker night, movie night or an evening with friends on the patio, these wings bring the sweet and the heat. By cooking the wings sous vide, you get fall-off-the-bone-tender meat, and the broiler crisps up the skin just perfectly. It's a much less messy and more reliable method than frying, and just might become your new favorite way to cook wings. Serve with your favorite dipping sauce, such as ranch, blue cheese or Spicy Mayo (page 62) — and lots of napkins.

**MAKES
4 SERVINGS**

**Sous vide time:
2 hours**

Tips

Liquid smoke is available in well-stocked grocery stores, often shelved with the barbecue sauces. It is potent, so we use only a touch to give a smoky flavor. If you don't have any on hand, use ¼ tsp (1 mL) smoked paprika or smoked sea salt, or reduce the hot pepper flakes to ¼ tsp (1 mL) and add ¼ tsp (1 mL) chipotle chile powder.

You can double the recipe, using 2 large freezer bags. Just be sure there is enough room in the water bath to allow the water to circulate around the bags.

To make wings ahead, prepare through step 3, then immerse bag in ice water to chill. Refrigerate in the sealed bag for up to 3 days or freeze for up to 3 months. Thaw in the refrigerator overnight, if frozen. Reheat in a 170°F (77°C) water bath for 30 minutes, then proceed with step 4.

- Preheat water bath to 170°F (77°C)
- Large resealable freezer bag
- Large rimmed baking sheet, lined with foil

½ tsp	hot pepper flakes	2 mL
	Salt	
½ tsp	freshly ground black pepper	2 mL
1 tbsp	pure maple syrup	15 mL
1 tbsp	whiskey	15 mL
¼ tsp	liquid smoke	1 mL
2 lbs	chicken wings, split, tips removed	1 kg

1. In a small bowl, combine hot pepper flakes, ½ tsp (2 mL) salt, black pepper, maple syrup, whiskey and liquid smoke.

2. Pat wings dry. Place wings in freezer bag and pour in sauce. Turn bag and gently massage wings to evenly coat with sauce. Arrange wings in a single layer. Remove excess air and seal bag.

3. Cook in preheated water bath for 2 hours. Remove bag from water bath and let rest for 5 minutes.

4. Meanwhile, preheat broiler with rack 4 inches (10 cm) from heat.

5. Carefully dump wings from bag into a colander set in the sink, letting excess liquid drain off. Arrange wings on prepared baking sheet, spacing them apart. Season both sides with salt.

6. Broil wings for 2 to 3 minutes, turning once, until golden brown and glazed. Serve immediately.

Variation

Buffalo Wings: For a classic Buffalo-style sauce, substitute 2 tbsp (30 mL) prepared Buffalo hot sauce for the maple-whiskey mixture. Omit the salt before broiling and toss the wings with more hot sauce after broiling, if desired (but be gentle, as they are very tender).

Hoisin-Glazed Chicken Meatballs

Meatballs are ever-popular appetizers and are often the first thing to get gobbled up. These meatballs with an Asian twist are a tasty treat, perfect for parties. Careful you don't eat them all before your guests arrive.

Tips

Food-safe disposable gloves are great for keeping your hands clean and preventing cross-contamination of food and surfaces, and are especially helpful with this sticky ground chicken mixture. Any time you handle raw poultry or meat, be sure to completely sanitize all tools and work surfaces when you are finished.

Chilling and freezing the moist, sticky chicken mixture is essential to shaping it into balls that hold their shape when sous vide cooking.

To make meatballs ahead, prepare through step 4 (skipping step 3) and freeze for up to 2 months. Preheat water bath as directed in step 3 and cook from frozen, increasing the cooking time to 2½ hours. Measure out the extra hoisin and chop the cilantro for glazing and garnishing the day you cook the meatballs.

If you're not a fan of cilantro, substitute chopped fresh flat-leaf (Italian) parsley or minced green onion.

- **Medium resealable freezer bag**
- **Baking sheet or plate, lined with plastic wrap**
- **Baking sheet, lined with foil**

1	large egg	1
1 lb	lean (85% to 90%) ground chicken	500 g
⅓ cup	quick-cooking rolled oats	75 mL
2 tbsp	chopped fresh cilantro, divided	30 mL
½ tsp	salt	2 mL
¼ tsp	hot pepper flakes	1 mL
3 tbsp	hoisin sauce, divided	45 mL
1	lime, cut into wedges	1

1. In a large bowl, using a fork, whisk egg until blended. Stir in chicken, oats, 1 tbsp (15 mL) cilantro, salt, hot pepper flakes and 2 tbsp (30 mL) hoisin sauce until well mixed. Cover and refrigerate for 1 hour.

2. Using a spoon or small ice cream scoop, divide chicken mixture into 16 equal portions, placing them on the plastic-lined baking sheet. Cover with plastic wrap and freeze for 1 hour.

3. Meanwhile, preheat water bath to 148°F (64°C).

4. Working quickly (the mixture gets sticky as it warms up), remove meat from freezer and roll each portion into a ball. Place meatballs in freezer bag, spacing them apart. Remove excess air and seal bag.

5. Cook in preheated water bath for 2 hours. Remove bag from water bath and let rest for 5 minutes.

6. Meanwhile, preheat broiler with rack 6 inches (15 cm) from heat.

7. In a large bowl, combine 2 tsp (10 mL) cilantro and the remaining hoisin sauce. Using a slotted spoon, carefully remove meatballs from bag, discarding liquid, and transfer to the bowl. Stir gently to coat completely. Arrange meatballs on the foil-lined baking sheet, spacing them apart.

8. Broil meatballs for 6 to 8 minutes or until bubbling and glazed. Serve in a warmed dish or platter, garnished with lime wedges and the remaining cilantro.

Sandwiches, Wraps and Salads

Roast Beef Sandwiches with Shaved Eye of Round, Caramelized Onions and Swiss Cheese

Take a tougher cut of meat like eye of round and turn it into a fabulously tender chunk of beef just perfect for thinly slicing and piling on a sandwich. This combination of beef, cheese and onions tastes like French onion soup, but in a sandwich.

MAKES 4 TO 6 SERVINGS

Sous vide time: 36 hours

Tips

The beef can be served warm immediately after cooking at the end of step 4, but it's much easier to slice thin once it's chilled. Use a very sharp knife and long, firm strokes to slice it very thin.

You can make the entire sandwich cold if you prefer; just skip the broiling steps.

- **Preheat water bath to 130°F (54.5°C)**
- **Medium resealable freezer bag**

1 lb	center-cut beef eye of round roast (3- to 4-inch/7.5 to 10 cm diameter), tied	500 g
1 tsp	freshly ground black pepper	5 mL
	Salt	
1 tbsp	vegetable oil	15 mL
4 to 6	crusty rolls or 5-inch (12.5 cm) lengths of baguette, split	4 to 6
8 to 12	thin slices Swiss cheese	8 to 12

Caramelized Onions

1 tbsp	vegetable oil	15 mL
1	medium onion, thinly sliced	1
½ tsp	pink peppercorns, crushed, or cracked black pepper	2 mL
¼ tsp	salt	1 mL
¼ tsp	dried rosemary, crumbled	1 mL

1. Pat roast dry and place on a plate. Rub pepper and ¼ tsp (1 mL) salt all over roast.

2. In a large skillet, heat oil over medium-high heat until shimmering. Sear roast on all sides until golden brown. Return to plate and let cool.

3. Place beef in freezer bag. Remove excess air and seal bag.

4. Cook in preheated water bath, covered, for 36 hours, replenishing water as necessary to keep meat immersed.

5. *Caramelized Onions:* Meanwhile, in a large skillet, heat oil over medium heat until shimmering. Add onion, pink peppercorns, salt and rosemary; cook, stirring, for about 5 minutes or until onion starts to soften. Reduce heat to medium-low and cook, stirring often, for about 30 minutes or until onion is very soft and golden brown. Transfer to a bowl or container and let cool. Cover and refrigerate until ready to use, for up to 5 days.

Variation

For a spicy touch, spread the cut sides of the toasted (or untoasted) rolls with Spicy Mayo (page 62) before adding the onions and cheese.

6. Remove bag from water bath and immerse in ice water to cool completely. Refrigerate for at least 1 hour, until chilled, or for up to 5 days.

7. Just before serving, preheat broiler with rack 6 inches (15 cm) from heat. Remove caramelized onions from refrigerator.

8. Remove roast from bag, discarding any liquid, and transfer to a cutting board. Thinly slice beef across the grain.

9. Place rolls, cut side up, on a baking sheet. Broil for about 2 minutes or until lightly toasted. Spoon caramelized onions onto bottoms of toasted rolls and arrange cheese slices on cut side of roll tops. Broil for 2 to 3 minutes or until cheese is melted and onions are warmed.

10. Pile shaved beef on top of onions, sprinkle with salt and top with cheesy roll tops. Serve immediately.

Serving Suggestion

• Add sliced tomatoes, pickles, lettuce, barbecue sauce or mayonnaise to up your sandwich game.

Coffee Barbecue Pulled Pork Sandwiches with Apple Slaw

This coffee barbecue sauce is one we created years ago when we owned our gourmet food store, where we sold brewed coffee, among many other things. Rather than tossing unsold coffee out, we simmered it in this zesty sauce, and it became a huge hit for pulled pork. Even people who don't enjoy drinking coffee love this dish. The sous vide creates a tender, flavorful pork, with a perfect texture for shredding, and the sauce cooks right in without the need to babysit the pork while it's cooking (other than topping up the water), which makes it great for entertaining.

MAKES 8 SERVINGS

Sous vide time: 14 hours

Tips

To brew the coffee for the barbecue sauce, use twice as much coffee as you would for a typical cup. If you want to avoid caffeine, use a good-quality brewed decaffeinated coffee, making sure to brew it double-strength to add a good, deep flavor to the sauce.

For the slaw, use a tart-sweet apple, such as Cortland, Empire, Granny Smith, Crispin or McIntosh. To julienne, cut thin lengthwise slices of unpeeled apple, parallel to the core, working all around the core. Stack a few slices at a time, cut side down, on the cutting board and cut them into thin, matchstick-size strips.

- Long metal skewer
- Large resealable freezer bag

Coffee Barbecue Sauce

1/2 cup	packed brown sugar	125 mL
2 tbsp	dry mustard	30 mL
1/2 tsp	ground ginger	2 mL
1 1/2 cups	strong brewed coffee (see tip)	375 mL
1/2 cup	light (fancy) molasses	125 mL
1/2 cup	apple cider vinegar	125 mL
1/4 cup	ketchup	60 mL
	Salt and freshly ground black pepper	
1 tsp	hot pepper sauce	5 mL
3 lb	boneless pork shoulder (butt) roast	1.5 kg
8	kaiser, ciabatta or other buns, split	8

Apple Slaw

1 tsp	ground coriander	5 mL
1/2 tsp	dry or Dijon mustard	2 mL
Pinch	salt	Pinch
	Freshly ground black pepper	
1/2 cup	mayonnaise or whipped salad dressing	125 mL
2 tbsp	apple cider vinegar	30 mL
1	large apple, julienned (see tip)	1
2 cups	shredded green cabbage or coleslaw mix	500 mL

1. *Barbecue Sauce:* In a deep saucepan, combine brown sugar, mustard, ginger, coffee, molasses, vinegar and ketchup. Bring to a boil over medium heat, stirring to dissolve sugar. Reduce heat and boil gently, stirring often, for about 20 minutes or until reduced by about half. Remove from heat. Stir in 1/4 tsp (1 mL) salt, pepper to taste and hot pepper sauce. Let cool completely.

Tip

To make ahead, prepare through step 6 (without making the slaw), then place the shredded pork in an airtight container or bowl and toss with the reserved barbecue sauce; let cool, cover and refrigerate for up to 3 days or freeze for up to 3 months. Refrigerate or freeze the reserved cooking liquid separately. Thaw overnight in the refrigerator, if necessary. Make the slaw up to 1 day ahead, then, when ready to serve, heat pork as directed in step 7.

Variation

Use a 4-lb (2 kg) bone-in pork shoulder blade roast and increase the cooking time to 16 hours.

2. Preheat water bath to 160°F (71°C).

3. Pat pork dry. Using the skewer, pierce roast several times all over. Place roast in freezer bag and pour in ¾ cup (175 mL) of the barbecue sauce. Turn bag and gently massage pork to evenly coat with marinade. Remove excess air and seal bag. Transfer the remaining barbecue sauce to a jar or other airtight container and refrigerate while cooking pork.

4. Cook pork in preheated water bath, covered, for 14 hours, replenishing water as necessary to keep meat immersed. The pork should be tender; if it isn't, return bag to water bath and cook, checking for doneness every 30 minutes. Remove bag from water bath and let stand for 15 minutes.

5. *Apple Slaw:* Meanwhile, in a large bowl, whisk together coriander, mustard, salt, pepper to taste, mayonnaise and vinegar. Add apple and cabbage, tossing to coat. Cover and refrigerate for at least 1 hour, to blend the flavors, or for up to 24 hours.

6. Remove pork from bag, reserving cooking liquid, and transfer to a bowl. Pour liquid into a measuring cup or jar and skim off and discard any fat that floats to the top. Set aside. Using your hands or two forks, shred pork into bite-size pieces, discarding fat.

7. In a large saucepan or skillet, combine shredded pork and reserved barbecue sauce, tossing to coat. Heat over medium heat, stirring gently, until bubbling hot, adding just enough reserved cooking liquid to moisten pork as desired. Season to taste with salt and pepper. Serve hot pork on buns, topped with apple slaw.

Sweet Shrimp Po'boy Sandwiches with Spicy Mayo

Typically, Louisiana-style po'boy sandwiches are made with battered and fried seafood. This sous vide version strays from tradition with tender shrimp with more of a poached texture, but the spicy mayo and tangy slaw are odes to the original. Serve crispy fries or chips on the side to add crunch. The shrimp are so tasty and have such a fabulous texture, they make a terrific appetizer on their own, too.

**MAKES
4 SERVINGS**

**Sous vide time:
15 minutes**

Tips

If jumbo shrimp aren't available, large will work in this recipe with the same cooking time. Avoid very large (extra-jumbo or colossal) shrimp, which tend to have a firmer, sometimes tough, texture. On the other hand, if the shrimp are too small, they may get tough in the time it takes to cook and pasteurize them.

You can use 2½ cups (625 mL) shredded coleslaw mix from a bag in place of the carrot and cabbage. You can even change up the flavor by using a broccoli or kale slaw, if you like. But don't skip the pickles — they're an essential po'boy ingredient.

- **Preheat water bath to 140°F (60°C)**
- **Medium resealable freezer bag**

2 tbsp	packed brown sugar	30 mL
Pinch	dried thyme	Pinch
Pinch	cayenne pepper	Pinch
2 tbsp	bourbon	30 mL
1 lb	jumbo (21/25 count) shrimp, thawed, peeled and deveined	500 g
4	soft buns, split	4
¼	lemon	¼
	Salt	

Tangy Slaw

1	medium carrot, shredded	1
2 cups	shredded green cabbage	500 mL
¼ cup	finely chopped drained pickles (sweet or dill)	60 mL
2 tbsp	pickle brine	30 mL
	Salt and freshly ground black pepper	

Spicy Mayo

¼ cup	mayonnaise	60 mL
1 tbsp	hot pepper sauce (such as Frank's)	15 mL

1. In freezer bag, combine sugar, thyme, cayenne and bourbon; gently shake and swish the bag to dissolve the sugar. Pat shrimp dry and add to bag. Turn bag and gently massage shrimp to evenly coat with marinade. Refrigerate for 15 minutes.

2. *Tangy Slaw:* Meanwhile, in a medium bowl, combine carrot, cabbage, pickles and brine. Season to taste with salt and pepper. Let stand at room temperature while the shrimp marinates and cooks.

Tip

To make ahead, prepare the shrimp as directed in steps 1 and 4, then immerse the bag in ice water to chill. Refrigerate in the sealed bag for up to 3 days. Make the spicy mayo, cover and refrigerate separately. The day you plan to serve the sandwiches, prepare the slaw up to 4 hours ahead. Serve cold.

Variation

In place of the bourbon, use another whiskey or rum. Or for a nonalcoholic version, use unsweetened pineapple juice.

3. *Spicy Mayo:* In a small bowl, combine mayonnaise and hot pepper sauce. Cover and refrigerate while the shrimp marinates and cooks.

4. Cook shrimp in preheated water bath for 15 minutes.

5. Meanwhile, if desired, preheat broiler with rack 6 inches (15 cm) from heat and toast cut sides of buns.

6. Remove bag from water bath. Using a slotted spoon, remove shrimp from bag, discarding liquid, and transfer to a medium bowl. Squeeze lemon over shrimp and season lightly with salt; toss to combine.

7. Spread spicy mayo on cut sides of buns. Pile shrimp and slaw on bun bottoms, then sandwich with bun tops. Serve immediately.

Serving Suggestions

- Make a splash at your next appetizer potluck. Marinate and cook the shrimp as directed, then chill them (see tip). Make the spicy mayo but skip the slaw. Serve the shrimp on a bed of ice, with the mayo for dipping, as a change from the traditional cocktail shrimp.

- Make 12 mini po'boy sliders, using small slider buns or dinner rolls. After assembling, secure the buns with toothpicks or bamboo skewers.

Lamb Meatballs with Yogurt Greek Salad in Pitas

Cooking meatballs sous vide, then finishing them under the broiler or in a skillet, produces super-tender and juicy meatballs with perfect browning on the outside — without the mess of frying or the trickiness of getting them perfectly cooked in the center without being dry. The Greek-inspired seasoning works equally well with lamb or beef, and the meatballs make a hearty pita pocket with a chunky vegetable salad dressed with yogurt.

Tips

Ground meat that is about 85% to 90% lean is best for these meatballs. There is enough fat to keep them moist and tender, but not so much that they fall apart or become greasy.

It's easier to arrange meatballs in a few smaller bags than in one large one, to keep them spaced apart, which helps them keep their shape. If they are touching in the bag, they stick together and cook up in some very odd shapes.

- Baking sheet, lined with plastic wrap or parchment paper
- 3 medium resealable freezer bags
- Baking sheet, lined with foil and lightly oiled

1	large egg	1
1	clove garlic, minced	1
2 tsp	grated lemon zest	10 mL
1 tsp	dried oregano	5 mL
½ tsp	freshly ground black pepper (approx.)	2 mL
Pinch	hot pepper flakes	Pinch
	Salt	
1½ lbs	lean ground lamb or beef (see tip)	750 g
¼ cup	dry bread crumbs	60 mL
4 to 6	medium (6- to 7-inch/15 to 18 cm) pitas with pocket	4 to 6

Yogurt Greek Salad

½ cup	plain Greek yogurt	125 mL
2 tbsp	extra virgin olive oil (approx.)	30 mL
1	large tomato, seeded and chopped	1
½	red or yellow bell pepper, chopped	½
1 cup	chopped cucumber	250 mL
¼ cup	chopped red onion (optional)	60 mL
2 tbsp	quartered pitted kalamata or other black olives	30 mL
	Salt and freshly ground black pepper	

1. In a large bowl, using a fork, whisk together egg, garlic, lemon zest, oregano, black pepper, hot pepper flakes and 1 tsp (5 mL) salt. Add lamb and bread crumbs, mixing with the fork just until evenly blended (do not overwork).

Tip

To make meatballs ahead, prepare through step 6, then immerse bags in ice water to chill. Refrigerate in the sealed bags for up to 3 days or freeze for up to 6 months. Thaw in the refrigerator overnight, if frozen. Reheat in a 140°F (60°C) water bath for 30 minutes, until warmed through, then proceed with step 7.

Variation

Instead of using the broiler to brown the meatballs, heat a large nonstick skillet over medium-high heat. Brush or spray a thin layer of oil over skillet. Add meatballs, in batches as necessary, and sear, turning to brown all sides, for 2 to 3 minutes, then transfer to a plate. Adjust heat and oil pan between batches as necessary.

2. Heat a small skillet over medium heat. Make a patty with about 2 tsp (10 mL) of the meat mixture and cook, turning once, for about 5 minutes or until no longer pink. Taste for seasoning. Add more salt and pepper to the meat mixture, if necessary, being careful not to overwork the meat.

3. Shape heaping tablespoonfuls (15 mL) of meat mixture into 1½-inch (4 cm) balls and place on plastic wrap–lined baking sheet, spacing them apart. Freeze for 15 to 30 minutes or until firm but not solid.

4. Meanwhile, preheat water bath to 140°F (60°C).

5. Place about 8 meatballs in each freezer bag, spacing them apart. Remove excess air and seal bags.

6. Cook in preheated water bath for 2 hours.

7. *Salad:* Meanwhile, in a medium bowl, whisk together yogurt and oil. Add tomato, red pepper, cucumber, red onion (if using) and olives. Toss to coat, adding a little more oil, if necessary, to thin the yogurt. Season to taste with salt and pepper. Set aside while you finish the meatballs.

8. Remove bag from water bath and let rest for 5 minutes.

9. Preheat broiler with rack 4 inches (10 cm) from heat.

10. Using tongs or a slotted spoon, remove meatballs from bag, discarding liquid, and arrange on foil-lined baking sheet, spacing them apart. Broil, turning once, for 4 to 6 minutes or until browned.

11. Cut about one-third off top of pitas, open pockets and stuff the trimmed-off portion into the bottom of each pita. Fill with meatballs and salad. Serve immediately.

Fresh Fajitas with Carne Asada and Avocado Pineapple Salsa

Carne asada translates as "grilled meat" and there is no definitive authentic version for the marinade, it seems. The only consensus I can find is that it must be flavorful while letting the beefy taste shine through. This version is based on one from Canada Beef that I cooked for a TV segment several years ago, and it's been a favorite for entertaining ever since. Now, with sous vide cooking for the first stage and a quick finish on a hot grill, it's even more convenient to make for guests. *~ Jennifer*

**MAKES
4 SERVINGS**

Sous vide time:
4 hours

Tips

If you don't have steak sauce on hand, the Sweet and Tangy Barbecue Sauce on page 123 makes a good substitute, or try a not-too-sweet bottled barbecue sauce. Use ¼ cup (60 mL) sauce and add 1 tbsp (15 mL) Worcestershire sauce for an extra punch of flavor.

We prefer a flaky sea salt, such as fleur de sel, freshly ground sea salt or kosher salt, for seasoning meats after sous vide cooking, for the pleasant, clean burst of salt flavor it contributes, but you can use any salt you have on hand.

The longer you let the steak marinate, the more the flavors will infuse into the meat.

- **Large resealable freezer bag**
- **Barbecue grill**

1 tsp	chili powder	5 mL
1 tsp	dried oregano	5 mL
½ tsp	garlic powder	2 mL
½ tsp	ground cumin	2 mL
¼ cup	steak sauce (such as HP sauce)	60 mL
1½ lb	beef flank steak	750 g
	Salt and freshly ground black pepper	
	Vegetable oil or cooking spray	
4	large (10-inch/25 cm) flour tortillas	4

Avocado Pineapple Salsa

1	large tomato, chopped	1
½	red bell pepper, chopped	½
1 cup	diced pineapple	250 mL
2 tbsp	finely chopped red onion	30 mL
½ tsp	grated lime zest	2 mL
2 tbsp	freshly squeezed lime juice	30 mL
½ tsp	hot pepper sauce (approx.)	2 mL
	Salt	
1	medium avocado	1

1. In a small bowl, combine chili powder, oregano, garlic powder, cumin and steak sauce.
2. Place steak in freezer bag and pour in marinade. Turn bag and gently massage steak to evenly coat with sauce. Remove excess air and seal bag. Refrigerate for at least 4 hours or up to 1 day.
3. Preheat water bath to 130°F (54.5°C) for medium-rare (see variation, page 23).
4. Cook steak in preheated water bath, covered, for 4 hours.

5. *Salsa:* Meanwhile, in a medium bowl, combine tomato, red pepper, pineapple, onion, lime zest, lime juice, hot pepper sauce and $1/2$ tsp (2 mL) salt. Cover and let stand at room temperature for up to 2 hours. Just before serving, chop avocado and fold into salsa.

6. Remove bag from water bath and let rest for 10 minutes.

7. Preheat barbecue grill to high, leaving one burner off.

8. Remove steak from bag, discarding liquid, and transfer to a plate. Gently pat dry (don't remove all of the seasoning, just the excess liquid). Season on both sides with salt and pepper.

9. Oil grill and place steak on hot side of grill. Grill, turning once, for 1 to 2 minutes per side or until well marked. Transfer to a cutting board and let rest for 5 minutes.

10. Meanwhile, stack tortillas on a large piece of foil and heat on unlit side of barbecue for 5 to 10 minutes, turning once, until warmed.

11. Cut steak across the grain into thin slices. Fill warm tortillas with sliced steak and salsa in a line down the center, fold up bottom and fold in sides. Serve immediately.

Variations

Other beef cuts, such as tri-tip or blade steak, can be used in place of the flank steak. Follow the basic cooking instructions on pages 22–23.

Substitute $1^1/_2$ lbs (750 g) boneless skinless chicken breasts or thighs for the steak. Use the same marinade and follow the basic cooking instructions on pages 28–29.

To use a grill pan instead of a barbecue grill to finish the steak, preheat pan over medium-high heat until hot and almost smoking (turn on your hood vent or open the windows). Lightly oil pan and sear steak, turning once, for 1 to 2 minutes per side or until sizzling and marked. Warm the tortillas in foil in a 350°F (180°C) oven.

Chili Lime Fish Soft Tacos with Tomato Corn Salsa

I love fish tacos but am not a fan of fried foods, which is how most fish tacos are made. This simple sous vide technique cooks the fish to a flaky, moist, tender texture, and the spice rub adds a punch of flavor without overpowering the fish. Chop the ingredients for the salsa while the fish cooks, for a fresh finishing touch. ~ *Jennifer*

MAKES 4 SERVINGS

Sous vide time: 45 minutes

Tips

For the corn, use thawed frozen corn kernels, drained canned corn or freshly cooked corn cut off the cob. If you have corn on the cob, add a deeper flavor by grilling the corn. Lightly brush 2 cobs with oil and cook on a barbecue grill over medium heat, turning often, for about 12 minutes; let cool, then cut kernels off the cob to add to the salsa.

To make the fish ahead, prepare through step 3, then immerse the bag in ice water to chill. Refrigerate in the sealed bag for up to 3 days. Reheat in a 140°F (60°C) water bath for 15 to 30 minutes, until hot. Or remove fish from bag, place it on a foil-lined baking sheet and broil for 1 to 2 minutes, turning once, until hot.

- Preheat water bath to 140°F (60°C)
- Medium resealable freezer bag

1 lb	skinless white fish fillet(s), such as cod, haddock, catfish or tilapia (about ½ inch/1 cm thick)	500 g
2 tsp	chili powder	10 mL
1 tsp	grated lime zest	5 mL
¼ tsp	ground cumin	1 mL
⅛ tsp	garlic powder	0.5 mL
Pinch	salt	Pinch
1 tbsp	vegetable oil	15 mL
2 tbsp	freshly squeezed lime juice	30 mL
8	small (6-inch/15 cm) corn tortillas	8

Tomato Corn Salsa

2	medium tomatoes, chopped	2
1	small clove garlic, minced	1
½	orange or red bell pepper, finely chopped	½
½	jalapeño pepper, minced	½
1 cup	corn kernels (see tip)	250 mL
2 tbsp	chopped fresh cilantro	30 mL
2 tbsp	freshly squeezed lime juice	30 mL
	Salt and freshly ground black pepper	

1. Rinse fish and pat dry. Place on a plate. In a small bowl, combine chili powder, lime zest, cumin, garlic powder, salt and oil. Spread spice mixture all over fish.
2. Place fish, in a single layer if necessary, in freezer bag and scrape in any remaining spice mixture. Remove excess air and seal bag.
3. Cook in preheated water bath for 45 minutes.

Tips

This recipe can easily be doubled or tripled. You can cook up to 2 lbs (1 kg) of fish fillets in a large freezer bag, as long as they fit in a single layer, or use multiple bags. If cooking for a crowd, instead of warming the tortillas in the skillet, stack them on a large piece of foil, lightly moistening each tortilla with water as you stack, and cover tightly, then warm in a 350°F (180°C) oven for about 10 minutes.

The salsa can be made 2 to 3 hours ahead of serving and held, covered, at room temperature, but it does tend to get juicy. If you do make it ahead, use a slotted spoon to add the salsa to the tacos so they don't get too sloppy.

4. *Salsa:* Meanwhile, place tomatoes in a fine-mesh sieve and shake gently over the sink to drain off excess juice. Transfer tomatoes to a medium bowl. Add garlic, bell pepper, jalapeño, corn, cilantro and lime juice, tossing to combine. Season to taste with salt and pepper. Let stand at room temperature while the fish cooks.

5. About 10 minutes before serving, heat a dry skillet over medium heat. Add one tortilla at a time and heat, turning once, for 30 to 60 seconds per side, or until warmed and a few brown spots appear. Transfer to a large piece of foil and cover to keep warm. Repeat with the remaining tortillas, adjusting heat as necessary to prevent burning.

6. Remove bag from water bath. Using a slotted spatula, remove fish from bag, discarding liquid, and transfer to a clean plate. Drizzle with lime juice. Using a fork, flake fish into large chunks.

7. Fill warm tortillas with fish and top with salsa. Serve immediately.

Variations

In place of the fish, use 1 lb (500 g) large (31/40 count) shrimp, peeled and deveined. Cook in a 140°F (60°C) water bath for 15 minutes.

In place of the Tomato Corn Salsa, try Mango Salsa (page 181) or Tangy Slaw (page 62).

Spiced Boneless Blade Steak with Roasted Garlic Caesar Salad

Inspired by classic Montreal steak spice and creamy pan-roasted garlic dressing, this recipe provides a big, bold burst of flavor that goes great with cold, crispy romaine lettuce. Tenderizing a "lesser" cut of meat with a longer time in the bath, while still keeping it medium-rare, is one of the wonders of sous vide cooking.

MAKES 4 SERVINGS

Sous vide time: 2 hours

Tips

We've found that the optimal doneness for a flavorful, tender steak is medium-rare. However, if you prefer, you can adjust the temperature according to the variation on page 23 for a different doneness.

If you have conventionally roasted garlic (when you roast a whole bulb) on hand, use 3 cloves mashed with 1 tbsp (15 mL) olive oil, and skip step 4.

- **Preheat water bath to 130°F (54.5°C) for medium-rare (see tip)**
- **Large resealable freezer bag**
- **Barbecue grill**

1 tbsp	sweet paprika	15 mL
1 tsp	freshly ground black pepper	5 mL
1 tsp	crushed pink peppercorns	5 mL
1 tsp	hot pepper flakes	5 mL
1 tsp	ground coriander	5 mL
½ tsp	garlic powder	2 mL
	Salt	
1¼ lb	boneless beef blade steak, about 1 inch (2.5 cm) thick	625 g
	Vegetable oil or cooking spray	

Roasted Garlic Caesar Salad

1 tbsp	chopped garlic (about 3 cloves)	15 mL
1 tbsp	olive oil	15 mL
½ cup	mayonnaise	125 mL
¼ tsp	hot pepper sauce	1 mL
8 cups	chopped romaine lettuce	2 L
¼ cup	freshly grated Parmesan cheese	60 mL

1. In a small bowl, combine paprika, black pepper, pink peppercorns, hot pepper flakes, coriander, garlic powder and 1 tsp (5 mL) salt.

2. Place steak on a plate and rub both sides with spice mixture. Place in freezer bag, and add any remaining spice mixture. Remove excess air and seal bag.

3. Cook in preheated water bath for 2 hours.

4. *Salad:* Meanwhile, in a small skillet, combine garlic and oil. Cook over low heat, stirring occasionally, for 10 to 15 minutes or until garlic has started to turn a deep golden color (do not let burn). Remove from heat, scrape into a small bowl and let cool.

5. Remove bag from water bath and let rest for 10 minutes. Meanwhile, preheat barbecue grill to medium-high.

6. Remove steak from bag, discarding liquid, and transfer to a plate. Gently pat dry, without removing spice mixture, and season on both sides with salt.

7. Oil grill and place steak on grill. Grill, turning once, for 1 to 2 minutes per side or until sizzling and marked. Transfer steak to cutting board and let rest for 5 minutes.

8. Add mayonnaise and hot pepper sauce to the garlic mixture and whisk to combine.

9. In a large bowl, toss romaine with about half the garlic dressing. Add more dressing, as desired. Divide salad among four serving bowls.

10. Thinly slice steak across the grain. Top each salad with sliced steak, dividing evenly, and sprinkle with Parmesan. Serve immediately, passing any extra dressing at the table.

Variations

To use a grill pan instead of a barbecue grill to finish the steak, preheat pan over medium-high heat until hot and almost smoking (turn on your hood vent or open the windows). Lightly oil pan and sear steak, turning once, for 1 to 2 minutes per side or until sizzling and marked.

Grilled or roasted tomatoes or bell peppers make an excellent addition to this salad.

If you're a fan of croutons, add a handful to each salad with the steak. Alternatively, double the garlic and oil, and brush half on baguette slices, then toast the baguette slices alongside the steak.

Grilled Lamb Chops with White Bean and Arugula Salad

We have each been on a trip to France, but not together (yet), and both of us have fond memories of the fragrant lamb and robust salads served there. Those memories inspired this salad, with flavors and fragrances reminiscent of the south of France. It just begs for a sunny terrace and a glass of rosé. By marinating the lamb ahead, cooking it sous vide, then finishing it on the grill, it makes for an easy entertaining dish. Feel free to double or triple the recipe for a group.

MAKES 2 SERVINGS

Sous vide time: 1½ hours

Tips

For even more flavor, use 1 cup (250 mL) cooked Provençal White Beans (page 157) in place of the plain beans.

If you find arugula too strong, substitute spinach or spring mix salad greens.

The longer you let the lamb chops marinate, the more the flavors will infuse into the meat — give it up to a day if you have the time. You can make the salad a day ahead, cover and refrigerate it, then let it come up to room temperature while you cook the lamb, but it's best to chop and add the tomato just before serving.

- **Medium resealable freezer bag**
- **Barbecue grill**

Lamb Chops

¼ tsp	garlic powder	1 mL
	Salt and freshly ground black pepper	
1 tbsp	olive oil	15 mL
1 tsp	red wine vinegar	5 mL
½ tsp	Dijon mustard	2 mL
4	lamb loin chops (about 1 lb/500 g total), each about 1½ inches (4 cm) thick	4
	Vegetable oil or cooking spray	

White Bean and Arugula Salad

1	medium tomato, chopped	1
½ cup	chopped cucumber	125 mL
1 tsp	chopped fresh basil (or ½ tsp/2 mL chopped fresh rosemary)	5 mL
1 cup	rinsed drained canned or cooked white kidney (cannellini) beans	250 mL
1 tbsp	extra virgin olive oil	15 mL
1 tsp	red wine vinegar	5 mL
	Salt and freshly ground black pepper	
2 cups	baby arugula	500 mL

1. *Lamb Chops:* In a small bowl, combine garlic powder, ¼ tsp (1 mL) each salt and pepper, oil, vinegar and mustard.

2. Place lamb chops in freezer bag and pour in marinade. Turn bag and gently massage chops to evenly coat with marinade, then arrange chops in a single layer. Remove excess air and seal bag. Refrigerate for at least 2 hours or up to 1 day.

Tips

We've found that the optimal doneness for flavorful, tender lamb chops is medium-rare. However, if you prefer rare lamb chops, preheat water bath to 120°F (49°C); for medium, preheat to 139°F (59°C); and for medium-well, preheat to 149°F (65°C). We do not recommend cooking tender cuts well-done. Lamb chops cooked rare will not be pasteurized; if food safety is a concern, and especially for those with compromised immune systems, cook meat to at least medium-rare.

To double or triple the recipe, use a large resealable freezer bag, or use 2 or 3 medium bags with 4 chops per bag.

3. Preheat water bath to 130°F (54.5°C) for medium-rare (see tip).

4. Cook lamb in preheated water bath for 1$\frac{1}{2}$ hours. Remove bag from water bath and let rest for 10 minutes.

5. *Salad:* Meanwhile, in a small bowl, combine tomato, cucumber, basil, beans, oil and vinegar. Season to taste with salt and pepper. Let stand at room temperature for up to 2 hours.

6. Preheat barbecue grill to medium-high.

7. Remove lamb from bag, discarding liquid, and place on a plate. Pat dry and season on both sides with salt and pepper.

8. Oil grill and place lamb on grill. Grill, turning once, for 1 to 2 minutes per side or until sizzling and marked.

9. Divide arugula between two serving plates and spoon half the tomato mixture over each, drizzling the remaining vinaigrette from the bowl over the salad. Add 2 hot lamb chops to each plate. Serve immediately.

Variations

To use a grill pan instead of a barbecue grill to finish the chops, preheat pan over medium-high heat until hot and almost smoking (turn on your hood vent or open the windows). Lightly oil pan and sear chops, turning once, for 1 to 2 minutes per side or until sizzling and marked.

Substitute two 4-oz (125 g) boneless skinless chicken breasts or 4 thighs (8 oz/250 g total) for the lamb chops. Marinate as directed and follow the sous vide cooking directions on pages 28–29.

Add $\frac{1}{4}$ cup (60 mL) crumbled goat cheese or sheep's milk cheese to the salad.

Basil Chicken and Mediterranean Tomato Salad

Most summers, I grow weird and wonderful varieties of heirloom tomatoes in our garden, along with loads of basil. Together, they define the flavor of summer to me, and I never tire of them. If you don't grow your own, check out farmers' markets and well-stocked grocery stores for the different tomato varieties to make this delightful salad. Pair with tender, juicy chicken, fragrant with basil, for a summer lunch or dinner. ~ *Jennifer*

<table>
<tr><td>

MAKES 4 SERVINGS

Sous vide time: 1½ hours

Tips

The different colors and shapes of tomatoes add interest to this salad, but if you don't have the specific types called for, just use what you can find. It's also delicious made with traditional red tomatoes on their own.

Cubed fresh or regular mozzarella or crumbled feta or soft goat cheese can be substituted for the bocconcini.

</td><td>

- **Preheat water bath to 151°F (66°C)**
- **Mini chopper or small food processor**
- **Medium resealable freezer bag**

Basil Chicken

⅓ cup	lightly packed fresh basil leaves	75 mL
¼ cup	olive oil	60 mL
2	boneless skinless chicken breasts (each about 8 oz/250 g)	2
	Salt and freshly ground black pepper	

Mediterranean Tomato Salad

12	yellow teardrop or green cherry tomatoes, halved	12
12	red grape or purple cherry tomatoes, halved	12
½ cup	drained small bocconcini cheese, halved	125 mL
½ cup	drained mixed black and/or green olives (optional)	125 mL
2 tbsp	balsamic vinegar	30 mL
	Salt and freshly ground black pepper	
3	plum (Roma) tomatoes, sliced	3
3	small yellow tomatoes, sliced	3
4 cups	spring mix salad greens	1 L

</td></tr>
</table>

1. *Chicken:* In mini chopper, combine basil and oil; purée until smooth.

2. Transfer 2 tbsp (30 mL) of the basil purée to a large bowl (cover remaining purée and set aside at room temperature). Add chicken to the bowl and turn to coat completely with the purée. Season lightly with salt and pepper. Place chicken in a single layer in freezer bag and scrape in any remaining purée. Remove excess air and seal bag.

3. Cook in preheated water bath for 1½ hours. Remove bag from water bath and let rest for 10 minutes.

You can serve this family-style by arranging the tomatoes, sliced chicken and greens on separate platters and letting diners serve themselves at the table. Or, for a buffet meal, arrange as directed on one large platter instead of individual plates.

4. *Salad:* Meanwhile, in a medium bowl, combine teardrop tomatoes, grape tomatoes, bocconcini, olives (if using), the remaining basil purée and vinegar. Season to taste with salt and pepper. Toss gently to coat.

5. Arrange sliced plum and yellow tomatoes in a ring just inside the lip of four dinner plates, dividing equally. Using a slotted spoon, divide tomato and cheese mixture evenly on top of the ring of tomatoes.

6. Toss greens in the bowl, using the remaining juice from the tomato mixture as a vinaigrette. Divide lettuce evenly among the plates, piling in the center of the ring of tomatoes.

7. Remove chicken from bag, discarding liquid, and transfer to a cutting board. Slice across the grain and arrange gently over lettuce. Season to taste with salt and pepper. Serve immediately.

Variation

For an even heartier salad, add 1 cup (250 mL) cooked Provençal White Beans (page 157) with the tomato mixture in step 4.

Rare Ahi Tuna with Napa Cabbage Slaw and Sesame Orange Vinaigrette

Sous vide is a sure-fire (sure-fireless?) way to cook tuna to the perfect doneness every time — much appreciated when you're splurging on high-quality sushi-grade tuna, which is definitely recommended for this salad. It's particularly nice for a special occasion; while it takes only minutes to prepare, it's sure to dazzle guests. The richness of the tuna is complemented by the acidity of the vinaigrette and the crispy slaw.

MAKES 4 SERVINGS

Sous vide time: 10 minutes

Tips

Toast sesame seeds in a small skillet over medium heat, stirring constantly, for 4 to 5 minutes or until golden brown and fragrant. Immediately transfer to a bowl and let cool.

Ten minutes for the tuna in the water bath will provide a cooked rare (pink) center. If you prefer it a little less pink (medium), cook for 20 minutes; or cook for 30 minutes for well-done, with no pink. In our tests, all three versions came out tender, moist and full of flavor when cooked at 129°F (54°C).

- Preheat water bath to 129°F (54°C)
- Medium resealable freezer bag

Sesame Orange Vinaigrette

2 tsp	grated orange zest	10 mL
¼ tsp	salt	1 mL
¼ tsp	freshly ground black pepper	1 mL
2 tbsp	olive oil	30 mL
2 tbsp	sesame oil	30 mL
2 tbsp	rice vinegar	30 mL

Napa Cabbage Slaw

4 cups	thinly sliced napa cabbage	1 L
1 cup	thinly sliced red bell pepper	250 mL
1 tbsp	thinly sliced green onion	15 mL
1 tbsp	chopped fresh cilantro	15 mL

Tuna

1 to 2 tbsp	sesame oil (approx.)	15 to 30 mL
12 oz	sushi-grade ahi tuna, cut into 4 equal portions	375 g
	Salt and freshly ground black pepper	
1 tbsp	toasted sesame seeds (see tip)	15 mL

1. *Vinaigrette:* In a measuring cup, whisk together orange zest, salt, pepper, olive oil, sesame oil and vinegar. Set 2 tbsp (30 mL) aside for tuna.

2. *Slaw:* In a large bowl, combine cabbage, red pepper, green onion and cilantro. Add the remaining vinaigrette and toss gently. Let stand at room temperature while you prepare the tuna.

Instead of assembling on individual plates, serve family-style on a large platter.

Jennifer, the home economist, suggests to peel and slice up the orange after grating off the zest and serve it as garnish, rather than letting the zested orange languish in the crisper!

3. *Tuna:* In a large skillet, heat 1 tbsp (15 mL) sesame oil over medium-high heat until shimmering. Pat tuna dry and season all over with salt and pepper. Working with one piece at a time, add tuna to hot skillet and sear, turning once, for about 30 seconds per side or just until browned. Transfer to a plate and repeat with remaining tuna, adding more oil and adjusting heat between batches as necessary. Let cool.

4. Transfer tuna to freezer bag and add reserved vinaigrette, turning bag to coat tuna evenly, then arrange tuna in a single layer. Remove excess air and seal bag.

5. Cook in preheated water bath for 10 minutes or to desired doneness (see tip, page 76). Remove bag from water bath and let rest for 10 minutes.

6. Remove tuna from bag, discarding liquid, and transfer to a cutting board. Divide slaw equally among four serving plates, mounding in the center. Thinly slice each piece of tuna and arrange on top of slaw. Sprinkle with toasted sesame seeds. Serve immediately.

Rainbow Beet Salad with White Cheddar and Balsamic Reduction

I like to add drama to a plate with a combination of colorful ingredients, but I always make sure the flavors complement each other. This light salad balances sweet, sour, bitter and salty, and shows off gorgeous contrasting colors for a vibrant starter to any dinner party. ~ Jay

MAKES 4 SERVINGS

Sous vide time: 1 hour

Tips

The different colors of the beets will bleed if you cook them in a bag together, so it's important to keep them separate. If you're using all one color of beet, you can cook 2 cups (500 mL) of slices in one medium freezer bag.

When cooking sous vide, uniform slices of hard vegetables, such as beets, are particularly important for even cooking. Do your best to cut the slices all the same thickness.

You can refrigerate the drained beets and the reduced balsamic dressing in separate airtight containers for up to 1 day before assembling the salad.

Variations

A shredded hard, aged goat's cheese or crumbled soft goat's cheese makes an excellent alternative to the Cheddar.

Substitute arugula or spinach for the mixed greens.

- **Preheat water bath to 190°F (88°C)**
- **2 medium resealable freezer bags**

1 cup	sliced peeled golden beets (1 to 2 beets, cut into ¼-inch/0.5 cm slices)	250 mL
2 tbsp	olive oil, divided	30 mL
	Salt and freshly ground black pepper	
1 cup	sliced peeled red or candy cane beets (1 to 2 beets, cut into ¼-inch/ 0.5 cm slices)	250 mL
1 tbsp	balsamic vinegar	15 mL
2 cups	mixed salad greens	500 mL
½ cup	shaved or shredded sharp (old) white Cheddar cheese	125 mL

1. In a medium bowl, combine golden beets, half the oil and ¼ tsp (1 mL) each salt and pepper. Transfer beet mixture to one freezer bag, arranging in a single layer. Remove excess air and seal bag.

2. In the same bowl (no need to clean it), repeat with the red beets, the remaining oil, and ¼ tsp (1 mL) each salt and pepper. Transfer to the second freezer bag, arranging in a single layer. Remove excess air and seal bag.

3. Cook both bags of beets in preheated water bath, covered, for 1 hour. The beets should be tender when pierced with a fork; if they aren't, return bags to water bath and cook, checking for doneness every 15 minutes. Remove bags from water bath and immerse in ice water to cool completely.

4. Drain golden beets through a fine-mesh sieve set over a small saucepan, reserving cooking juices; transfer beets to a bowl. Repeat with the red beets, combining the juices; transfer red beets to a separate bowl. Set beets aside.

5. Add vinegar to reserved cooking juices in saucepan and bring to a boil over medium heat. Reduce heat and boil gently until reduced by half and slightly syrupy. Remove from heat and let cool.

6. Arrange beets on a serving platter or individual serving plates. Top with salad greens and cheese. Gently drizzle balsamic reduction over top. Season to taste with salt and pepper. Serve immediately.

Warm Potato Salad with Red Wine Vinaigrette

With a light vinaigrette dressing, this simple salad is perfect for summer evenings to accompany steak, fish, chicken or burgers, or serve it on a bed of greens as a starter. It's easy to make and it keeps well.

MAKES 4 TO 6 SERVINGS

Sous vide time: 1½ hours

Tip

Combining the potatoes with the vinaigrette while they're still warm helps them absorb the liquid and soak in the flavor.

Variations

Add 2 tbsp (30 mL) chopped or sliced radishes and/or ½ cup (125 mL) diced red or yellow bell pepper with the potatoes in step 4.

Add 1 medium tomato, seeded and chopped, and ¼ cup (60 mL) crumbled feta cheese just before serving.

To turn this salad into a meal, just before serving add 1 spicy sausage, removed from casing, cooked and crumbled, and 1 hard-cooked egg, chopped, per serving.

- **Preheat water bath to 190°F (88°C)**
- **Medium resealable freezer bag**

1 lb	baby potatoes (about 3 cups/750 mL)	500 g
¼ tsp	dried tarragon	1 mL
	Salt and freshly ground black pepper	
¼ cup	olive oil	60 mL
1 tbsp	red wine vinegar	15 mL

1. Place potatoes in freezer bag, arranging in a single layer. Remove excess air and seal bag.
2. Cook in preheated water bath, covered, for 1½ hours. The potatoes should be tender when pierced with a fork; if they aren't, return bag to water bath and cook, checking for doneness every 15 minutes.
3. Meanwhile, in a medium bowl, combine tarragon, ¼ tsp (1 mL) each salt and pepper, oil and vinegar.
4. Remove bag from water bath. Using a slotted spoon, transfer potatoes to dressing in bowl and toss gently to coat. Let cool slightly to serve warm, or cover and refrigerate for about 1 hour, until chilled, or for up to 3 days. Season to taste with salt and pepper just before serving.

"Baked" Potato Salad

This salad takes us on a trip down memory lane to potatoes wrapped in foil and baked, then topped with tangy sour cream and salty, smoky bacon. It is just begging to be served alongside a thick, hot slice of roast beef or a steak, burgers or cold shaved roast beef.

<table>
<tr><td>MAKES 4 TO
6 SERVINGS</td></tr>
</table>

**Sous vide time:
1½ hours**

Tips

Baby (sometimes called mini) potatoes often come in a bag of mixed colors: red, white, yellow and or blue/purple, and they give a nice visual effect and contribute different flavors to this salad. Of course, the recipe works just as well with a single color of potato, too.

Full-fat or lower-fat sour cream is best for this recipe, or you can use plain Greek yogurt instead. Avoid fat-free products, as they tend to have a gelatinous texture that doesn't coat the warm potatoes well.

If you're making this ahead, add the bacon the day you plan to serve it (a few hours ahead is fine) for the best texture. If you're enjoying leftovers after a day or two, the bacon will be a little softer but still tasty.

- **Preheat water bath to 190°F (88°C)**
- **Medium resealable freezer bag**

1 lb	mixed color baby potatoes (about 3 cups/ 750 mL)	500 g
4	slices bacon, cooked crisp and crumbled	4
	Salt and freshly ground black pepper	
¼ cup	sour cream	60 mL
1 tbsp	white vinegar	15 mL
	Chopped fresh chives or green onions (optional)	

1. Place potatoes in freezer bag, arranging in a single layer. Remove excess air and seal bag.

2. Cook in preheated water bath, covered, for 1½ hours. The potatoes should be tender when pierced with a fork; if they aren't, return bag to water bath and cook, checking for doneness every 15 minutes. Remove bag from water bath and let cool for 15 minutes.

3. Meanwhile, in a medium bowl, combine bacon, a pinch of salt, ¼ tsp (1 mL) pepper, sour cream and vinegar.

4. Using a slotted spoon, transfer potatoes to dressing in bowl and toss gently to coat. Let cool slightly to serve warm, or cover and refrigerate for about 1 hour, until chilled, or for up to 2 days. Season to taste with salt and pepper and sprinkle with chives (if using) just before serving.

Variations

This salad is as flexible as a baked potato. Try adding shredded cheese; chopped herbs, such as fresh basil, thyme or a touch of rosemary; or add a dash of hot sauce. Be creative.

Beef and Veal

Steak with Mushrooms in Brown Butter and Thyme

Once you've prepared your steak of choice, the accompaniment is both simple and classic. The secret is to get the pan hot enough to brown the butter, but not so hot as to burn it. Serve with hot frites or oven-baked potato wedges. A little baguette to soak up the butter is a good idea.

MAKES 1 TO 2 SERVINGS

Tips

Regular white (button) mushrooms are delicious in this recipe or, to vary the flavor, use oyster mushrooms, sliced portobellos or halved or quartered shiitake mushroom caps.

The mushrooms will absorb butter during the cooking process, so reserving half of the butter to add at the end ensures that you get a lovely butter coating on the cooked mushrooms and to drizzle over the steak.

Use dried herbs sparingly when adding them to a recipe that is cooked for a short time, or near the end of a recipe. Like perfume, a little can be enchanting, too much can be overwhelming.

2 tbsp	butter, divided	30 mL
1	boneless beef steak (6 to 8 oz/175 to 250 g), cooked sous vide (see page 20 or 22)	1
	Salt and freshly ground black pepper	
4	large mushrooms, quartered (about 1 cup/ 250 mL, 2 oz/60 g)	4
Pinch	dried thyme	Pinch

1. In a medium skillet (preferably cast-iron), melt 1 tbsp (15 mL) butter over medium heat until it starts to bubble and turn light brown.

2. Remove cooked steak from bag, discarding liquid, and pat dry. Season on both sides with salt and pepper. Add steak to skillet and sear, turning once, for about 2 minutes per side or until golden brown. Transfer steak to a cutting board and tent with foil.

3. Return skillet to medium heat and add mushrooms and thyme; cook, stirring constantly, for about 5 minutes or until mushrooms are tender and golden brown. Add the remaining butter and cook, stirring, for about 1 minute or until butter is browned and mushrooms are coated.

4. Cut steak into 2 equal pieces (or thinly slice across the grain, if desired) and transfer to plate(s). Pour mushrooms and butter over steak.

Garlic Soy Rib Steak

A quick and easy marinade adds some zing to an already flavorful and tender steak. Serve with rice and an Asian-influenced stir-fry, or sliced on a salad.

MAKES 2 SERVINGS

Sous vide time: 1½ hours

Tips

We prefer a flaky sea salt, such as fleur de sel, freshly ground sea salt or kosher salt, for seasoning meats after sous vide cooking, for the pleasant, clean burst of salt flavor it contributes, but you can use any salt you have on hand.

The longer you let the steak marinate, the more the flavors will infuse into the meat.

We've found that the optimal doneness for a flavorful, tender steak is medium-rare. However, if you prefer, you can adjust the temperature according to the variation on page 21 for a different doneness.

- Medium resealable freezer bag
- Barbecue grill

2 tbsp	reduced-sodium soy sauce	30 mL
2 tbsp	olive oil	30 mL
2 tbsp	freshly squeezed lemon juice	30 mL
¼ tsp	garlic powder	1 mL
	Freshly ground black pepper	
12 oz	boneless beef rib steak, about ¾ inch (2 cm) thick	375 g
	Salt	
	Vegetable oil or cooking spray	

1. In a small bowl, combine soy sauce, oil, lemon juice, garlic powder and ⅛ tsp (0.5 mL) pepper.
2. Place steak in freezer bag and pour in marinade. Turn bag and gently massage steak to evenly coat with marinade. Remove excess air and seal bag. Refrigerate for at least 2 hours or up to 1 day.
3. Preheat water bath to 130°F (54.5°C) for medium-rare (see tip).
4. Cook steak in preheated water bath for 1½ hours. Remove bag from water bath and let rest for 10 minutes.
5. Meanwhile, preheat barbecue grill to medium-high.
6. Remove steak from bag, discarding liquid, and transfer to a plate. Pat dry and season on both sides with salt and pepper.
7. Oil grill and place steak on grill. Grill, turning once, for 1 to 2 minutes per side or until sizzling and marked.

Variation

To use a grill pan instead of a barbecue grill to finish the steak, preheat pan over medium-high heat until hot and almost smoking (turn on your hood vent or open the windows). Lightly oil pan and sear steak, turning once, for 1 to 2 minutes per side or until sizzling and marked.

Argentinian Flank Steak with Chimichurri

This steak is served with the traditional sauce used as both a marinade and accompaniment for grilled meats in Argentina. Serve it off the grill with spicy roasted potatoes and grilled vegetables. If there's any left over, refrigerate it overnight and slice it very thin for use on a salad or in a tortilla wrap sandwich.

**MAKES
4 SERVINGS**

Sous vide time:
4 hours

Tips

Some people dislike the taste of cilantro. To avoid it, simply substitute an equal amount of parsley.

If you like things hot, replace with jalapeño with a hotter pepper, such as a serrano pepper. Scotch bonnets and habanero peppers are at the upper end of most people's tolerance level, so try half — or a whole one, if you're daring.

We've found that the optimal doneness for a flavorful, tender steak is medium-rare. However, if you prefer, you can adjust the temperature according to the variation on page 23 for a different doneness.

Variation

To broil steak instead of grilling, preheat broiler with rack 6 inches (15 cm) from heat. Place steak on a wire rack set over a foil-lined rimmed baking sheet, or on a broiler pan. Broil for 3 to 4 minutes per side or until sizzling.

- **Food processor or immersion blender**
- **Medium resealable freezer bag**
- **Barbecue grill**

1	jalapeño pepper, seeded and cut into chunks	1
1	clove garlic	1
¼ cup	lightly packed fresh parsley leaves	60 mL
¼ cup	lightly packed fresh cilantro leaves and tender stems	60 mL
1 tbsp	fresh oregano leaves	15 mL
	Salt and freshly ground black pepper	
½ cup	olive oil	125 mL
⅓ cup	red wine vinegar	75 mL
1 lb	beef flank steak	500 g
	Vegetable oil or cooking spray	

1. In food processor or in a tall cup using immersion blender, combine jalapeño, garlic, parsley, cilantro, oregano, ¼ tsp (1 mL) each salt and pepper, oil and vinegar; pulse to finely chop, then process until fairly smooth.

2. Place steak in freezer bag and pour in ¼ cup (60 mL) of the chimichurri. Turn bag and gently massage steak to evenly coat with sauce. Remove excess air and seal bag. Refrigerate for at least 4 hours or up to 1 day. Transfer the remaining chimichurri to a jar, cover and refrigerate until serving.

3. Preheat water bath to 130°F (54.5°C) for medium-rare (see tip).

4. Cook steak in preheated water bath, covered, for 4 hours. Remove bag from water bath and let rest for 10 minutes.

5. Meanwhile, preheat barbecue grill to medium-high.

6. Remove steak from bag, discarding liquid, and transfer to a plate. Gently pat dry (don't remove all of the chimichurri, just the excess liquid). Season lightly on both sides with salt and pepper.

7. Oil grill and place steak on grill. Grill, turning once, for about 2 minutes per side or until sizzling and marked.

8. Transfer steak to a cutting board and slice thinly across the grain. Serve with the remaining chimichurri.

Bacon-Wrapped Beef Tenderloin with Brandy Cream Sauce

Beef tenderloin has much less fat content than most other cuts of meat. The bacon adds flavor and moisture, and the brandy cream gives this dish a level of decadence suitable for special occasions. Serve with polenta, asparagus and a warm tomato and arugula salad.

MAKES 2 SERVINGS

Sous vide time: 2½ hours

Tips

If your cream sauce gets too thick, thin it out by adding water, 1 tbsp (15 mL) at a time.

This recipe can easily be doubled; use a large resealable freezer bag or divide the steaks into 2 medium bags. Sear the steaks in batches, if necessary to avoid crowding the pan, in step 5.

Variation

If you prefer grilled steaks, you can finish them on a barbecue grill preheated to medium-high. Sear for about 2 minutes — just long enough to add grill marks and heat steaks. To make the sauce, brown the butter slightly in the skillet over medium heat, then proceed with step 6.

- **Preheat water bath to 130°F (54.5°C)**
- **Medium resealable freezer bag**

2	6-oz (175 g) center-cut beef tenderloin steaks, about 1½ inches (4 cm) thick	2
2	slices bacon	2
	Salt and freshly ground black pepper	
1 tbsp	butter	15 mL

Brandy Cream Sauce

1	clove garlic, minced	1
2 tbsp	brandy	30 mL
⅓ cup	heavy or whipping (35%) cream	75 mL
	Salt and freshly ground black pepper	

1. Pat steaks dry. Wrap a slice of bacon around each steak, like a label on a tin can.
2. Place steaks in freezer bag, spacing them apart. Remove excess air and seal bag.
3. Cook in preheated water bath for 2½ hours. Remove bag from water bath and let rest for 10 minutes.
4. Remove steaks from bag, discarding liquid, and transfer to a plate. Pat dry and season on both sides with salt and pepper.
5. Heat a large, heavy skillet over medium heat. Add butter and swirl to coat pan. Sear steaks, turning once, for about 2 minutes per side or until golden brown. Using tongs, transfer steaks to warmed plates, leaving butter in pan. Tent steaks with foil and let rest.
6. *Brandy Cream Sauce:* Return skillet to medium-low heat. Add garlic and cook, stirring, for about 2 minutes or until golden brown and fragrant. Add brandy, stirring to scrape up any brown bits stuck to pan. Simmer until about half of the brandy has evaporated. Stir in cream and bring to a gentle simmer; simmer, stirring often, for 3 to 4 minutes or until sauce is thick enough to lightly coat the back of a spoon. Season to taste with salt and pepper. Spoon sauce over steaks.

Pepper-Crusted Beef Tenderloin Roast with Horseradish Crème Fraîche

Crème fraîche gives you the rich texture of sour cream and a subtle tangy taste. Horseradish is a classical pairing with roast beef. This is a very nice entrée for a celebratory dinner. Serve it with oven-roasted baby red potatoes and asparagus spears.

MAKES 4 SERVINGS

Sous vide time: 3½ hours

Tips

Leftover roast can be cooled, then wrapped and refrigerated for up to 4 days. Cover and refrigerate crème fraîche separately. Serve cold, or reheat slices by searing them in a skillet over medium-high heat, turning once, for about 1 minute per side.

We prefer a flaky sea salt, such as fleur de sel, freshly ground sea salt or kosher salt, for seasoning meats after sous vide cooking, for the pleasant, clean burst of salt flavor it contributes, but you can use any salt you have on hand.

Variation

If you want to use this beef hot or cold for sandwiches, instead of making the crème fraîche, substitute an equal amount of mayonnaise for the cream; use right away or refrigerate for up to 5 days.

- **Preheat water bath to 130°F (54.5°C)**
- **Large resealable freezer bag**

1¼ lb	center-cut beef tenderloin roast, tied	625 g
1 tsp	freshly ground black pepper	5 mL
¼ tsp	salt	1 mL
1 tbsp	vegetable oil	15 mL

Crème Fraîche

½ cup	heavy or whipping (35%) cream	125 mL
1 tbsp	freshly squeezed lemon juice	15 mL
1 tbsp	prepared horseradish	15 mL

1. Pat roast dry. In a small bowl, combine pepper and salt. Spread evenly over entire roast.
2. Place roast in freezer bag. Remove excess air and seal bag.
3. Cook in preheated water bath for 3½ hours.
4. *Crème Fraîche:* Meanwhile, in a small bowl, combine cream, lemon juice and horseradish. Cover and let stand at room temperature.
5. Remove roast from bag, discarding liquid, and transfer to a cutting board. Tent with foil and let rest for 10 minutes.
6. In a large skillet, heat oil over medium heat until shimmering. Pat beef dry and remove butcher's twine. Sear on all sides until golden brown.
7. Return beef to cutting board and cut across the grain into 4 equal slices (or thinly slice, if desired). Serve with crème fraîche on the side.

Serving Suggestion

- For a fancy breakfast, omit the crème fraîche and serve this roast with a poached egg and spicy Hollandaise Sauce (see variation, page 177).

Super-Slow Whiskey, Garlic and Brown Sugar Beef Brisket

Whether it's in soup, beef dips or gravy, beef with caramelized garlic is a classic combination. This rich-flavored slow-cooked brisket is just as good the next day in sandwiches or quesadillas. It's a bit of a surprise to see a slow-cooked brisket still pink throughout, and it's a pleasant surprise when you feel how tender and moist it is.

MAKES 10 TO 12 SERVINGS

Sous vide time: 36 hours

Tips

If you'd prefer a smaller roast, most butcher shops will cut them to size; you can use the same method, seasoning and cooking time.

When cooking for this length of time, covering the sous vide container improves heat efficiency and slows down water evaporation (see page 16).

When using wine or spirits in sous vide cooking, make sure to simmer the mixture long enough to remove the alcohol before adding it to the cooking bag; otherwise, it can leave a medicinal, almost bitter aftertaste.

Leftover brisket can be cooled, wrapped and refrigerated for up to 4 days or frozen for up to 3 months. Thaw in the refrigerator overnight, if frozen.

- **Preheat water bath to 130°F (54.5°C)**
- **Extra-large resealable freezer bag**

3½ lb	beef brisket flat, trimmed	1.75 kg
½ tsp	salt	2 mL
¼ tsp	freshly ground black pepper	1 mL
1 tbsp	vegetable oil	15 mL
1	clove garlic, finely chopped	1
2 tsp	whiskey	10 mL
¼ cup	packed brown sugar	60 mL

1. Pat brisket dry and rub all over with salt and pepper. In a large skillet, heat oil over medium heat until shimmering. Sear brisket on all sides until golden brown. Transfer to a plate and set aside.

2. Reduce heat to low. Add garlic to skillet and cook, stirring, for 2 to 3 minutes or until golden brown and tender. Add whiskey and cook, stirring, until nearly evaporated. Stir in brown sugar until moistened and crumbly. Remove from heat and let cool.

3. Rub sugar mixture into surface of brisket. Place beef in freezer bag and add any remaining sugar mixture. Remove excess air and seal bag.

4. Cook in preheated water bath, covered, for 36 hours, replenishing water as necessary to keep meat immersed. Remove bag from water bath and let rest for 15 minutes.

5. Remove brisket from bag, discarding liquid, and transfer to a cutting board. Cut beef across the grain into thin slices.

Serving Suggestions

- In summer, transfer the cooked brisket to a medium-high preheated barbecue grill, over indirect heat, and mop with your favorite barbecue sauce; cover grill to glaze for about 10 minutes, then let rest for 5 minutes before slicing. Serve with grilled vegetables and roasted potatoes.

- Thinly sliced cold brisket makes a great sandwich. Jay's favorite is with red pepper jelly, provolone cheese and arugula on sourdough bread.

Korean Bulgogi-Style Short Ribs

These short ribs are a great example of how sous vide cooking makes a tender dish out of an inexpensive cut of meat. Serve them with sticky rice and stir-fried vegetables. For the adventurous, add a little kimchi on the side.

**MAKES
4 SERVINGS**

Sous vide time:
24 hours

Tips

Be very gentle when removing the cooked short ribs from the bag so they don't fall apart. It helps to lay the bag on a cutting board or rimless baking sheet and gently lift the strips of ribs with a large, slotted spatula from the bag and onto the lined baking sheet.

This seasoning is mildly spiced. You can increase or decrease the Sriracha to your own comfort level for hot food.

When cooking for this length of time, covering the sous vide container improves heat efficiency and slows down water evaporation (see page 16). If using a stick-style immersion sous vide circulator, be sure to leave a vent for steam to escape well away from the stick, to avoid excess moisture building around the appliance.

- **Preheat water bath to 135°F (57°C)**
- **Large resealable freezer bag**
- **Rimmed baking sheet, lined with foil**

1	medium onion, finely chopped	1
1	garlic clove, minced	1
¼ cup	packed brown sugar	60 mL
2 tbsp	reduced-sodium soy sauce	30 mL
1 tbsp	unseasoned rice vinegar	15 mL
½ tsp	grated lime zest	2 mL
1 tbsp	freshly squeezed lime juice	15 mL
1 tsp	toasted sesame oil	5 mL
1 tsp	Sriracha	5 mL
2 lbs	sliced beef short ribs, ½ inch (1 cm) thick	1 kg

1. In a medium bowl, combine onion, garlic, brown sugar, soy sauce, vinegar, lime zest, lime juice, sesame oil and Sriracha.

2. Place short ribs in freezer bag and pour in marinade. Turn bag and gently massage ribs to evenly coat with marinade. Remove excess air and seal bag.

3. Cook in preheated water bath, covered, for 24 hours, replenishing water as necessary to keep meat immersed. Remove bag from water bath and let rest for 10 minutes.

4. Meanwhile, preheat broiler with rack 6 inches (15 cm) from heat.

5. Carefully remove ribs from bag, discarding liquid, and transfer to prepared baking sheet.

6. Broil ribs, rotating pan as necessary, for 4 minutes or until browned. Carefully flip ribs over and broil for 2 to 3 minutes or until lightly browned.

Variation

Instead of broiling, you can finish these ribs on a barbecue grill preheated to high. A hot slotted vegetable grilling grate would be helpful to keep the ribs from falling apart.

Swiss Steaks in Sweet Tomato Sauce

If you're old enough to remember electric frying pans as a newfangled appliance, you might have had something similar to this dish, inspired by my own childhood memories. Mashed potatoes and cooked peas are still the perfect accompaniments. ~ *Jay*

MAKES 4 SERVINGS

Sous vide time: 12 hours

Tips

The steaks will be ready to eat after about 12 hours in the water bath and, for convenience, can be held for up to 6 more hours without affecting the texture.

You might find top round steaks already pounded thin at the butcher shop or grocery store. To pound out your own steaks, place them between large pieces of plastic wrap on a cutting board on a sturdy counter. Using the flat side of a meat mallet (or the bottom of a saucepan), firmly strike steak, starting in the center and working outward in each direction until desired thickness is reached (about ¼ inch/0.5 cm thick for this recipe).

For the pineapple, one snack-size (4½ oz/142 mL) can gives you just the right amount.

- **Preheat water bath to 130°F (54.5°C)**
- **Large resealable freezer bag**

1½ lbs	boneless beef top round steak, cut into 8 pieces and pounded (see tip)	750 g
2 tbsp	vegetable oil, divided	30 mL
½	red onion, finely chopped	½
1	red bell pepper, chopped	1
1	clove garlic, minced	1
¼ cup	drained canned pineapple chunks	60 mL
½ tsp	dried oregano	2 mL
½ tsp	hot pepper flakes	2 mL
	Salt and freshly ground black pepper	
1 cup	drained canned diced tomatoes	250 mL

1. Pat steaks dry. In a large skillet, heat 1 tbsp (15 mL) oil over medium-high heat until shimmering. Add steaks, in batches, and sear, turning once, for about 2 minutes per side or until browned. Transfer to a bowl and let cool. Repeat with the remaining beef, adding oil and adjusting heat as necessary between batches. Set aside.

2. Reduce heat to medium-low and add any remaining oil to skillet. Add onion and cook, stirring, for about 3 minutes or until softened. Add red pepper and cook, stirring, for about 2 minutes or until fragrant. Add garlic, pineapple, oregano, hot pepper flakes and ½ tsp (2 mL) each salt and pepper; cook, stirring, for 2 minutes or until fragrant.

3. Stir in tomatoes. Increase heat to medium and bring to a boil, stirring often. Boil for 2 to 3 minutes or until peppers are tender. Remove from heat and let cool.

4. Transfer meat and sauce to freezer bag. Remove excess air and seal bag.

5. Cook in preheated water bath, covered, for 12 hours, replenishing water as necessary to keep meat immersed. The beef should be tender; if it isn't, return bag to water bath and cook, checking for doneness every 30 minutes. Remove bag from water bath and let rest for 5 minutes.

6. Using a slotted spatula, transfer steaks to a deep platter or serving dish. Season sauce with salt and pepper to taste. Pour sauce over steaks.

Tomato and White Wine Braised Osso Buco

Osso buco prepared by Jennifer's mom, Patricia, is my favorite meal of all time. She serves this ultimate comfort dish with silky Parmesan risotto. Don't forget to scoop the tasty marrow out of the middle of the bone when you're finished. A piece of baguette helps mop up every last drop of succulent sauce. ~ *Jay*

MAKES 4 SERVINGS

Sous vide time: 24 hours

Tips

When cooking for this length of time, covering the sous vide container improves heat efficiency and slows down water evaporation (see page 16). If using a stick-style immersion sous vide circulator, be sure to leave a vent for steam to escape well away from the stick, to avoid excess moisture building around the appliance.

Leftovers aren't always great, but we found this dish to be even better the next day.

- **Preheat water bath to 158°F (70°C)**
- **Large resealable freezer bag**

3 tbsp	olive oil, divided	45 mL
4	1-inch (2.5 cm) thick slices veal shank (about 2½ lbs/1.25 kg total)	4
1	medium onion, finely chopped	1
1	stalk celery, finely chopped	1
1	medium carrot, finely chopped	1
1	clove garlic, minced	1
⅓ cup	dry white wine	75 mL
1¾ cups	canned tomatoes (preferably San Marzano), with juice, coarsely chopped (half a 28-oz/796 mL can)	425 mL
	Salt and freshly ground black pepper	
¼ cup	chopped fresh parsley	60 mL

1. In a large skillet, heat 2 tbsp (30 mL) oil over medium-high heat until shimmering. Add 2 veal shanks and sear, turning once, for 4 to 5 minutes, until browned on both sides. Transfer to a plate and repeat with the remaining shanks. Set aside.

2. Reduce heat to medium-low and add the remaining oil to skillet. Add onion, celery and carrot; cook, stirring, for about 5 minutes or until softened. Add garlic and cook, stirring, for about 2 minutes or until fragrant. Add wine and cook, stirring and scraping up any brown bits stuck to pan, for 2 minutes or until most of the wine has evaporated.

3. Remove from heat and stir in tomatoes. Stir in ½ tsp (2 mL) each of salt and pepper.

To make osso buco ahead, prepare through step 5, then immerse bag in ice water to chill. Refrigerate in the sealed bag for up to 3 days, or freeze for up to 6 months. Thaw overnight in the refrigerator, if frozen. Remove veal from sauce and reduce sauce as directed in step 7, adding veal shanks once the sauce has thickened. Simmer for 5 to 10 minutes or until veal is heated through.

4. Transfer shanks to freezer bag and pour in sauce. Turn bag and gently massage meat to evenly coat with sauce. Remove excess air and seal bag.

5. Cook in preheated water bath, covered, for 24 hours, replenishing water as necessary to keep meat immersed. The veal should be fork-tender; if it isn't, return bag to water bath and cook, checking for doneness every 30 minutes. Remove bag from water bath.

6. Using a slotted spoon, remove shanks from sauce and place in a deep serving dish. Tent with foil and keep warm.

7. Pour sauce into a large saucepan and bring to a boil over medium-high heat. Reduce heat and boil gently, stirring occasionally, for about 10 minutes or until reduced to desired consistency. Season to taste with salt and pepper.

8. Remove foil from serving dish and pour hot sauce over veal shanks. Garnish with parsley and serve immediately.

Three-Chile Chunky Beef and Bean Chili

A steaming bowl of chili is one of the first things I crave when the weather turns cold in the fall, and it's definitely a recipe we enjoy in football season (watching games, that is). This one, with chili powder, smoky chipotle and jalapeño, is a warmer-upper for sure. The great thing about cooking this sous vide is, once it's in the water bath, you don't have to worry about checking on it. You can even cook it overnight so it's ready for the next day any time you need a warming meal. ~ *Jennifer*

MAKES 6 SERVINGS

Sous vide time: 12 hours

Tips

This chili has a moderate amount of heat, with a touch of smoky flavor from the chipotle. If you prefer a mild chili, omit the chipotle or the jalapeño; if you prefer a more fiery chili, increase the chipotle to ½ tsp (2 mL) or add some hot pepper sauce to taste just before serving.

The chili will be ready to eat after about 12 hours in the water bath and, for convenience, can be held for up to 6 more hours without affecting the texture.

- **Preheat water bath to 140°F (60°C)**
- **Large resealable freezer bag**

2 tbsp	vegetable oil, divided	30 mL
1¼ lbs	stewing beef, cut into 1-inch (2.5 cm) chunks	625 g
1	medium onion, chopped	1
1	clove garlic, minced	1
2 tbsp	chili powder	30 mL
1 tsp	ground cumin	5 mL
½ tsp	dried oregano	2 mL
¼ tsp	chipotle pepper powder	1 mL
	Salt	
1	red bell pepper, chopped	1
2 tsp	minced seeded jalapeño pepper	10 mL
1	can (28 oz/796 mL) diced tomatoes, with juice	1
1	can (14 to 19 oz/398 to 540 mL) red kidney beans, drained and rinsed	1
	Sour cream, shredded Cheddar cheese and tortilla chips (optional)	

1. In a large skillet, heat 1 tbsp (15 mL) oil over medium-high heat until shimmering. Add half the beef and brown on all sides, stirring often. Using a slotted spoon, transfer to a large bowl. Repeat with the remaining beef, adding oil and adjusting heat between batches as necessary. Set aside.

2. Reduce heat to medium-low and add any remaining oil to skillet. Add onion and cook, stirring, for about 3 minutes or until softened. Add garlic, chili powder, cumin, oregano, chipotle powder and ½ tsp (2 mL) salt; cook, stirring, for about 2 minutes or until garlic is fragrant. Add red pepper and jalapeño; cook, stirring, for 2 minutes or until red pepper starts to soften. Remove from heat.

Tips

The chili can be served directly from the water bath, but if you like it piping hot, pour it into a large pot and bring it to a simmer over medium-high heat, stirring gently, until bubbling hot.

To make chili ahead, prepare through step 5, then immerse bag in ice water to chill. Refrigerate in the sealed bag for up to 3 days, or freeze for up to 6 months. Thaw overnight in the refrigerator, if frozen. Reheat in a large saucepan over medium heat, stirring often. Alternatively, heat in the sealed bag in a 140°F (60°C) water bath for 30 to 60 minutes.

3. Set a sieve over a large measuring cup or bowl and drain tomatoes. Measure $1/2$ cup (125 mL) juice; set the remainder aside for another use. Pour measured juice into skillet and stir to scrape up any brown bits stuck to pan.

4. Transfer beef and any accumulated juices to freezer bag. Add onion mixture, tomatoes and beans, stirring to combine. Remove excess air and seal bag.

5. Cook in preheated water bath, covered, for 12 hours, replenishing water as necessary to keep meat immersed. The beef should be tender; if it isn't, return to water bath and cook, checking for doneness every 30 minutes. Remove bag from water bath.

6. Season chili to taste with salt. Ladle into warmed serving bowls and, if desired, garnish with sour cream, cheese and tortilla chips.

Variations

For an added smoky chile flavor, when poblano peppers are in season, grill 2 large poblano peppers over high heat (or broil on a baking sheet), turning often, until blackened on all sides. Transfer to a bowl, cover and let cool, then peel off skins and discard core and stems. Coarsely chop the peppers and stir into chili just before serving.

Three-Chile Pork and Black Bean Chili: Substitute 1-inch (2.5 cm) chunks of trimmed boneless pork shoulder for the beef and use black beans instead of red kidney beans. Increase the water bath temperature to 144°F (62°C).

Beef and Ale Ragoût

I'm a fan of richly flavored, dark craft beers, in the glass and for cooking. In this comforting dish, a classic in winter, the dark beer adds a hearty depth of flavor that you sometimes miss with sous vide cooking, since sauces cook without evaporating. Serve with a crusty sourdough bread or fresh-baked biscuits to soak up the juice. *~ Jennifer*

Tips

The stew will be ready to eat after about 12 hours in the water bath and, for convenience, can be held for up to 6 more hours without affecting the texture.

The ragoût can be served directly from the water bath, but if you like it piping hot, pour it into a large pot and bring it to a simmer over medium-high heat, stirring gently, until bubbling hot.

- **Preheat water bath to 190°F (88°C)**
- **Large resealable freezer bag**

3 cups	sliced white potatoes (about 4 medium)	750 mL
2 cups	mushrooms, quartered	500 mL
1½ cups	chopped carrots (2 to 3)	375 mL
1 cup	sliced halved peeled white turnips	250 mL
2 tbsp	vegetable oil (approx.), divided	30 mL
6	pearl onions, peeled (or 12, if small)	6
1	bottle (12 oz/341 mL) dark ale, divided	1
	Salt and freshly ground black pepper	
¼ tsp	dried rosemary	1 mL
2 lbs	stewing beef, cut into 1-inch (2.5 cm) chunks	1 kg
3 tbsp	tomato paste	15 mL

1. In freezer bag, combine potatoes, mushrooms, carrots and turnips; set aside.

2. In a large skillet, heat 1 tbsp (15 mL) oil over medium-high heat until shimmering. Add pearl onions and cook, stirring, for about 3 minutes or until golden brown. Remove from heat and add half the ale, stirring to scrape up any brown bits stuck to pan. Stir in ½ tsp (2 mL) salt, ¼ tsp (1 mL) pepper and rosemary.

3. Add ale mixture to bag of vegetables. Remove excess air and seal bag.

4. Cook in preheated water bath for 60 to 70 minutes or until potatoes and carrots are tender. Remove bag from water bath and set aside.

5. Decrease water bath temperature to 140°F (60°F).

6. In the same large skillet (no need to clean it), heat 1 tbsp (15 mL) oil over medium-high heat until shimmering. Add half the beef and brown on all sides, stirring often. Transfer to a large bowl. Repeat with the remaining beef, adding oil and adjusting heat as necessary between batches. Set aside.

Tip

This ragoût is even better when made ahead. Prepare through step 9, then immerse bag in ice water to chill. Refrigerate in the sealed bag for up to 3 days. Using a slotted spoon, remove beef from sauce and set aside. In a large saucepan, bring sauce and vegetables to a boil over medium heat, stirring often. Add beef, reduce heat and simmer, stirring often, for 5 to 10 minutes or until beef is heated through. Alternatively, heat in the sealed bag in a 140°F (60°C) water bath for about 30 minutes; it's best to then heat until bubbling in a saucepan (see tip, page 94) to make sure it's piping hot.

7. Reduce heat to medium-low and add the remaining ale to skillet. Add tomato paste and cook, stirring, for about 3 minutes or until combined. Remove from heat.

8. Add beef mixture to vegetables in bag. Remove excess air and seal bag.

9. Cook in preheated water bath, covered, for 12 hours, replenishing water as necessary to keep meat immersed. The beef should be tender; if it isn't, return to water bath and cook, checking for doneness every 30 minutes. Remove bag from water bath.

10. Season ragoût to taste with salt and pepper. Ladle into warmed serving bowls.

Variations

In place of the white turnips, use $1\frac{1}{2}$-inch (4 cm) chunks of rutabaga or coarsely chopped parsnips, cutting them slightly larger than the carrots, as they will soften more quickly than carrots.

Beef Bourguignon: In step 2, replace the ale with $\frac{3}{4}$ cup (175 mL) no-salt-added ready-to-use beef broth. Before step 6, cook 3 slices of bacon in the skillet; remove the bacon to drain on a paper towel, then proceed with step 6. Use $\frac{3}{4}$ cup (175 mL) dry red wine (preferably a Burgundy, another Pinot Noir or a Pinot blend) in place of the beer in step 7. Crumble the bacon and add it to the freezer bag with the beef mixture in step 8.

Curry Beef and Pumpkin Stew

This simple curry dish is influenced by African flavors, including peanuts, often called groundnuts. The richness of the sauce is complemented by the mild heat and goes well with rice or cooked millet. Serve sautéed zucchini and bell peppers on the side.

**MAKES
6 SERVINGS**

Sous vide time:
12 hours

Tips

The stew will be ready to eat after about 12 hours in the water bath and, for convenience, can be held for up to 6 more hours without affecting the texture.

This stew is even better when made ahead, and can be frozen. Prepare through step 4, then immerse bag in ice water to chill. Refrigerate in the sealed bag for up to 3 days, or freeze for up to 6 months. Thaw overnight in the refrigerator, if frozen. Using a slotted spoon, remove beef from sauce and set aside. In a large saucepan, bring sauce to a boil over medium heat, stirring often. Add beef, reduce heat and simmer, stirring often, for 5 to 10 minutes or until beef is heated through. Alternatively, heat in the sealed bag in a 140°F (60°C) water bath for about 30 minutes.

- **Preheat water bath to 140°F (60°C)**
- **Large resealable freezer bag**

2 tbsp	vegetable oil, divided	30 mL
1½ lbs	stewing beef, cut into 1-inch (2.5 cm) chunks	750 g
1	medium onion, chopped	1
1½ tsp	curry powder or paste	7 mL
1 cup	canned pumpkin purée (not pie filling)	250 mL
½ cup	coconut milk (see tip, page 50)	125 mL
½ cup	water	125 mL
¼ cup	peanut butter (smooth or crunchy)	60 mL
¼ cup	freshly squeezed lime juice	60 mL
½ tsp	freshly ground black pepper	2 mL
	Salt	
1 tbsp	chopped fresh cilantro	15 mL
1	lime, cut into wedges	1

1. In a large skillet, heat 1 tbsp (15 mL) oil over medium-high heat until shimmering. Add half the beef and brown on all sides, stirring often. Using a slotted spoon, transfer beef to a large bowl. Repeat with the remaining beef, adding oil and adjusting heat as necessary between batches. Set aside.

2. Reduce heat to medium-low and add any remaining oil to skillet. Add onion and cook, stirring, for about 3 minutes or until softened. Add curry powder and cook, stirring, for about 2 minutes or until fragrant. Add pumpkin, coconut milk, water, peanut butter, lime juice, pepper and ½ tsp (2 mL) salt; cook, stirring, for 2 minutes or until smooth. Pour over beef in bowl and stir to coat.

3. Transfer meat mixture to freezer bag. Remove excess air and seal bag.

4. Cook in preheated water bath, covered, for 12 hours, replenishing water as necessary to keep meat immersed. The beef should be tender; if it isn't, return bag to water bath and cook, checking for doneness every 30 minutes. Remove bag from water bath.

5. Season curry to taste with salt. Ladle into warmed serving bowls and garnish each serving with cilantro and a lime wedge.

Broccoli and Cheddar Strata (page 42)

Lettuce Wraps with Shrimp in Spicy Peanut Sauce (page 50)

Maple Whiskey Glazed Chicken Wings (page 55)

Fresh Fajitas with Carne Asada and Avocado Pineapple Salsa (page 66)

Rainbow Beet Salad with White Cheddar and Balsamic Reduction (page 78)

Argentinian Flank Steak with Chimichurri (page 84)

Super-Slow Whiskey, Garlic and
Brown Sugar Beef Brisket (page 87)

Chile Citrus Pork Tenderloin (page 100)

Pork Loin Stuffed with Apples and Prunes, with Grainy Mustard Cream Sauce (page 102)

Cherry Chipotle Barbecue Back Ribs (page 106)

Piri Piri–Style Flattened Chicken (page 120)

Berbere Spice–Rubbed
Chicken Thighs (page 126)

Salmon Fillet with Lemon Dill Butter (page 136)

Red Curry Quinoa with Squash and Black Beans (page 144)

Fingerling Potatoes with Olive Oil and Herbs (page 154)

Mason Jar Lemon Pudding Cakes (page 166)

Pork and Lamb

Herb and Mustard Pork Chops

This recipe is easily adapted to your favorite herbs as the seasons change. Sage goes well with autumn and winter foods, while basil makes a nice spring or summer match. These chops partner well with nearly any potato, sweet potato or rice dish.

**MAKES
2 SERVINGS**

Sous vide time:
1½ hours

Tips

Use boneless center-cut or rib chops for this recipe, for the most even doneness and texture when cooked sous vide.

Keep an eye on the chops while they're under the broiler. It only takes a moment for the marinade to go from nicely done to burnt because of the honey.

This recipe can easily be doubled; use 2 medium bags or 1 large bag for 4 chops.

- **Preheat water bath to 140°F (60°C)**
- **Medium resealable freezer bag**
- **Baking sheet, lined with foil**

½ tsp	dried sage or basil	2 mL
¼ tsp	dried thyme	1 mL
¼ tsp	salt	1 mL
¼ tsp	freshly ground black pepper	1 mL
1 tbsp	Dijon mustard	15 mL
1 tbsp	liquid honey	15 mL
2	boneless pork loin chops, about ¾ inch (2 cm) thick	2

1. In a medium bowl, combine sage, thyme, salt, pepper, mustard and honey. Add pork chops and turn to coat completely.

2. Place pork chops in freezer bag, arranging in a single layer, and scrape in any remaining mustard mixture. Remove excess air and seal bag.

3. Cook in preheated water bath for 1½ hours. Remove bag from water bath and let rest for 10 minutes.

4. Meanwhile, preheat broiler with rack 6 inches (15 cm) from heat.

5. Remove chops from bag, discarding liquid, and place on prepared baking sheet.

6. Broil chops, turning once, for 2 to 3 minutes per side or until glazed and lightly browned.

Cajun-Spiced Pork Chops

This Cajun-inspired dish adds some heat to a midweek favorite. Serve it up with red beans and rice, with some mango chutney on the side.

MAKES 2 SERVINGS

Sous vide time: 1½ hours

Tips

Use boneless center-cut or rib chops for this recipe, for the most even doneness and texture with this cooking method.

These chops are cooked at a lower temperature than other tender pork cuts to keep them nice and juicy once they are blackened. The final result will be a soft, just-pink inside with a crusted outside. If you prefer a firmer pork chop, increase the water bath temperature to 135°F (57°C).

Finishing these chops in a cast-iron pan will create some smoke. Make sure to have your exhaust vent on and open some windows. If your gas barbecue grill has a side burner, consider using the cast-iron pan outside.

This recipe can easily be doubled; use 2 medium bags or 1 large bag for 4 chops.

- **Preheat water bath to 130°F (54.5°C)**
- **Medium resealable freezer bag**
- **Cast-iron pan (see variation)**

1 tsp	sweet paprika	5 mL
1 tsp	freshly ground black pepper	5 mL
½ tsp	salt	2 mL
¼ tsp	garlic powder	1 mL
¼ tsp	dried oregano	1 mL
¼ tsp	dried thyme	1 mL
Pinch	cayenne pepper	Pinch
2	boneless pork loin chops, about ¾ inch (2 cm) thick	2

1. In a shallow dish, combine paprika, black pepper, salt, garlic powder, oregano, thyme and cayenne. Add pork chops and turn to coat completely, rubbing evenly with the spices.

2. Place pork chops in freezer bag, arranging in a single layer, and add any remaining spice mixture. Remove excess air and seal bag.

3. Cook in preheated water bath for 1½ hours. Remove bag from water bath and let rest for 10 minutes.

4. Heat the cast-iron pan over medium-high heat until very hot and almost smoking. Remove chops from bag, discarding liquid, and place in hot pan. Sear, turning once, for 1 to 2 minutes per side or until spice rub is blackened.

Variations

If you don't have a cast-iron pan or prefer to use a barbecue grill, preheat barbecue grill to high, oil grill and place chops on grill. Grill, turning once, for 1 to 2 minutes per side or until sizzling and marked (they won't fully blacken as they do in the pan).

The spice rub also works well with chicken and fish. See page 28 or 32 for basic cooking instructions.

Chile Citrus Pork Tenderloin

Pork tenderloin is a meat that easily goes from perfectly cooked to overdone. Sous vide cooking allows you to hit that sweet spot every time. A quick finish on the grill gives the outside some color and traditionally cooked texture. This dish pairs well with a fruit salsa or chutney to complement the heat. If you like heat, add a little more chipotle powder.

| | MAKES 4 SERVINGS | |

Sous vide time: 1½ hours

Tip

This tenderloin is delicious cold for sandwiches, canapés or on a salad. At the end of step 3, immerse bag in ice water to chill, then refrigerate the sealed bag for up to 3 days. You can mark the pork on the grill as directed in step 6 before slicing, or skip that step.

Variations

For a milder version, replace the chipotle chile powder with an equal amount of ancho chile powder or regular chili powder.

Instead of grilling the cooked tenderloin, you can finish it in a hot cast-iron pan over medium-high heat. Cooking it in a cast-iron pan will create some smoke. Make sure to have your exhaust vent on and open some windows. If your barbecue grill has a side burner, consider using the cast-iron pan outside.

- **Preheat water bath to 140°F (60°C)**
- **Medium resealable freezer bag**
- **Barbecue grill**

1 tsp	chipotle powder	5 mL
	Salt	
2 tbsp	freshly squeezed lemon juice	30 mL
2 tbsp	freshly squeezed lime juice	30 mL
1	pork tenderloin (about 1 lb/500 g), trimmed and cut in half crosswise (see tip, page 101)	1
	Freshly ground black pepper	
	Vegetable oil or cooking spray	

1. In a shallow bowl, combine chipotle powder, ¼ tsp (1 mL) salt, lemon juice and lime juice. Add tenderloin pieces and turn to coat completely.

2. Place tenderloin pieces in freezer bag, spacing them apart, and pour in the remaining juice mixture. Remove excess air and seal bag.

3. Cook in preheated water bath for 1½ hours. Remove bag from water bath and let rest for 10 minutes.

4. Meanwhile, preheat barbecue grill to medium-high.

5. Remove tenderloin from bag, discarding liquid, and transfer to a plate. Gently pat dry (don't remove all of the seasoning, just the excess liquid). Lightly season all over with salt and pepper.

6. Oil grill and place tenderloin on grill. Grill, turning two or three times, for about 2 minutes per side or until sizzling and marked. Transfer pork to a cutting board and slice crosswise into medallions.

Serving Suggestion

- For fajitas, cut the hot tenderloin crosswise into thin slices, then stack and cut into thin strips and serve in warmed tortillas with sautéed or grilled bell peppers and onion. If the pork is chilled, add it to sautéing vegetables in a skillet for the last minute or two to warm up.

Garlic, Sage and Thyme–Rubbed Pork Tenderloin

Because of its low fat content, pork tenderloin is a very neutral-tasting meat that easily takes on whatever flavor profile you wish to assign it. In this case, we've used a classic herb combination to give this dish a rich but subtle flavor that goes well with potatoes, rice, pasta or salad. It would be nicely highlighted by roasted or grilled apples as a garnish.

MAKES 4 SERVINGS

**Sous vide time:
1½ hours**

Tips

We cut the tenderloin in half crosswise to fit it in a medium bag without bending it. If your full-length tenderloin will fit in a large bag or a vacuum-seal pouch, you can leave it whole to cook — it won't affect the timing.

Pork tenderloin can easily become overcooked on the grill. Preheat the grill well, so it's nice and hot, and don't grill for too long or you'll dry the pork out.

This tenderloin is delicious cold for sandwiches, canapés or on a salad. At the end of step 3, immerse bag in ice water to chill, then refrigerate the sealed bag for up to 3 days. You can mark the pork on the grill as directed in step 6 before slicing, or skip that step.

- **Preheat water bath to 140°F (60°C)**
- **Medium resealable freezer bag**
- **Barbecue grill**

½ tsp	dried sage	2 mL
½ tsp	dried thyme	2 mL
¼ tsp	garlic powder	1 mL
	Salt and freshly ground black pepper	
1	pork tenderloin (about 1 lb/500 g), trimmed and cut in half crosswise	1
	Vegetable oil or cooking spray	

1. In a shallow bowl, combine sage, thyme, garlic powder and ¼ tsp (1 mL) each salt and pepper. Add tenderloin pieces and turn to coat completely.

2. Place tenderloin pieces in freezer bag, spacing them apart, and add any remaining herb mixture. Remove excess air and seal bag.

3. Cook in preheated water bath for 1½ hours. Remove bag from water bath and let rest for 10 minutes.

4. Meanwhile, preheat barbecue grill to medium-high.

5. Remove tenderloin from bag, discarding liquid, and transfer to a plate. Gently pat dry (don't remove all of the seasoning, just the excess liquid). Lightly season all over with salt and pepper.

6. Oil grill and place tenderloin on grill. Grill, turning two or three times, for about 2 minutes per side or until sizzling and marked.

7. Transfer pork to a cutting board and slice crosswise into medallions.

Variation

To grill pork medallions instead of the larger piece, reduce the water bath temperature to 130°F (54.5°C) and cook as directed through step 3. Preheat the barbecue as directed. Cut the pork tenderloin into 1-inch (2.5 cm) thick medallions and grill for 1 to 2 minutes per side.

Pork Loin Stuffed with Apples and Prunes, with Grainy Mustard Cream Sauce

Combining the classic European flavors of pork and fruit, this simple yet elegant pork loin roast makes a wonderful dinner entrée. Serve it with spätzle or gnocchi, and braised red cabbage.

**MAKES
4 SERVINGS**

Sous vide time:
3 hours

Tips

Choose apples that keep their shape and flavor when cooked, such as Empire, Crispin (Mutsu), Idared or Granny Smith.

In place of prunes, substitute dried cranberries or dried tart or sweet cherries, or use a mixture of dried fruit, keeping the amount at ⅓ cup (75 mL) total.

- **Preheat water bath to 137°F (58°C)**
- **Butcher twine**
- **Large resealable freezer bag**

2 tbsp	vegetable oil, divided	30 mL
⅓ cup	finely chopped onion	75 mL
1	crisp cooking apple (unpeeled), diced	1
⅓ cup	chopped pitted prunes	75 mL
½ tsp	grainy Dijon mustard	2 mL
1½ lb	boneless center-cut pork loin roast, butterflied (see tip)	750 g
	Salt and freshly ground black pepper	

Grainy Mustard Cream Sauce

¾ cup	heavy or whipping (35%) cream	175 mL
1 tbsp	grainy Dijon mustard	15 mL
1 tsp	pure maple syrup	5 mL
	Salt and freshly ground black pepper	

1. In a large skillet, heat 1 tbsp (15 mL) oil over medium heat. Add onion and cook, stirring, for about 5 minutes or until softened. Add apple, prunes and mustard; reduce heat to medium-low and cook, stirring occasionally, for about 5 minutes or until apple is tender. Remove from heat and let cool completely.

2. Pat pork dry and spread roast open, cut side up, on a cutting board. Lightly season the cut side with salt and pepper. Spread cooled fruit mixture evenly across surface of roast. Starting at one short edge, gently roll up the roast into a cylinder, jelly roll–style. Tie with butcher twine.

3. In clean skillet, heat the remaining oil over medium heat until shimmering. Working carefully to avoid losing stuffing, transfer roast to the pan and sear until golden brown on all sides. Transfer to a plate and let cool for 5 minutes.

Tips

For a more elegant plate presentation, first pour the sauce on the plate, then lay the sliced pork on top, nestled up against the accompanying side dishes.

This pork roast is best served right after cooking, but elements can be prepared ahead. The apple filling can be prepared, covered and refrigerated for up to 2 days; let warm at room temperature for 15 to 30 minutes to remove the chill before filling the roast. Do not stuff the roast ahead. The cream sauce can be cooked, cooled and refrigerated in an airtight container for up to 2 days. While the roast is resting, reheat the sauce in a saucepan over medium-low heat, stirring often, until hot.

4. Place pork roast in freezer bag. Remove excess air and seal bag.

5. Cook in preheated water bath for 3 hours. Remove pork from bag, discarding liquid, and transfer to a cutting board. Tent with foil and let rest for 15 minutes.

6. *Cream Sauce:* Meanwhile, in a small saucepan, combine cream, mustard and maple syrup. Bring to a simmer over medium heat, stirring often. Reduce heat and simmer gently, stirring often, for about 5 minutes or until reduced by one-third. Season to taste with salt and pepper.

7. Cut roast crosswise into thick slices and serve with cream sauce.

How to Butterfly a Pork Loin

Ask your butcher to butterfly the pork loin for you, or you can easily do it yourself. To do so, cut off any strings. Place the loin on a cutting board, fat side down, with one narrow end closest to you. Hold a large knife parallel to the cutting board and, starting on the right side of the loin, about one-third of the way up from the board, cut almost but not all the way through to the left side, leaving about ¾ inch (2 cm) intact. Open the loin up like a book, with the thicker side to the left, and press flat. Starting in the center of the opened loin, cut in half on the left side, almost but not all the way through, then press open. You should now have a rectangle with three sections of approximately equal thickness.

Porchetta-Style Roast Pork Loin

Traditionally, a porchetta roast has loads of garlic and herbs stuffed in the middle. There are as many versions as there are families. This one is inspired by the Italian classic and is rich with basil and garlic, but is modified to better suit sous vide cooking. Sous vide leaves it moist and juicy in the middle, while finishing it on the barbecue makes for a rich, smoky flavor on the outside. Heads up: leftovers make a really good sandwich.

MAKES 6 TO 8 SERVINGS

Sous vide time: 3 hours

Tips

Sometimes pork loin roasts come with two single loins tied together as one roast, making what's called a double roast. For this recipe, be sure to use a single loin roast; it should be tied into a neat, uniformly thick roast. We love the rib end for its slightly richer flavor, but any loin cut will work.

As herbs come into season, you can mix them with the basil, keeping the total amount at about ½ cup (125 mL). Sage, parsley, rosemary and fennel seeds are all complementary flavors.

To chill the roast, at the end of step 7, let it cool slightly, then return it to the freezer bag. Remove excess air and seal bag. Immerse bag in ice water to chill, then refrigerate for up to 3 days.

- **Preheat water bath to 140°F (60°C)**
- **Mini chopper or small food processor**
- **Large resealable freezer bag**
- **Barbecue grill**

½ cup	packed fresh basil leaves	125 mL
1 tsp	garlic powder	5 mL
	Salt and freshly ground black pepper	
¼ cup	olive oil (approx.)	60 mL
3 to 3½ lb	boneless pork loin roast, tied (see tip)	1.5 to 1.75 kg

1. In mini chopper, combine basil, garlic powder, ½ tsp (2 mL) salt, ½ tsp (2 mL) pepper and oil; purée until a smooth paste forms. If it seems too thick, add more oil, a little at a time, puréeing until oil is incorporated and paste is the desired consistency.

2. Transfer purée to a large bowl. Pat pork dry, add to purée and turn to completely coat the roast.

3. Place roast in freezer bag and scrape in any remaining purée. Remove excess air and seal bag.

4. Cook in preheated water bath for 3 hours. Remove bag from water bath and let rest for 10 minutes.

5. Meanwhile, preheat barbecue grill to high.

6. Remove roast from bag, discarding liquid, and transfer to a plate. Lightly season all over with salt and pepper.

7. Place roast on grill. Grill, rolling roast gently to brown all sides, for about 2 minutes per side or until sizzling and marked. Reduce heat to low (or move roast to cool side of grill) and let stand on grill for 5 minutes.

8. Transfer pork to a cutting board. Use scissors to remove butcher twine, then cut across the grain into thin or medium-thick slices.

Serving Suggestions

- Serve a spicy aïoli or basil pesto alongside the hot roast, or with slices of hot or cold roast on a crusty bun for a sandwich.
- Dice leftover roast and add to a corn chowder or minestrone soup.

Honey Sriracha Pork Belly

Pork belly — uncured bacon — is popular in cultures around the world. This version is balanced between the heat of Sriracha sauce and the sweetness of honey.

MAKES 6 TO 8 SERVINGS

Sous vide time: 12 hours

Tips

High-fat foods, such as this pork belly, float in the water bath, so weighing down the bag with a heavy spoon, ladle or other heatproof, waterproof weighty utensil is important to keep the bag immersed.

When cooking for this length of time, covering the sous vide container improves heat efficiency and slows down water evaporation (see page 16).

To make ahead, prepare through step 4, then immerse bag in ice water to chill. Refrigerate in the sealed bag for up to 5 days, then proceed with step 5.

- Preheat water bath to 155°F (68°C)
- Large resealable freezer bag

1 tsp	ground ginger	5 mL
½ tsp	garlic powder	2 mL
3 tbsp	Sriracha	45 mL
1 tbsp	liquid honey	15 mL
1 tbsp	reduced-sodium soy sauce	15 mL
2¼ lb	pork belly (1 slab)	1.125 kg

1. In a large bowl, whisk together ginger, garlic powder, Sriracha, honey and soy sauce.
2. Cut pork belly crosswise into 4 equal pieces. Add to bowl and toss to coat evenly.
3. Transfer pork belly pieces to freezer bag and add any remaining sauce. Remove excess air and seal bag.
4. Place in preheated water bath and weigh down bag with a heavy spoon. Cook, covered, for 12 hours, replenishing water as necessary to keep pork immersed.
5. Remove pork belly from bag, discarding liquid, and transfer to a cutting board. Pat pork dry with a paper towel. Cut each piece of pork belly across the grain into 4 equal slices.
6. Heat a large skillet over medium heat. In batches as necessary to avoid crowding the pan, sear pork belly slices, turning, for 2 to 3 minutes per side or until golden brown (be careful, as pork will splatter). Transfer to a plate lined with paper towels. Adjust heat as necessary between batches to prevent burning.

Serving Suggestions

- This pork belly is wonderful sliced thin and served in noodle soups, on sandwiches or simply topped with a soft poached egg.
- Because of its richness, this pork belly is particularly tasty accompanied by tangy vinegar-based coleslaw or spicy kimchi.

Cherry Chipotle Barbecue Back Ribs

Ribs benefit from a long, slow cooking method, making them an ideal candidate for sous vide. You can cook them overnight, then chill for the day and warm them up and do the final glaze just before serving. The homemade barbecue sauce with tangy cherries and smoky heat puts these ribs over the top — in the best way possible.

**MAKES
4 SERVINGS,
ABOUT 2½ CUPS
(625 ML) SAUCE**

**Sous vide time:
12 hours**

Tips

To peel tomatoes, bring a pot of water to a boil over high heat. Working with 2 or 3 tomatoes at a time, plunge them into boiling water for 30 seconds. Immediately transfer to a bowl of very cold water and let cool. Cut out cores and peel off skins.

The secret to super-tender ribs (with any cooking method) is to remove the membrane from the bone side. Place ribs on a cutting board. Using the tip of a knife and starting at one end of the ribs, lift the thin membrane that covers the bone. Using a paper towel to help grip, peel off the membrane and discard; trim off any excess fat.

- **Immersion blender or blender**
- **2 extra-large resealable freezer bags**
- **Barbecue grill**

Cherry Chipotle Barbecue Sauce

2 tbsp	butter	30 mL
1	small onion, finely chopped	1
1	clove garlic, minced	1
½ tsp	salt	2 mL
½ tsp	dry mustard	2 mL
½ tsp	ground ginger	2 mL
½ tsp	chipotle chile powder	2 mL
¼ tsp	freshly ground black pepper	1 mL
Pinch	celery seeds	Pinch
5	plum (Roma) tomatoes (about 1¼ lbs/ 625 g total), peeled, seeded and chopped	5
2 cups	pitted sweet cherries (about 12 oz/ 375 g), halved (thawed, if frozen)	500 mL
⅔ cup	packed brown sugar	150 mL
¼ cup	apple cider vinegar	60 mL
2 tbsp	tomato paste	30 mL
2	racks pork back ribs, trimmed (see tip)	2

1. *Barbecue Sauce:* In a deep pot, melt butter over medium heat. Add onion and cook, stirring, for 3 minutes or until softened. Add garlic, salt, mustard, ginger, chipotle powder, pepper and celery seeds; cook, stirring, for 2 minutes or until spices are fragrant.

2. Stir in tomatoes, cherries, brown sugar, vinegar and tomato paste; bring to a boil, stirring often. Reduce heat and boil gently, stirring often, for about 30 minutes or until tomatoes and cherries are very soft and sauce is thick. Reduce heat and stir more often as the sauce thickens to prevent burning.

Tips

The barbecue sauce actually benefits from being made at least a few days ahead. Transfer cooled sauce to a clean jar or airtight container, cover tightly and refrigerate for up to 1 month or freeze for up to 3 months. Thaw overnight in the refrigerator, if necessary.

To make ribs ahead, prepare through step 7, then immerse bags in ice water to chill. Refrigerate in the sealed bags for up to 3 days or freeze for up to 3 months (storing extra sauce separately). Thaw in the refrigerator overnight, if frozen. Reheat in a 144°F (62°C) water bath for 30 minutes, then proceed with step 8.

3. Using an immersion blender in the pot, purée sauce until smooth (or transfer sauce to an upright blender to purée, then return to the pot). Bring sauce to a simmer over medium heat, stirring often. Reduce heat and simmer, stirring often (watch carefully, as sauce will splatter), for 10 to 15 minutes or until sauce is thick. Let cool (see tip).

4. Preheat water bath to 144°F (62°C).

5. Place ribs on a cutting board. Cut each rack in half (or to a length that will fit in freezer bags). Spread about 1 cup (250 mL) barbecue sauce evenly over ribs. Cover and refrigerate the remaining barbecue sauce.

6. Place ribs in freezer bags, arranging in a single layer. Remove excess air and seal bags.

7. Cook in preheated water bath, covered, for 12 hours, replenishing water as necessary to keep meat immersed. The ribs should be fork-tender; if they aren't, return bag to water bath and cook, checking for doneness every 30 minutes. Remove bags from water bath.

8. Preheat barbecue grill to medium-high.

9. Warm the remaining barbecue sauce slightly in the microwave on Medium (50%) or in a saucepan over medium-low heat.

10. Remove ribs from bags, discarding liquid, and transfer to a cutting board. Pat ribs dry. Cut into 2- or 3-rib portions.

11. Place ribs on preheated grill. Grill, turning once, for 1 to 2 minutes per side or until lightly browned. Brush both sides with barbecue sauce. Grill, turning once and brushing with sauce, for 2 to 3 minutes per side or until hot and glazed. Serve extra sauce on the side, as desired.

Variations

To broil ribs instead of grilling, preheat broiler with rack 6 inches (15 cm) from heat. Line a large rimmed baking sheet with foil and place cut rib portions on sheet. Brush both sides of ribs with barbecue sauce. Broil, turning once, for 3 to 4 minutes per side or until hot and glazed.

Tart Cherry Chipotle Barbecue Sauce: If red tart (sour) cherries are available, use them in place of sweet cherries and increase the brown sugar to ¾ cup (175 mL). If using the pre-pitted cherries in buckets, use 1½ cups (375 mL) packed drained cherries and ¼ cup (60 mL) of the juice.

Shortcut Barbecue Ribs: Instead of making your own sauce, use 2 cups (500 mL) good-quality bottled barbecue sauce. Choose a thick, flavorful sauce that isn't too sugary. A thin sauce will create too much liquid and lack flavor; a sugary sauce will become too sweet when cooking sous vide and will burn when grilling.

Thai Coconut Red Curry Ribs

These ribs are a sous vide variation on one of my favorite recipes from the *Complete Curry Cookbook*, which I co-wrote with Byron Ayanoglu. The complex flavors of the zesty sauce infuse into the ribs during the long, slow cooking. I love to serve them as a centerpiece of a Thai-inspired meal with steaming jasmine rice and green mango salad. ~ *Jennifer*

**MAKES
4 SERVINGS**

**Sous vide time:
12 hours**

Tips

When using only part of a can of coconut milk, as in this recipe, be sure to shake the can before opening, then, before measuring the milk, use a small whisk to thoroughly incorporate the cream layer that tends to float to the top. Extra coconut milk can be refrigerated in an airtight container for up to 5 days or frozen for up to 6 months.

This amount of red curry paste gives a bit of a hot kick to the sauce, but not too much. For more heat, increase the paste to 1½ to 2 tbsp (22 to 30 mL). Or, for a mild version, use 1½ tsp (7 mL). You can always add a little splash of Asian hot sauce to the reserved sauce before glazing the ribs if you find you want a little more kick.

- **2 extra-large resealable freezer bags**
- **Barbecue grill**

¾ cup	well-stirred coconut milk, divided	175 mL
2	cloves garlic, minced	2
2 tbsp	minced gingerroot	30 mL
1 tbsp	Thai red curry paste	15 mL
2 oz	block tamarind	60 mL
¼ cup	packed brown sugar or palm sugar	60 mL
2 tbsp	fish sauce	30 mL
1 tsp	grated lime zest	5 mL
1 tbsp	freshly squeezed lime juice	15 mL
2	racks pork back ribs, trimmed (see tip, page 109)	2

1. In a small saucepan, heat 2 tbsp (30 mL) coconut milk over medium heat until bubbling. Add garlic, ginger and curry paste; cook, stirring, for about 1 minute or until softened and fragrant.

2. Add tamarind, brown sugar, the remaining coconut milk and fish sauce; bring to a boil, stirring and mashing tamarind. Reduce heat and boil gently, stirring often, for about 15 minutes or until reduced by about one-third.

3. Strain tamarind mixture through a fine-mesh sieve into a bowl, pressing to push as much pulp through as possible; discard solids. Stir in lime zest and lime juice. Let cool completely.

4. Preheat water bath to 144°F (62°C).

5. Place ribs on a cutting board. Cut each rack in half (or to a length that will fit in freezer bags).

6. Place ribs in freezer bags and pour one-quarter of the tamarind sauce into each bag. Turn bags and gently massage ribs to evenly coat with sauce. Arrange ribs in a single layer. Remove excess air and seal bags. Cover and refrigerate the remaining sauce.

Tips

The secret to super-tender ribs (with any cooking method) is to remove the membrane from the bone side. Place ribs on a cutting board. Using the tip of a knife and starting at one end of the ribs, lift the thin membrane that covers the bone. Using a paper towel to help grip, peel off the membrane and discard; trim off any excess fat.

To make ribs ahead, prepare through step 7, then immerse bags in ice water to chill. Refrigerate in the sealed bags for up to 3 days or freeze for up to 3 months (storing extra sauce separately). Thaw in the refrigerator overnight, if frozen. Reheat in a 144°F (62°C) water bath for 30 minutes, then proceed with step 8.

7. Cook ribs in preheated water bath, covered, for 12 hours, replenishing water as necessary to keep meat immersed. The ribs should be fork tender; if they aren't, return bag to water bath and cook, checking for doneness every 30 minutes. Remove bags from water bath.

8. Preheat barbecue grill to medium-high.

9. Warm the remaining sauce slightly in the microwave on Medium (50%) or in a saucepan over medium-low heat.

10. Remove ribs from bags, discarding liquid, and transfer to a cutting board. Pat ribs dry. Cut into 2- or 3-rib portions.

11. Place ribs on preheated grill. Grill, turning once, for 1 to 2 minutes per side or until lightly browned. Brush both sides with sauce. Grill, turning once, for 2 to 3 minutes per side, until hot and glazed. Serve any extra sauce on the side.

Variation

To broil ribs instead of grilling, preheat broiler with rack 6 inches (15 cm) from heat. Line a large rimmed baking sheet with foil and place cut rib portions on sheet. Broil for 3 to 4 minutes per side or until lightly browned. Brush both sides of ribs with sauce. Broil, turning once, for 2 to 3 minutes per side or until hot and glazed.

Retro Sweet-and-Sour Spareribs

When I was growing up, my mom, who is a fabulous cook, made everything from scratch, so we didn't eat much takeout. But on occasion, my dad picked up Chinese takeout and, as we dug in to that big paper bag, we knew there would always be a container of those sticky, glazed sweet-and-sour ribs. This glaze is as close as I could get to that '70s version of my memory, and the sous vide makes them melt-in-your-mouth tender. ~ *Jennifer*

**Sous vide time:
12 hours**

Tips

Don't be tempted to use fresh pineapple for this recipe, as it contains the enzyme bromelain, which breaks down protein (it's used to make meat tenderizer) and makes these ribs too mushy with the long cooking time. (Ask us how we know!) The sous vide does a great job of making them tender without the enzyme, which has been deactivated in canned pineapple.

If you can find the narrow strips of sliced ribs (sometimes called riblets), use 4 rack-length strips for this recipe and broil the strips whole (or halved to fit on the baking sheet), then cut them into sections and proceed as directed.

- **Preheat broiler with rack 4 inches (10 cm) from heat**
- **Rimmed baking sheet, lined with foil**
- **2 large resealable freezer bags**

1	can (14 to 15 oz/398 to 425 mL) pineapple tidbits (see tip)	1
½ cup	granulated sugar or packed brown sugar	125 mL
1 tsp	ground ginger	5 mL
½ tsp	garlic powder	2 mL
⅓ cup	reduced-sodium soy sauce	75 mL
2 tbsp	unseasoned rice vinegar or cider vinegar	30 mL
2	racks pork side or back ribs, trimmed (see tips, page 111)	2
4 tsp	cornstarch	20 mL
1 tbsp	cold water	15 mL
	Additional reduced-sodium soy sauce or salt	

1. Drain pineapple, reserving juice. Measure 1 cup (250 mL) pineapple tidbits and ¼ cup (60 mL) juice. Store extra pineapple and juice in an airtight container in the refrigerator for another use.

2. In a small saucepan, combine sugar, ginger, garlic powder, soy sauce and vinegar. Bring to a boil over medium heat, stirring to dissolve sugar. Reduce heat and boil gently, stirring often, for 2 minutes. Remove from heat and stir in ¼ cup (60 mL) pineapple. Let cool completely. Transfer the remaining pineapple and the ¼ cup (60 mL) juice to an airtight container and refrigerate while cooking ribs.

3. Preheat water bath to 144°F (62°C).

4. Cut ribs into 3- or 4-rib portions and arrange on prepared baking sheet, spacing them apart. Broil, turning once, for 4 to 5 minutes per side or until lightly browned. Let cool completely.

Tips

The secret to super-tender ribs (with any cooking method) is to remove the membrane from the bone side. Place ribs on a cutting board. Using the tip of a knife and starting at one end of the ribs, lift the thin membrane that covers the bone. Using a paper towel to help grip, peel off the membrane and discard; trim off any excess fat.

To make ribs ahead, prepare through step 6, then immerse bags in ice water to chill. Refrigerate in the sealed bags for up to 3 days or freeze for up to 3 months. Thaw in the refrigerator overnight, if frozen. Reheat in a 144°F (62°C) water bath for 30 minutes, then proceed with step 7.

5. Place ribs in freezer bags and pour in sauce, dividing equally. Turn bags and gently massage ribs to evenly coat with sauce. Arrange ribs in a single layer. Remove excess air and seal bags.

6. Cook in preheated water bath, covered, for 12 hours, replenishing water as necessary to keep meat immersed. The ribs should be fork-tender. If they aren't, return bag to water bath and cook, checking for doneness every 30 minutes. Remove bags from water bath.

7. Using tongs, remove ribs from bags, reserving sauce, and transfer to a warmed serving dish. Cover dish with foil to keep warm.

8. Pour reserved sauce into a glass measuring cup. Spoon off and discard as much fat from sauce as possible.

9. Pour sauce into a small saucepan and add the remaining pineapple and pineapple juice. Bring to a boil over medium-high heat.

10. In a small bowl, whisk together cornstarch and water. Pour into saucepan, whisking. Boil, whisking constantly, for about 3 minutes or until sauce is thickened and glossy. Season to taste with soy sauce. Pour over ribs. Serve immediately.

Serving Suggestion

• For the complete retro experience, serve with steamed white rice or fried rice and stir-fried snow peas or broccoli. Don't forget the packaged fortune cookies.

Mediterranean Lamb Shoulder Chops with Tomatoes, Olives and Capers

Sous vide cooking helps transform a cut usually destined for cold-weather braising into a refreshing dish custom-made for the bounty of summer's harvest. Let the vegetables marinate while the lamb cooks, plate it up at the last minute with a simple side of rice or pasta, and you've got a perfect dish for no-fuss entertaining.

MAKES 4 SERVINGS

Sous vide time: 24 hours

Tip

If you prefer to warm the tomato mixture before serving, transfer it to a medium resealable freezer bag and add it to the water bath about 15 minutes before the lamb is done. Leave it in while the lamb rests and grills, or reheat in a saucepan over medium-low heat, stirring often.

- Preheat water bath to 140°F (60°C)
- Large resealable freezer bag
- Barbecue grill

2 tbsp	olive oil (approx.), divided	30 mL
4	bone-in lamb shoulder blade chops, ½ inch (1 cm) thick (about 2 lbs/1 kg total)	4
	Salt and freshly ground black pepper	
¼ cup	dry white wine	60 mL
1	medium tomato, chopped	1
½ cup	quartered drained marinated artichoke hearts	125 mL
¼ cup	pitted kalamata olives	60 mL
1 tsp	drained capers	5 mL
¼ cup	chopped fresh parsley	60 mL
	Vegetable oil or cooking spray	

1. In a large skillet, heat 1 tbsp (15 mL) olive oil over medium heat until shimmering. Pat lamb dry and season both sides with salt and pepper. Add lamb chops to skillet, in batches as necessary, and sear, turning once, for 3 to 4 minutes or until browned on both sides. Transfer to a plate and let cool slightly. Repeat with the remaining chops, adding olive oil and adjusting heat as necessary between batches. (Reserve skillet.)

2. Place lamb chops in freezer bag, arranging in a single layer. Remove excess air and seal bag.

3. Cook in preheated water bath, covered, for 24 hours, replenishing water as necessary to keep meat immersed.

Variations

Instead of white wine, you can use 1 tbsp (15 mL) freshly squeezed lemon juice and 1 tbsp (15 mL) water; reduce the boiling time to 30 seconds.

For a real kick, substitute 2 tbsp (30 mL) ouzo for the white wine; reduce the boiling time to 30 seconds. Also serve some ouzo over ice as a beverage — perfect on a summer day.

To use a grill pan instead of a barbecue grill to finish the chops, preheat pan over medium-high heat until hot and almost smoking (turn on your hood vent or open the windows). Lightly oil pan and sear chops, turning once, for 1 to 2 minutes per side or until sizzling and marked.

4. Return skillet to medium heat. Add wine and bring to a boil, scraping up any brown bits stuck to pan. Boil for 1 minute. Add tomato, artichokes, olives and capers; cook, stirring occasionally, for 3 to 4 minutes or until tomatoes just start to soften. Remove from heat and stir in parsley. Transfer to an airtight container, let cool and refrigerate until required, for up to 2 days.

5. Remove lamb from water bath and let rest for 10 minutes. Remove tomato mixture from the fridge and let stand at room temperature.

6. Meanwhile, preheat barbecue grill to high.

7. Remove lamb from bag, discarding liquid, and pat dry.

8. Oil grill and place lamb chops on grill. Grill, turning once, for 1 to 2 minutes per side or until sizzling and marked. Place on serving plates or a platter and garnish with tomato mixture.

Serving Suggestion

- To make a side salad for the lamb (or another meal), the tomato and artichoke mixture can easily be doubled and combined with cooled cooked pasta and a little crumbled feta cheese.

Beer-Braised Lamb Shanks

Great for a wintry night, these lamb shanks are rich with the earthy flavors of root vegetables and malty beer. Serve with mashed potatoes or polenta, to soak up all the juicy goodness, and buttered green peas.

**MAKES
4 SERVINGS**

Sous vide time:
24 hours

Tips

If you don't have pink peppercorns, you can use ½ tsp (2 mL) cracked black peppercorns instead, though the pink ones do add an interesting, woodsy flavor to the lamb.

The lamb will be fall-off-the-bone tender, so be sure to handle the shanks gently when transferring them from the bag to the saucepan and when stirring while the sauce is reducing, to prevent them from falling apart. If they are falling apart too much (or look like they're about to), use a slotted spoon to remove them from the sauce while you simmer it down, and keep the shanks warm in a covered dish.

Like many braised dishes, these shanks actually taste better the next day. Remove them from the water bath after step 4 and immerse bag in ice water to chill. Refrigerate in the sealed bag for up to 3 days. When ready to serve, proceed with step 5, simmering until the lamb is piping hot and the sauce is thickened.

- **Preheat water bath to 165°F (74°C)**
- **Large resealable freezer bag**

2 tbsp	olive oil	30 mL
4	lamb shanks (about 2 lbs/1 kg total)	4
1 cup	finely chopped onion	250 mL
1 cup	finely chopped carrots	250 mL
1 cup	diced parsnips or turnips	250 mL
1 cup	beer (preferably dark or amber ale)	250 mL
	Salt	
1 tsp	dried rosemary, crumbled	5 mL
¼ tsp	pink peppercorns, crushed	1 mL
	Freshly ground black pepper	

1. In a large skillet, heat oil over medium heat until shimmering. Pat lamb shanks dry. Sear on all sides until golden brown. Transfer to a plate and let cool.

2. Add onion to the skillet and cook, stirring, for 2 to 3 minutes or until lightly browned. Add carrots and parsnips; cook, stirring occasionally, for 3 to 4 minutes or until starting to soften. Add beer, 1 tsp (5 mL) salt, rosemary and peppercorns; bring to a boil. Reduce heat and simmer for 3 to 4 minutes.

3. Place lamb shanks and vegetables in freezer bag. Remove excess air and seal bag.

4. Cook in preheated water bath, covered, for 24 hours, replenishing water as necessary to keep meat immersed.

5. Transfer lamb, vegetables and cooking liquid from bag to a large, deep saucepan. Bring to a boil over medium heat. Reduce heat and simmer, stirring gently occasionally, for 10 to 15 minutes or until sauce has thickened to gravy consistency. Season to taste with salt and pepper.

Serving Suggestion

- Make lamb poutine: Before step 5, transfer the shanks to a large bowl and break the meat into large chunks; discard bones. Transfer sauce and vegetables to the saucepan and bring to a boil. Whisk 2 tbsp (30 mL) all-purpose flour with 2 tbsp (30 mL) beer, then whisk into sauce; simmer until gravy is thick, then return meat to the gravy. Cook up a pile of french fries, arrange them on a platter, top with lamb and gravy, then sprinkle with cheese curds.

Dijon and Rosemary Leg of Lamb

This French-inspired lamb roast is ideal for festive occasions and is simple to prepare. Sous vide ensures that it's cooked perfectly all the way through. Serve with fluffy mashed potatoes and steamed haricots verts or asparagus to complete the experience.

MAKES 6 TO 8 SERVINGS

Sous vide time: 10 hours

Tips

Some lamb roasts come tied in a fine mesh elastic netting, but that tends to make a very dense roast. For this recipe, it's best to use a roast tied with butcher string at about 1-inch (2.5 cm) intervals along its length, rather than the netting.

No mortar and pestle? Crush peppercorns on a cutting board with the bottom of a saucepan.

For a silkier sauce, after step 8, purée it with an immersion blender until smooth.

Leftover lamb roast can be cooled, wrapped and refrigerated for up to 4 days. Serve cold or reheat by slicing it a little thicker and searing the slices in a skillet over medium-high heat, turning once, for about 1 minute per side.

- Preheat water bath to 139°F (59°C)
- Large resealable freezer bag

1 tbsp	vegetable oil	15 mL
2½ lb	boneless lamb leg roast, tied (see tip)	1.25 kg
2 tbsp	Dijon mustard	30 mL
¼ tsp	pink peppercorns, crushed	1 mL
¼ tsp	dried rosemary, crumbled	1 mL
	Salt and freshly ground black pepper	
	Water (if necessary)	
¼ cup	butter	60 mL
¼ cup	all-purpose flour	60 mL
2 tbsp	dry red wine	30 mL

1. In a large skillet, heat oil over medium heat until shimmering. Pat lamb dry. Sear on all sides until golden brown. Transfer to a plate and let cool.

2. In a small bowl, combine mustard, peppercorns, rosemary and ¼ tsp (1 mL) each salt and pepper. Spread evenly over entire lamb roast.

3. Place lamb roast in freezer bag. Remove excess air and seal bag.

4. Cook in preheated water bath, covered, for 10 hours, replenishing water as necessary to keep meat immersed.

5. Remove lamb roast from bag, reserving liquid, and transfer to a cutting board. Tent with foil and let rest while you prepare the sauce.

6. Pour reserved liquid through a fine-mesh sieve and measure 2 cups (500 mL), adding water if necessary.

7. In a small saucepan, melt butter over medium heat. Reduce heat to low and whisk in flour. Cook, stirring constantly, for 5 to 6 minutes or until flour is bubbling and lightly browned. Gradually pour in wine, whisking to make a paste.

8. Add about one-quarter of the lamb juices, a little at a time, whisking until sauce is blended and smooth. Pour in the remaining lamb juices, stirring constantly. Bring to a simmer over medium heat; reduce heat and simmer, stirring often, for 5 to 6 minutes or until sauce is slightly thickened. Season to taste with salt and pepper.

9. Cut off strings and cut lamb across the grain into thin slices. Serve on a platter with sauce on the side.

Greek-Style Leg of Lamb with Lemon and Oregano

This traditional Mediterranean-style boneless lamb roast is great for summer nights on the patio. Serve it with roasted potatoes, Greek salad and warm pita bread.

Tips

Some lamb roasts come tied in a fine mesh elastic netting, but that tends to make a very dense roast. For this recipe, it's best to use a roast tied with butcher string at about 1-inch (2.5 cm) intervals along its length, rather than the netting.

Leftover lamb roast can be cooled, wrapped and refrigerated for up to 4 days. Serve cold or reheat by slicing it a little thicker and searing the slices in a skillet over medium-high heat, turning once, for about 1 minute per side.

Variation

Instead of broiling, you can brown the cooked roast on a barbecue grill preheated to medium-high. Oil grill and place lamb on grill. Grill, turning often, for about 5 minutes per side or until brown and sizzling. While grilling the roast, cut a couple of lemons in half and grill, cut side down, then serve them alongside the roast to squeeze over top.

- **Preheat water bath to 139°F (59°C)**
- **Large resealable freezer bag**
- **Baking sheet, lined with foil**

3 tbsp	olive oil, divided	45 mL
2½ lb	boneless lamb leg roast, tied (see tip)	1.25 kg
	Salt and freshly ground black pepper	
2	small cloves garlic, finely minced	2
1½ tsp	dried oregano	7 mL
2 tbsp	freshly squeezed lemon juice	30 mL

1. In a large skillet, heat 1 tbsp (15 mL) oil over medium heat until shimmering. Pat lamb dry and season all over with salt and pepper. Sear on all sides until golden brown. Transfer to a plate and let cool.

2. In a large bowl, combine garlic, oregano, lemon juice and the remaining oil. Add lamb roast and turn to coat evenly.

3. Place lamb roast in freezer bag and scrape in any remaining oil mixture. Remove excess air and seal bag.

4. Cook in preheated water bath, covered, for 10 hours, replenishing water as necessary to keep meat immersed. Remove bag from water bath and let rest for 10 minutes.

5. Meanwhile, preheat broiler with rack 8 inches (20 cm) from heat.

6. Remove lamb roast from bag, discarding liquid, and pat dry. Place on prepared baking sheet.

7. Broil lamb, turning often, for 3 to 5 minutes per side or until crisp and golden brown. Transfer lamb to a cutting board. Cut off strings and cut lamb across the grain into thin slices.

Poultry

Coq au Vin

In North America, we have Julia Child to thank for introducing classic French recipes such as coq au vin to us, and now you can thank your sous vide machine for giving you a fuss-free, simplified way to cook it. The rich sauce permeates the chicken while it cooks, but you still taste the meat itself, which can sometimes get lost with traditional cooking methods. Serve with fluffy mashed potatoes — and a glass of wine, of course.

MAKES 4 TO 6 SERVINGS

Sous vide time:
3½ hours

Tips

A Pinot Noir, either from France or a French-style wine, is the traditional wine for this dish, as it lends a rich wine flavor and doesn't overpower the chicken, while giving a lighter color than some bigger reds do. If you prefer an even lighter-colored dish, and a lighter taste, use an unoaked Chardonnay or a Pinot Gris.

Air-chilled chicken is a must when cooking sous vide to make sure you get a rich chicken flavor rather than a watery one.

- **Preheat water bath to 148°F (64°C)**
- **Large resealable freezer bag**
- **Large rimmed baking sheet, lined with foil**

3	slices bacon, chopped	3
1 tbsp	olive oil	15 mL
2	cloves garlic, minced	2
1	small onion, finely chopped	1
1 cup	chopped mushrooms	250 mL
¼ tsp	dried thyme (or 1 sprig fresh thyme)	1 mL
	Salt and freshly ground black pepper	
2 tbsp	brandy or cognac	30 mL
1	bay leaf	1
½ cup	light dry red wine (such as Pinot Noir) or dry white wine	125 mL
½ cup	ready-to-use chicken broth	125 mL
1 tbsp	tomato paste	15 mL
3 to 4 lb	whole chicken	1.5 to 2 kg
2 tbsp	all-purpose flour	30 mL
2 tbsp	butter, softened	30 mL
	Chopped fresh parsley	

1. In a large skillet, cook bacon over medium-high heat until crisp. Using a slotted spoon, transfer bacon to a bowl and set aside. Drain off all but 1 tbsp (15 mL) fat from pan.

2. Reduce heat to medium and add oil to bacon fat in skillet. Add garlic, onion, mushrooms, thyme, ¼ tsp (1 mL) salt and ½ tsp (2 mL) pepper; cook, stirring, for about 5 minutes or until onion is soft and mushrooms release their liquid and start to brown.

3. Add brandy and boil, stirring, until evaporated. Add bay leaf and wine; bring to a boil, scraping up any brown bits stuck to pan. Remove from heat and stir in broth and tomato paste. Let cool completely.

To make ahead, prepare chicken through step 6, then immerse bag in ice water to chill. Refrigerate in the sealed bag for up to 2 days. Using a slotted spoon, remove chicken from sauce and set aside. In a large saucepan, bring sauce to a boil over medium heat, stirring often. Add chicken, reduce heat and simmer, stirring often, for 5 to 10 minutes or until chicken is heated through. Remove the chicken with a slotted spoon and proceed with step 7. Alternatively, heat in the sealed bag in a 140°F (60°C) water bath for 30 minutes, then proceed with step 7.

4. Meanwhile, place chicken, breast side down, on a large cutting board, with the neck farthest away from you. Using a sharp knife or kitchen shears, cut along the right side of the back bone, starting at the tail and working up to the neck. Repeat on the left side to remove the back bone (reserve for stock or discard). Cut leg quarters from body and cut at the joint into thighs and drumsticks. Cut wings from body. Flip breast over so bone is facing up and cut along the breast bone into two halves. Cut each breast on a slight diagonal into 2 pieces.

5. Transfer chicken to freezer bag and pour in sauce. Add half the bacon; wrap and refrigerate the remaining bacon. Arrange chicken pieces in a single layer. Remove excess air and seal bag.

6. Cook in preheated water bath for 3½ hours. Remove from water bath and let rest for 5 minutes.

7. Meanwhile, preheat broiler with rack 6 inches (15 cm) from heat. Remove reserved bacon from refrigerator.

8. Using a slotted spoon, remove chicken pieces from bag, reserving liquid, and place, skin side up, on prepared baking sheet.

9. Broil chicken for 5 to 7 minutes or until skin is golden brown and crispy. Transfer to a warmed deep serving dish and cover with foil to keep warm.

10. Meanwhile, pour cooking liquid into a medium saucepan and bring to a boil over medium heat. In a small bowl, combine flour and butter, mashing with a spoon to make a paste. Dollop paste into boiling liquid while whisking. Boil, whisking, for about 5 minutes or until sauce is thickened. Season to taste with salt and pepper. Pour over chicken and sprinkle with reserved bacon and parsley.

Variation

If you're of the school who feels pearl onions are essential to coq au vin, peel 8 oz (250 g) pearl onions and reserve an extra 1 tbsp (15 mL) bacon fat at the end of step 1. Before proceeding with step 2, add pearl onions to the 1 tbsp (15 mL) fat in the skillet and cook, stirring, for about 3 minutes or until golden brown. Using a slotted spoon, transfer onions to a bowl, then proceed with step 2, adding the reserved bacon fat and oil to the pan. Return the browned onions to the skillet at the end of step 2.

Piri Piri–Style Flattened Chicken

Cooking a whole chicken sous vide was one of our most pleasant surprises as we started experimenting with this technique. The white and dark meats are unbelievably moist and tender — cooked to perfection every time — not something easily done with roasting or grilling. Inspired by the Portuguese classic, this version of flattened chicken has just enough heat to raise your internal temperature but not so much as to be intimidating.

Sous vide time:
3½ hours

Tips

If you're comfortable spatchcocking a chicken (the technical term for splitting the chicken, removing the backbone and flattening a chicken), do it yourself. Otherwise, most butchers will do it for you if you call ahead.

If you don't have an immersion blender, you can use a mini chopper or small food processor to purée the garlic mixture. Alternatively, you can grate the garlic on a Microplane-style zester and stir it together with the remaining ingredients in the bowl.

This recipe is medium-hot to spicy. For a more authentic piri piri sauce, add 1 or 2 seeded halved small bird's eye chiles or 1 jalapeño pepper with the garlic, or add 1 to 2 tsp (5 to 10 mL) bottled piri piri sauce with the lemon juice. For a milder version, omit the cayenne or the hot pepper flakes.

To marinate the chicken ahead, prepare through step 3 and refrigerate for up to 1 day before cooking.

- **Preheat water bath to 148°F (64°C)**
- **Immersion blender (see tip)**
- **Extra-large resealable freezer bag**
- **Large rimmed baking sheet, lined with foil**

1	clove garlic, halved	1
1 tsp	cayenne pepper	5 mL
1 tsp	sweet paprika	5 mL
1 tsp	hot pepper flakes	5 mL
¼ tsp	dried oregano	1 mL
¼ tsp	salt	1 mL
¼ tsp	freshly ground black pepper	1 mL
3 tbsp	olive oil	45 mL
2 tbsp	freshly squeezed lemon juice	30 mL
3 to 4 lb	whole chicken, flattened (see tip)	1.5 to 2 kg

1. In a deep cup or bowl, combine garlic, cayenne, paprika, hot pepper flakes, oregano, salt, pepper, oil and lemon juice. Using the immersion blender, purée until smooth.
2. Place chicken in a large bowl and pour in garlic mixture, turning to evenly coat chicken.
3. Transfer chicken to freezer bag and add any remaining garlic mixture. Arrange so skin side is up and chicken is flattened. Remove excess air and seal bag.
4. Cook in preheated water bath for 3½ hours. Remove bag from water bath, gently place in sink and let stand for 5 minutes.
5. Preheat broiler with rack 6 inches (15 cm) from heat.
6. Open bag (still resting in sink; see tip, page 121) and carefully lift bag to slide chicken, skin side up, onto prepared baking sheet; discard liquid.
7. Broil chicken for 5 to 7 minutes or until skin is golden brown and crispy. Cut chicken into leg, wing and breast portions.

Serving Suggestion

- This makes an excellent summer meal served with potato salad, such as Warm Potato Salad with Red Wine Vinaigrette (page 79) and fresh vegetables with dip.

Tandoori Flattened Chicken

Tandoori is traditionally cooked in a hot tandoor, or clay oven, but this variation allows you to have rich, juicy chicken meat with skin crisped at the last minute under the broiler. With a prepared tandoori paste, it is so easy to make but delivers as much flavor as if you worked in the kitchen for hours.

MAKES 4 TO 6 SERVINGS

Sous vide time: 3½ hours

Tips

For a little extra zip, squeeze fresh lemon or lime wedges over the chicken when serving.

Air-chilled chicken is a must when cooking sous vide to make sure you get a rich chicken flavor rather than a watery one.

Be gentle when transferring the cooked chicken to the baking sheet: it is fall-off-the-bone tender. Reduce splashing of the hot liquid by keeping the bag in the sink and sliding the chicken onto the baking sheet.

Variation

Herbes de Provence Flattened Chicken: Instead of the tandoori paste and yogurt, combine 1 tsp (5 mL) dried herbes de Provence, ¼ tsp (1 mL) salt, 2 tbsp (30 mL) freshly squeezed lemon juice and 1 tbsp (15 mL) extra virgin olive oil; coat, marinate and cook the chicken as directed.

- **Extra-large resealable freezer bag**
- **Large rimmed baking sheet, lined with foil**

¼ cup	tandoori paste	60 mL
2 tbsp	plain yogurt (not fat-free)	30 mL
3 to 4 lb	whole chicken, flattened (see tip, page 120)	1.5 to 2 kg
	Salt and freshly ground black pepper	

1. In a large bowl, combine tandoori paste and yogurt. Add chicken and turn to coat, spreading the sauce with a spatula as necessary.

2. Transfer chicken to freezer bag and add any remaining tandoori mixture. Arrange so skin side is up and chicken is flattened. Remove excess air and seal bag. Place in a shallow baking dish and refrigerate for at least 3 hours or overnight.

3. Preheat water bath to 148°F (64°C).

4. Cook chicken in preheated water bath for 3½ hours. Remove bag from water bath, gently place in sink and let stand for 5 minutes.

5. Meanwhile, preheat broiler with rack in center of oven.

6. Open bag (still resting in sink; see tip) and carefully lift bag to slide chicken, skin side up, onto prepared baking sheet; discard liquid. Season to taste with salt and pepper.

7. Broil chicken for 7 to 9 minutes or until skin is charred and crispy. Cut chicken into leg, wing and breast portions.

Serving Suggestions

- Serve hot chicken with basmati rice, raita and naan, along with your favorite curried vegetables.
- Leftover tandoori chicken makes a great sandwich wrap. Combine chicken, minted yogurt, lettuce and sliced cucumbers in your favorite flour tortilla or naan.

Garlic and Lemon Chicken Breasts

Cooking chicken with the bones still in and the skin on imparts extra flavor to the finished product. This recipe is wonderful as an entrée for dinner or served cold as part of a salad or in a stuffed pita sandwich with your favorite accompaniments.

MAKES 2 TO 4 SERVINGS

Sous vide time: 3 hours

Tips

Garlic added raw to foods cooked sous vide can become strong and bitter, and we tend to use garlic powder in many recipes to avoid this. For this simple chicken recipe, we want a pungent garlic flavor, but do make sure to use only a medium clove (about 1 tsp/5 mL minced). Use only hand-minced fresh garlic, not garlic pressed through a garlic press or minced in a food processor, and not pre-minced garlic from a jar — all of which can be too harsh in flavor. Cut the clove in half before mincing and pick out any green sprout inside (this also causes bitterness).

To make chilled chicken ahead for use in salad or sandwiches, prepare through step 3, then immerse bag in ice water to chill. Refrigerate in the sealed bag for up to 3 days. Skip the broiling steps and remove the skin before serving cold.

- **Preheat water bath to 148°F (64°C)**
- **Medium resealable freezer bag**
- **Baking sheet, lined with foil**

1	clove garlic, minced	1
½ tsp	grated lemon zest	2 mL
1 tbsp	freshly squeezed lemon juice	15 mL
	Salt and freshly ground black pepper	
2	large bone-in skin-on chicken breasts (each about 12 oz/375 g)	2

1. In a large bowl, combine garlic, lemon zest, lemon juice and ¼ tsp (1 mL) each salt and pepper. Add chicken breasts, turning to coat evenly.
2. Place chicken in freezer bag, arranging in a single layer, and add any remaining garlic mixture. Remove excess air and seal bag.
3. Cook in preheated water bath for 3 hours. Remove bag from water bath and let rest for 10 minutes.
4. Meanwhile, preheat broiler with rack 6 inches (15 cm) from heat.
5. Remove chicken from bag, discarding liquid, and place, skin side up, on prepared baking sheet. Season to taste with salt and pepper.
6. Broil chicken for 7 to 8 minutes or until skin is golden brown and crispy.

Variation

If you prefer to grill the chicken breasts, you can finish them on a barbecue grill preheated to medium. Oil grill and place chicken on grill. Grill, skin side up, covered, for 3 to 4 minutes to dry off the skin and heat the chicken, then flip over to the skin side for about 3 minutes — just long enough to add grill marks.

Sweet and Tangy Barbecue Sauce Chicken

These evenly cooked, tender chicken breasts, glazed with an easy homemade barbecue sauce, will become your go-to choice, not just for summer, but all year round.

MAKES 4 SERVINGS

Sous vide time: 3 hours

Tips

This recipe can be multiplied to feed a crowd. Double, triple or quadruple the sauce recipe (using a larger pot for larger batches), and use one large freezer bag per 4 to 6 chicken breasts (as long as they fit without overlapping). Make sure you cook only as many bags as will allow the water to circulate thoroughly around them.

To make ahead and serve chilled, cover and refrigerate extra sauce in step 3 and serve with chicken later or reserve for another use (it will keep up to 1 month in the fridge). Cook chicken as directed through step 5, then immerse bag in ice water to chill. Refrigerate in the sealed bag for up to 3 days or freeze for up to 3 months. Thaw in the refrigerator overnight, if frozen. Skip the grilling steps and serve cold.

Variation

Use 8 boneless skinless chicken thighs and increase the water bath temperature to 148°F (64°C).

- **Large resealable freezer bag**
- **Barbecue grill**

1 tbsp	packed brown sugar	15 mL
1 tsp	dry mustard	5 mL
½ tsp	chili powder	2 mL
½ tsp	garlic powder	2 mL
½ tsp	freshly ground black pepper	2 mL
1 cup	ketchup	250 mL
¼ cup	apple cider vinegar	60 mL
1 tbsp	vegetable oil	15 mL
1 tbsp	light (fancy) or dark (cooking) molasses	15 mL
½ tsp	hot pepper sauce	2 mL
4	boneless skinless chicken breasts (each about 6 oz/175 g)	4
	Vegetable oil or cooking spray	

1. In a deep saucepan, combine brown sugar, mustard, chili powder, garlic powder, pepper, ketchup, vinegar, oil, molasses and hot pepper sauce; bring to a boil over medium heat, stirring often. Reduce heat and boil gently, stirring often, for 15 to 20 minutes or until sauce is thick. (As the sauce thickens, reduce heat and stir more often to prevent burning.) Transfer to a large bowl and let cool.

2. Meanwhile, preheat water bath to 140°F (60°C).

3. Transfer half the barbecue sauce to a small bowl, cover and set aside at room temperature. Add chicken to the remaining sauce and turn to coat evenly.

4. Place chicken in freezer bag, arranging in a single layer, and add any remaining sauce. Remove excess air and seal bag.

5. Cook in preheated water bath for 3 hours. Remove bag from water bath and let rest for 5 minutes.

6. Meanwhile, preheat barbecue grill to medium.

7. Remove chicken from bag, discarding liquid, and transfer to a plate.

8. Oil grill and place chicken on grill. Grill, turning once, for 1 to 2 minutes per side or until lightly browned. Brush both sides with the reserved barbecue sauce. Grill, turning once and brushing with sauce, for 1 to 2 minutes per side or until hot and glazed. Serve extra sauce on the side, as desired.

Chicken Legs with Lemon and Rosemary

Chicken thighs become fall-off-the-bone tender with sous vide cooking. This simple seasoning partners particularly well with summery foods and makes a nice dish to serve in cooler months with year-round-available ingredients. Pair it with grilled vegetables, roasted potatoes, potato salad or lightly dressed mixed greens.

MAKES 4 SERVINGS

Sous vide time: 4 hours

Tips

You'll need about 2 large (or 3 medium) lemons to get the zest for this recipe, but you'll need the juice from only 1 lemon. Squeeze extra lemon juice from the zested lemons and refrigerate in an airtight container for up to 5 days or freeze for up to 6 months.

Air-chilled chicken is a must when cooking sous vide to make sure you get a rich chicken flavor rather than a watery one.

- Preheat water bath to 148°F (64°C)
- Large resealable freezer bag
- Large rimmed baking sheet, lined with foil

1 tbsp	grated lemon zest	15 mL
3 tbsp	freshly squeezed lemon juice	45 mL
2 tbsp	extra virgin olive oil	30 mL
½ tsp	dried rosemary, crumbled	2 mL
	Salt and freshly ground black pepper	
4	bone-in skin-on chicken leg quarters (about 2 lbs/1 kg total)	4

1. In a large bowl, combine lemon zest, lemon juice, oil, rosemary and ½ tsp (2 mL) each salt and pepper. Add chicken to bowl, turning to coat evenly.

2. Place chicken in freezer bag, arranging in a single layer, and add any remaining lemon mixture. Remove excess air and seal bag.

3. Cook in preheated water bath, covered, for 4 hours. Remove bag from water bath and let stand for 5 minutes.

4. Meanwhile, preheat broiler with rack 6 inches (15 cm) from heat.

5. Using a slotted spoon, remove chicken pieces from bag, discarding liquid, and place, skin side up, on prepared baking sheet.

6. Broil chicken for 7 to 8 minutes or until skin is golden brown and crispy.

Variation

If you prefer to grill the chicken breasts, you can finish them on a barbecue grill preheated to medium. Oil grill and place chicken on grill. Grill, skin side up, covered, for 3 to 4 minutes to dry off the skin and heat the chicken, then flip over to the skin side for about 3 minutes — just long enough to add grill marks. For added zing, grill some lemon halves to squeeze over the finished chicken legs.

Mole-Style Chicken Thighs

Typically, mole is a sauce-laden dish featuring chiles and unsweetened chocolate, often with a tomato or citrus base. We've turned the traditional flavors into a spice rub so the chicken can easily be cooked sous vide and used for a number of dishes, such as tacos, nachos or soup, or simply served on its own with the traditional accompaniments of vegetable-studded rice, fresh salsa and refried beans.

**MAKES
4 SERVINGS**

**Sous vide time:
3½ hours**

Tips

For an extra-deep flavor, prepare the chicken through step 3 and refrigerate for at least 4 hours or up to 24 hours before cooking.

Air-chilled chicken is a must when cooking sous vide to make sure you get a rich chicken flavor rather than a watery one.

Variations

We like the flavor of bone-in chicken, but you can use boneless skinless chicken instead. Reduce the sous vide cooking time to 3 hours.

To broil chicken instead of grilling, preheat broiler with rack 4 inches (10 cm) from heat. Place chicken, smooth side up, on a foil-lined baking sheet. Broil for 4 minutes or until browned.

- Preheat water bath to 148°F (64°C)
- Large resealable freezer bag
- Large rimmed baking sheet, lined with foil (optional)

1 tbsp	vegetable oil	15 mL
2 tsp	ancho chile powder	10 mL
1 tsp	sweet paprika	5 mL
½ tsp	ground cumin	2 mL
⅛ tsp	ground cinnamon	0.5 mL
1 tbsp	unsweetened cocoa powder	15 mL
1 tbsp	ground almonds (optional)	15 mL
½ tsp	dried oregano	2 mL
¼ tsp	salt	1 mL
¼ tsp	garlic powder	1 mL
8	bone-in skinless chicken thighs (about 2¼ lbs/1.125 kg total)	8
	Vegetable oil or cooking spray (optional)	

1. In a small skillet, heat oil over medium-low heat. Add ancho powder, paprika, cumin and cinnamon; cook, stirring constantly, for about 2 minutes or just until fragrant and slightly darker. Transfer to a large bowl and stir in cocoa powder, ground almonds (if using), oregano, salt and garlic powder; let cool completely.

2. Add chicken to spice mixture in bowl, stirring to coat evenly.

3. Place chicken in freezer bag, arranging in a single layer, and add any remaining spice mixture. Remove excess air and seal bag.

4. Cook in preheated water bath for 3½ hours. Remove bag from water bath and let stand for 5 minutes.

5. If you want to brown the chicken, preheat barbecue grill to medium-high.

6. Remove chicken from bag, discarding liquid, and transfer to a plate or cutting board. If browning, gently pat chicken dry (without removing the spices). Otherwise, shred or chop chicken to use right away in recipes.

7. To brown, oil grill and place chicken on grill. Grill, turning once, for 1 to 2 minutes per side or until sizzling and marked.

Berbere Spice–Rubbed Chicken Thighs

This Ethiopian-inspired spice mixture lends a touch of the exotic to tender, juicy chicken thighs. It has a kick of heat along with the complex flavor of the myriad spices, which will complement an African-themed meal or simply add a boost to your usual chicken dinner. Serve with fruit-studded couscous and minted yogurt.

MAKES 4 SERVINGS

Sous vide time: 3½ hours

Tips

Replace the individual spices with 5 tsp (25 mL) prepared berbere spice mixture. Check the label and add the salt called for if your spice mixture does not include salt. Some prepared blends are very fiery, so you may want to try the recipe with 1 tbsp (15 mL) if you aren't sure just how hot yours is — or be daring and use the full amount!

Air-chilled chicken is a must when cooking sous vide to make sure you get a rich chicken flavor rather than a watery one.

- Preheat water bath to 148°F (64°C)
- Spice grinder or mortar and pestle
- Large resealable freezer bag
- Large rimmed baking sheet, lined with foil

1 tsp	coriander seeds	5 mL
¼ tsp	fenugreek seeds	1 mL
⅛ tsp	cumin seeds	0.5 mL
Pinch	cardamom seeds	Pinch
2 tsp	sweet paprika	10 mL
¼ tsp	salt	1 mL
¼ tsp	ground ginger	1 mL
¼ tsp	ground turmeric	1 mL
¼ tsp	freshly ground black pepper	1 mL
⅛ tsp	cayenne pepper	0.5 mL
⅛ tsp	ground allspice	0.5 mL
1 tbsp	olive oil	15 mL
8	bone-in skin-on chicken thighs (about 2½ lbs/1.25 kg total)	8

1. In spice grinder (or using mortar and pestle), grind coriander, fenugreek, cumin and cardamom seeds until powdered. Add paprika, salt, ginger, turmeric, black pepper, cayenne and allspice; pulse or stir to combine.

2. In a dry small skillet, toast spices over medium-low heat, stirring constantly, for about 5 minutes or just until fragrant and slightly darker. Transfer to a large bowl and stir in oil; let cool completely.

3. Add chicken to spice mixture in bowl, stirring to coat evenly.

Tip

To make chicken ahead for use chilled in salad or sandwiches, remove skin, if desired, before tossing chicken with spice mixture; prepare through step 5, then immerse bag in ice water to chill. Refrigerate in the sealed bag for up to 3 days. Skip the broiling steps.

4. Place chicken in freezer bag, arranging in a single layer, and add any remaining spice mixture. Remove excess air and seal bag.

5. Cook in preheated water bath for $3\frac{1}{2}$ hours. Remove bag from water bath and let stand for 5 minutes.

6. Meanwhile, preheat broiler with rack 6 inches (15 cm) from heat.

7. Remove chicken from bag, discarding liquid, and place, skin side up, on prepared baking sheet.

8. Broil chicken for about 5 minutes or until skin is golden brown and crispy.

Chicken and Tomato Salad

For a zesty salad on a hot summer evening, chop 2 large tomatoes, $\frac{1}{2}$ small red onion and 2 tbsp (30 mL) fresh mint and toss with 3 tbsp (45 mL) extra virgin olive oil and 2 tbsp (30 mL) white wine vinegar or freshly squeezed orange juice. Season with salt to taste, then add hot or chilled shredded Berbere Spice-Rubbed Chicken Thighs.

Butter Chicken

This is far from the traditional method of making butter chicken, but breaking with tradition sometimes leads to new discoveries! Cooking the chicken right in the sauce in the sous vide helps it absorb the spices, tang and zip while the chicken remains moist and becomes oh-so-tender. It's sure to satisfy that butter chicken craving (I suspect I'm not the only person who gets those) while being super-easy to make. ~ *Jennifer*

**MAKES
6 SERVINGS**

Sous vide time:
2½ hours

Tips

Air-chilled chicken is a must when cooking sous vide to make sure you get a rich chicken flavor rather than a watery one.

Prepared tandoori paste (and other curry paste) is very convenient to have on hand for a shortcut when making curries. It's available in jars in the Indian section of well-stocked supermarkets and in specialty stores. Tandoori and the similar tikka paste are quite mild compared to many curry blends, so they make for a good introduction to Indian foods.

- **Preheat water bath to 148°F (64°C)**
- **Large resealable freezer bag**

1½ lbs	boneless skinless chicken thighs	750 g
½ cup	plain yogurt (not fat-free)	125 mL
3 tbsp	tandoori or tikka curry paste, divided	45 mL
1 tbsp	vegetable oil	15 mL
1	small onion, chopped	1
1	clove garlic, minced	1
1 tbsp	minced gingerroot (or 1 tsp/5 mL ground ginger)	15 mL
1 tsp	ground cumin	5 mL
1 tsp	paprika	5 mL
Pinch	hot pepper flakes	Pinch
	Salt	
1½ cups	canned crushed (ground) tomatoes	375 mL
1 cup	heavy or whipping (35%) cream	250 mL
2 tbsp	freshly squeezed lime or lemon juice (optional)	30 mL
	Chopped fresh cilantro	

1. Cut chicken thighs into 1½-inch (4 cm) chunks, trimming off excess fat. In freezer bag, combine chicken, yogurt and 1 tbsp (15 mL) tandoori paste; massage to evenly coat chicken. Set aside for 15 minutes.

2. Meanwhile, in a medium saucepan, heat oil over medium heat. Add onion, reduce heat to medium-low and cook, stirring, for about 8 minutes or until soft and starting to turn golden. Add garlic, ginger, cumin, paprika, hot pepper flakes, ¼ tsp (1 mL) salt and the remaining tandoori paste; cook, stirring, for 2 minutes or until garlic is softened and spices are fragrant. Remove from heat and pour in tomatoes, stirring to scrape up any brown bits stuck to pan. Let cool.

Tip

To make ahead, prepare through step 4, then immerse bag in ice water to chill. Refrigerate in the sealed bag for up to 2 days. When ready to serve, use a slotted spoon to remove chicken from bag and set aside. Proceed with step 6, then add chicken to the thickened sauce and simmer, stirring gently, for about 5 minutes or until heated through. Alternatively, heat in the sealed bag in a 140°F (60°C) water bath for 30 minutes, then proceed with step 5.

3. Add tomato sauce to chicken in bag and stir to combine. Remove excess air and seal bag.

4. Cook in preheated water bath for $2\frac{1}{2}$ hours. The chicken should be fork-tender; if it isn't, return bag to water bath and cook, checking for doneness every 15 minutes.

5. Remove bag from water bath and, using a slotted spoon, transfer chicken to a warmed serving dish; cover to keep warm.

6. Pour sauce into clean saucepan, add cream and bring to a boil over medium-high heat, stirring often. Reduce heat and boil gently for 5 minutes or until slightly thickened. Remove from heat, stir in lime juice (if using) and season to taste with salt. Pour over chicken and garnish with cilantro.

Serving Suggestion

- Complete the meal with steamed basmati rice, sliced cucumbers or tender-crisp green beans and warm, buttery naan.

Orange and Garlic Duck Breast

Having spent several seasons cooking at a duck hunting camp, I have cooked a duck breast or two (hundred!) in my time, and it can be tricky to get just the right tender texture and doneness. When researching sous vide cooking, I came across many references touting it as a foolproof method for cooking duck breast. Having tried it, I am convinced and now cook duck breast sous vide for the restaurant guests at Viamede Resort. They're convinced, too. ~ Jay

....

**MAKES
2 SERVINGS**

Sous vide time:
2 hours

Tips

The two-stage browning process renders some of the fat from the duck breast to start, preventing the meat from being too greasy-tasting, and crisps up the skin at the end for optimal texture. It might seem fiddly, but it's worthwhile to do both. Be sure to brown the duck just before cooking sous vide and let it cool only while you prepare the sauce. For optimal food safety, poultry and meat should never be browned then held before cooking.

This water bath temperature gives you medium-rare to medium doneness, which we preferred for taste and texture; if you prefer rare duck, reduce the temperature to 129°F (54°C), but keep in mind that the duck will not be pasteurized, so this should be avoided if the food safety of undercooked duck is a concern for you.

- **Preheat water bath to 135°F (57°C)**
- **Medium resealable freezer bag**
- **Baking sheet, lined with foil**

2	boneless skin-on duck breasts (each about 8 oz/250 g)	2
	Salt	
¼ cup	finely chopped shallot or onion	60 mL
1	small clove garlic, minced	1
¼ tsp	freshly ground black pepper	1 mL
⅛ tsp	dried thyme (or 1 sprig fresh thyme)	0.5 mL
1 tsp	grated orange zest	5 mL
¼ cup	freshly squeezed orange juice, divided	60 mL
1 tsp	liquid honey	5 mL
1 tbsp	butter, cut into cubes	15 mL

1. Score skin of duck breasts in a crosshatch pattern, without cutting through to the meat. Season both sides lightly with salt.

2. Heat a medium heavy skillet over medium-high heat until very hot. Sear duck, skin side down, for about 3 minutes or until skin is well browned. Remove from heat. Using tongs, transfer duck to a plate, leaving fat in pan.

3. Let skillet cool slightly. Return to low heat, add shallot and cook, stirring, for 1 minute or until starting to soften. Add garlic, pepper and thyme; cook, stirring, for 30 seconds. Remove from heat and add orange zest, half the orange juice and honey, stirring to scrape up any brown bits stuck to pan.

4. Pat duck breasts dry and place in freezer bag, then pour in orange juice mixture. Squeeze bag gently to spread liquid over duck and arrange breasts side by side. Remove excess air and seal bag.

5. Cook in preheated water bath for 2 hours. Remove bag from water bath and let rest for 5 minutes.

Tips

You can double the recipe for more servings, just use two medium-size freezer bags and divide the sauce equally between the bags in step 4.

To make ahead, prepare through step 5, then immerse bag in ice water to chill. Refrigerate in the sealed bag for up to 3 days. Reheat in a 140°F (60°C) water bath for 30 minutes, then proceed with step 6.

Variation

Lemon Lavender Honey Duck Breast: Replace the orange zest and juice with lemon zest and juice, add a pinch of crumbled dried culinary lavender with the thyme, and increase the honey to 2 tsp (10 mL).

6. Meanwhile, preheat broiler with rack 4 inches (10 cm) from heat.

7. Remove duck breasts from bag, reserving liquid, and place, skin side up, on prepared baking sheet. Pat duck dry.

8. Broil duck for about 3 minutes or until skin is golden brown and crispy. Transfer to a cutting board and let rest while you reduce the sauce.

9. In a small saucepan, combine reserved cooking liquid and the remaining orange juice; bring to a boil over medium heat. Boil, stirring often, for about 5 minutes or until slightly reduced. Reduce heat and simmer, whisking in butter, a few pieces at a time, until blended. Season to taste with salt.

10. Cut duck breasts crosswise into thin slices and serve hot with sauce.

Serving Suggestion

- Serve with steamed broccoli, sautéed bell peppers and mashed or roasted potatoes or a rice pilaf.

Warm Orange Duck and Asparagus Salad

This duck also makes an impressive warm salad. Arrange mixed greens, such as arugula, frisée and baby kale, on serving plates with sliced oranges, steamed or roasted asparagus, and thin slices of red onions or radishes. Top with warm slices of duck breast drizzled with the orange sauce.

Sage and Butter Turkey Breast

If you love turkey but dislike the hassle of cooking an entire bird, this simple alternative turns out tender and flavorful. The light herb seasoning and butter let the taste of the turkey shine through, and sous vide cooking results in evenly cooked, moist white meat. Serve with mashed potatoes and cranberry sauce. Don't forget to leave a little turkey for sandwiches the next day.

MAKES 6 TO 8 SERVINGS

Sous vide time: 3½ hours

Tips

If you'd like to make gravy, reserve the cooking liquid from the bag and use your favorite gravy recipe, adding good-quality ready-to-use chicken broth or homemade chicken stock with a little dried sage or poultry seasoning to enhance the flavor.

To make turkey ahead for use chilled in sandwiches or salads, remove skin before tying, if desired, prepare through step 4, then immerse bag in ice water to chill. Refrigerate in the sealed bag for up to 3 days. Skip the broiling steps.

- **Preheat water bath to 151°F (66°C)**
- **Butcher twine**
- **Large resealable freezer bag**
- **Large rimmed baking sheet, lined with foil**

3 lb	boneless skin-on turkey breast	1.5 kg
½ tsp	dried sage, crumbled	2 mL
	Salt and freshly ground black pepper	
¼ cup	butter, cut into cubes	60 mL

1. Pat turkey dry. Using butcher twine, tie the breast into a cylindrical shape.

2. In a small bowl, combine sage and ¼ tsp (1 mL) each salt and pepper. Spread evenly over entire turkey breast.

3. Place turkey breast in freezer bag. Sprinkle butter around turkey. Remove excess air and seal bag.

4. Cook in preheated water bath for 3½ hours. Remove bag from water bath and let rest for 10 minutes.

5. Meanwhile, preheat broiler with rack 8 inches (20 cm) from heat.

6. Remove turkey from bag, discarding liquid, and place, skin side up, on prepared baking sheet. Pat dry and season to taste with salt and pepper.

7. Broil turkey, rotating the baking sheet often to brown evenly, for 8 to 10 minutes or until crisp and golden brown. Transfer turkey to a cutting board, cut off string and cut turkey crosswise into slices.

Serving Suggestion

- Slices of cold turkey make great sandwiches with chutney or cranberry sauce and slices of Brie cheese.

Fish and Seafood

Caribbean-Style Catfish

This dish brings the heat. Catfish fillets are firm and juicy, so they work well in this recipe. While I was able to find catfish at most of the grocery stores I visited, you could also use red snapper where available. Serve over rice, with a cold beer to temper the heat. *~ Jay*

Sous vide time:
30 minutes

Tips

If you're not a fan of really hot food, you can substitute a milder pepper for the Scotch bonnet. Half a jalapeño or Anaheim pepper make good alternatives. Or use a bell pepper and let the diners add their favorite bottled hot sauce at the table.

Any other firm white fish fillets will work in this recipe. Before you shop, check for sustainable choices at seafoodwatch.org or oceanwise.ca, or ask at your grocery store or fishmonger for the best options.

You can easily double or triple this recipe. Use a medium bag for every 2 fillets, or use a large bag for 3 or 4 fillets, keeping them in a single layer and spacing them slightly apart so they don't stick together as they cook.

- **Preheat water bath to 120°F (49°C)**
- **Medium resealable freezer bag**

1	tomato, diced	1
1	clove garlic, minced	1
½	Scotch bonnet pepper, seeded and minced	½
1 tbsp	minced gingerroot	15 mL
1 tbsp	dried parsley	15 mL
¼ tsp	salt	1 mL
¼ tsp	ground lemon pepper	1 mL
1 tbsp	freshly squeezed lime juice	15 mL
1 tsp	vegetable oil	5 mL
2	skinless catfish fillets (each 6 oz/175 g)	2
1 tbsp	butter	15 mL

1. In a small bowl, combine tomato, garlic, Scotch bonnet pepper, ginger, parsley, salt, lemon pepper, lime juice and oil.
2. Rinse catfish and pat dry. Place fish and tomato mixture in freezer bag, spacing fillets slightly apart. Remove excess air and seal bag.
3. Cook in preheated water bath for 30 minutes. Remove bag from water bath and let rest for 5 minutes.
4. Heat a nonstick skillet over medium-high heat. Gently transfer catfish and sauce to the hot pan, being cautious of splatter. Cook fish, without turning, for 3 minutes or until excess juice has evaporated. Remove from heat. Transfer fish and sauce to serving plates.
5. Melt butter in still-warm pan and drizzle over catfish.

Serving Suggestions

- Serve this spicy fish on a bed of brown rice, or cook up a recipe of rice and peas for a traditional Caribbean accompaniment.
- This fish makes a really good base for fish tacos. Add some coleslaw and a wedge of fresh lime to squeeze over top.

Arctic Char with Fennel and Orange

Arctic char resembles both trout and salmon, tasting almost like a cross between the two, and pairs well with the subtle licorice flavor of fennel and the fresh orange. You could pair this with a salad in the summer or a simple risotto in the winter.

MAKES 2 SERVINGS

Sous vide time: 1 hour

Tips

Fennel adds a touch of licorice flavor to the dish. If you're not fond of fennel, you can substitute celery or even carrots and use chopped fresh parsley for garnish (or just omit the garnish).

Keeping the skin on the char helps keep it from falling apart when you transfer it from the bag to serving plates.

For some added crunch, garnish with ¼ cup (60 mL) toasted cashews or almonds.

You can easily double, triple or quadruple this recipe. Add 2 to 3 fish pieces per medium bag, ensuring that they fit in a single layer, with room between each piece to keep them from sticking together as they cook. Try to keep pieces of a similar thickness in bags together.

- Preheat water bath to 180°F (82°C)
- Medium resealable freezer bag

1	small bulb fennel	1
1 tsp	olive oil	5 mL
¼ tsp	salt	1 mL
¼ tsp	freshly ground black pepper	1 mL
2	pieces skin-on Arctic char fillet (each 6 oz/175 g and about ¾ inch/2 cm thick)	2
1	large navel or blood orange, peeled and cut into segments	1

1. Trim fennel bulb, reserving about 4 fennel fronds. Cut fennel bulb in half lengthwise, trim out core and thinly slice fennel. You should have about 1 cup (250 mL). Break the fronds into small sprigs and set aside.

2. In freezer bag, combine fennel slices, oil, salt and pepper. Arrange fennel in an even layer. Remove excess air and seal bag.

3. Cook in preheated water bath for 35 minutes. The fennel should be tender; if it isn't, return bag to water bath and cook for 10 to 15 minutes longer. Remove bag from water bath.

4. Reduce water bath temperature to 120°F (49°C), adding a little cool water to speed up the process.

5. Rinse fish and pat dry. Open bag and lay it flat on the counter, then lay fish pieces on top of the fennel, spacing them slightly apart, with the flesh side touching the fennel. Remove excess air and seal bag.

6. Return bag to water bath and cook for 25 minutes. Remove bag from water bath and let rest for 5 minutes.

7. Remove fish and fennel from bag, discarding liquid, and transfer to serving plates. Top with fennel fronds and orange segments.

Salmon Fillet with Lemon Dill Butter

Sometimes simple is best. Whether it's for a weeknight meal or for entertaining, the classic pairing of lemon and dill accents the flavor of salmon perfectly. Serve tender-crisp green beans and a multigrain rice blend on the side.

**MAKES
2 SERVINGS**

Sous vide time:
45 minutes

Tip

You can easily double, triple or quadruple this recipe. Add 2 to 3 fish pieces per medium bag, ensuring that they fit in a single layer, with room between each piece to keep them from sticking together as they cook. Try to keep pieces of a similar thickness in bags together.

Variation

If you prefer a little browning color, transfer cooked salmon to a foil-lined baking sheet and pat dry. Preheat broiler with rack 4 inches (10 cm) from heat and broil salmon for 2 to 3 minutes or just until light golden.

- **Preheat water bath to 130°F (54.5°C)**
- **Medium resealable freezer bag**

2	pieces skin-on center-cut salmon fillet (each about 6 oz/175 g and 1 inch/2.5 cm thick)	2
	Salt and freshly ground black pepper	
½ tsp	grated lemon zest	2 mL
¼ tsp	chopped fresh dill	1 mL
1 tbsp	butter, cut into small pieces	15 mL
	Lemon wedges	

1. Rinse salmon and pat dry. Season flesh side with salt and pepper, then sprinkle with lemon zest and dill, dividing equally. Place fish pieces in freezer bag, spacing them slightly apart. Add butter on top of salmon. Remove excess air and seal bag.

2. Cook in preheated water bath for 45 minutes. Remove bag from water bath.

3. Remove salmon from bag, reserving liquid, and transfer to warmed plates. Drizzle with reserved cooking liquid and season to taste with more salt and pepper, if desired. Serve with lemon wedges to squeeze over top.

Serving Suggestion

- This salmon makes a nice addition to pasta with vegetables and a light cream sauce. Flake the salmon into large chunks, removing the skin, and add on top of hot pasta.

Rainbow Trout with Lemongrass and Ginger

Rainbow trout is typically fairly thin and can dry out if cooked just a minute or two too long by conventional methods. The sous vide keeps it perfectly moist, with a pleasantly firm texture, and allows the delicate seasonings to perfume the mild fish. This summery dish goes well with a mango and cucumber salad or fresh salad rolls. Serve it with jasmine rice.

MAKES 2 SERVINGS

Sous vide time: 25 minutes

Tips

Keeping the skin on the trout helps keep it from falling apart when you transfer it from the bag to the plate.

Use the thicker, lighter-colored end of the lemongrass for more flavor, trimming off the tough outer layers before chopping it. Lightly smash the chopped pieces with the flat side of the knife to help release more flavor. Simmer the top part of the lemongrass in a soup, or use it to add fragrance to rice as you cook it.

You can easily double or triple this recipe. Use individual bags for each fillet, or use a large bag for 2 fillets, keeping them in a single layer and spacing them apart slightly so they don't stick together as they cook.

- **Preheat water bath to 120°F (49°C)**
- **Medium resealable freezer bag**

1	skin-on rainbow trout fillet (12 oz/375 g)	1
1	4-inch (10 cm) piece lemongrass, chopped (see tip)	1
1 tbsp	minced gingerroot	15 mL
	Salt	
1/8 tsp	hot pepper flakes	0.5 mL
1/4 tsp	grated lime zest	1 mL
1 tbsp	freshly squeezed lime juice	15 mL

1. Rinse trout and pat dry. Place on a plate, with the flesh side up. In a small bowl, combine lemongrass, ginger, 1/4 tsp (1 mL) salt, hot pepper flakes, lime zest and lime juice. Spread lemongrass mixture over flesh side of fish.

2. Transfer trout to freezer bag. Remove excess air and seal bag.

3. Cook in preheated water bath for 25 minutes. Remove bag from water bath and let rest for 5 minutes.

4. Remove trout from bag, discarding liquid, and place on a clean plate. Pick off and discard lemongrass pieces. Season to taste with salt. Using a large spatula, divide the trout into 2 equal portions, lifting the fish off the skin.

Bouillabaisse Fish Soup in a Saffron Garlic Broth

This French-inspired soup is rich with the flavors of garlic and saffron. While you simmer the soup portion on the stovetop, the seafood cooks to perfection in the sous vide, which keeps it tender and moist — and the flavor of the seafood really comes through in the delicate broth. Serve it with a crusty baguette to mop up the drips at the bottom of the bowl.

MAKES 4 SERVINGS

Sous vide time: 30 minutes

Tips

Cut the fish, shrimp and scallops into approximately equal, bite-size chunks, large enough that you can see what they are, but small enough to fit on a spoon as you eat the soup.

Substitute other firm white fish for the cod and/or monkfish. Before you shop, check for sustainable choices at seafoodwatch.org or oceanwise.ca, or ask at your grocery store or fishmonger for the best options. Stay away from fragile fish, like trout and sole, as they will fall apart when added to the soup, and very oily fish that are too strong.

You can prepare the broth ahead through step 1, and it actually benefits from being made ahead. Let it cool and refrigerate in an airtight container for up to 3 days. While the fish cooks, reheat the broth in a saucepan over medium heat until simmering, then proceed with step 4.

- **Preheat water bath to 120°F (49°C)**
- **Medium resealable freezer bag**

1 tbsp	olive oil	15 mL
2	cloves garlic, minced	2
1 cup	finely diced potato	250 mL
1/2 cup	chopped red bell pepper	125 mL
1/2 cup	chopped trimmed fennel bulb	125 mL
1/4 tsp	saffron threads	1 mL
	Salt and freshly ground black pepper	
2 tbsp	freshly squeezed lemon juice	30 mL
1 tbsp	dry white wine	15 mL
4 cups	water	1 L
4 oz	skinless cod or haddock fillet, cut into chunks	125 g
4 oz	skinless monkfish fillet, cut into chunks	125 g
4 oz	shrimp, peeled, deveined and chopped	125 g
4 oz	sea scallops, hard side muscles trimmed off, chopped	125 g

1. In a large saucepan, heat oil over medium-high heat until shimmering. Add garlic and cook, stirring occasionally, for 2 to 3 minutes or until lightly browned. Add potato, red pepper, fennel, saffron, 3/4 tsp (3 mL) salt, 1/2 tsp (2 mL) pepper, lemon juice and wine; cook, stirring, for 3 to 4 minutes or until potato starts to soften. Add water and bring to a boil. Reduce heat and simmer for about 30 minutes or until potato is tender.

2. Meanwhile, place cod, monkfish, shrimp and scallops in freezer bag, pressing them into a single layer as much as possible. Remove excess air and seal bag.

3. Cook in preheated water bath for 30 minutes. Remove bag from water bath and let rest for 5 minutes.

4. Add cooked fish mixture, with liquid, to hot soup. Stir until combined. Season to taste with salt and pepper.

Gumbo-Style Fish Stew

An homage to the classic New Orleans staple, this fish stew invokes the trinity of celery, onions and peppers. Some versions include sausage or chicken, and the seafood is based on what's available at the market.

MAKES
4 SERVINGS

Sous vide time: 2 hours

Tips

If fresh okra isn't available, frozen will work equally well in this recipe. Let it thaw slightly, cut it into thick slices (if whole), then measure what you need for the recipe. Let thaw completely before adding to the pan.

You can make the gumbo ahead by completing step 2 (don't prep the seafood until the day you plan to cook it). Let gumbo cool and refrigerate in an airtight container for up to 3 days or freeze for up to 2 weeks. Thaw in the refrigerator overnight, if frozen. Reheat in the saucepan just until warmed, then proceed with step 1 and steps 3 to 7.

Garnish with chopped fresh parsley, if desired.

Variation

Add ½ cup (125 mL) chopped spicy cured sausage (such as andouille or chorizo) to the gumbo with the green pepper.

- **Preheat water bath to 180°F (82°C)**
- **2 medium resealable freezer bags**

8 oz	skinless cod fillet, cut into chunks	250 g
4 oz	shrimp, peeled and deveined	125 g
4 oz	sea scallops, hard side muscles trimmed off	125 g
1 tbsp	vegetable oil	15 mL
1	clove garlic, minced	1
1	small onion, finely chopped	1
1	stalk celery, finely chopped	1
1	green bell pepper, chopped	1
1	can (28 oz/796 mL) diced tomatoes, with juice	1
1 cup	thickly sliced okra	250 mL
½ tsp	hot pepper flakes	2 mL
¼ tsp	cayenne pepper	1 mL
¼ tsp	dried thyme	1 mL
	Salt and freshly ground black pepper	
4 cups	hot cooked rice	1 L

1. Place cod, shrimp and scallops in a freezer bag, pressing them into a single layer as much as possible. Remove excess air and seal bag. Set aside in the refrigerator.

2. In a large saucepan, heat oil over medium heat until shimmering. Add garlic, onion, celery and green pepper; cook, stirring, for about 5 minutes or until onion is translucent. Stir in tomatoes, okra, hot pepper flakes, cayenne, thyme and ½ tsp (2 mL) each salt and black pepper; cook, stirring, for 5 minutes. Remove from heat and let cool slightly.

3. Transfer gumbo to second freezer bag. Remove excess air and seal bag.

4. Cook gumbo in preheated water bath for 1½ hours.

5. Reduce water bath temperature to 135°F (57°C), adding a little cool water to speed up the process.

6. Add seafood bag to water bath alongside gumbo bag and cook for 30 minutes. Remove both bags from water bath and let rest for 5 minutes.

7. Place rice in bowls and spoon seafood, with liquid, over rice. Season gumbo with salt and pepper, then spoon over seafood.

Seafood Chowder

All too often seafood chowder is plagued with rubbery, dry nuggets of fish and seafood, or else you have to hunt through the entire bowl to find a single piece of fish. With this combo method of cooking, you make the soup base separately and use sous vide to cook the seafood perfectly, right when you need it. This simple yet hearty version has a slightly creamy base loaded with moist, tender seafood. Serve it with thick slices of sourdough bread or crackers.

**MAKES
4 SERVINGS**

Sous vide time:
30 minutes

Tips

You can add to or replace the fish or seafood ingredients with virtually any fish or shellfish, but avoid using oily fish, such as mackerel, as it will overpower the flavors.

You can make the soup ahead of time (don't prep the seafood until the day you plan to cook it). Complete step 3, then let it cool and refrigerate in an airtight container for up to 3 days. While cooking the seafood in steps 1 and 2, reheat the soup in a saucepan over medium heat until simmering, then proceed with step 4.

Variation

For a thicker chowder, whisk 2 tbsp (30 mL) all-purpose flour into the cold cream before adding it to the soup in step 5. Bring to a gentle boil over medium heat, stirring. Boil gently for about 5 minutes or until thickened, then proceed with step 6.

- **Preheat water bath to 120°F (49°C)**
- **Medium resealable freezer bag**
- **Immersion blender or blender**

4 oz	skinless haddock or tilapia fillet, cut into chunks	125 g
4 oz	shrimp, peeled, deveined and chopped	125 g
4 oz	sea scallops, hard side muscles trimmed off, chopped	125 g
1 tbsp	butter	15 mL
1	clove garlic, minced	1
1	small onion, finely chopped	1
2	medium potatoes, diced	2
	Salt and freshly ground black pepper	
1/8 tsp	dried thyme	0.5 mL
4 cups	water	1 L
1 cup	heavy or whipping (35%) cream	250 mL

1. Place haddock, shrimp and scallops in freezer bag, pressing them into a single layer as much as possible. Remove excess air and seal bag.

2. Cook in preheated water bath for 30 minutes. Remove bag from water bath and let rest for 5 minutes.

3. Meanwhile, in a large saucepan, melt butter over medium-high heat. Add garlic and onion; cook, stirring, for 3 to 5 minutes or until onion is translucent. Add potatoes, 1/2 tsp (2 mL) each salt and pepper, thyme and water; bring to a boil. Reduce heat and simmer for about 15 minutes or until potatoes are tender.

4. Remove pan from heat. Using an immersion blender in the pan, purée soup until smooth (or transfer soup to an upright blender, in batches as necessary, to purée, then return to the pan).

5. Return soup to low heat and stir in cream. Bring to a gentle simmer, stirring often (do not let boil).

6. Add cooked fish mixture, with liquid, to hot soup. Stir until combined. Season to taste with salt and pepper.

Vegetarian Mains

Montreal Steak–Spiced Cauliflower Steaks with Mango Salsa

Here's a vegetable dish that gives the sensation of a center-of-the-plate steak but without the meat. The steak spice doesn't make the cauliflower taste like meat, but does add a nice, deep flavor. Feel free to substitute another spice blend to change the flavor. The mango salsa adds color and a fresh taste that enhances the dish, or you can sub in your favorite steak condiment, such as steak sauce or barbecue sauce.

**MAKES
2 SERVINGS**

Sous vide time: 1 hour

Tips

Depending on the diameter of your steaks, you may need to use 2 large freezer bags and place 1 steak in each. If using smaller pieces (see tip below), you can fit a few steaks into each freezer bag; just be sure they don't overlap.

To get nice large steaks, you need the largest cauliflower possible, and there will be leftovers. You can cut smaller steaks from smaller heads, but they tend to fall apart. If you're not so concerned about the visual, cooking 4 or 6 smaller pieces (still 1 inch/2.5 cm thick) works just as well in this recipe.

Chop up extra cauliflower for crudités or use it to make soup. Wrap unused cauliflower in paper towels, place in a plastic bag and store in the refrigerator for up to 5 days.

- **Preheat water bath to 180°F (82°C)**
- **Large resealable freezer bag (see tip)**

1	large head cauliflower	1
1 tbsp	extra virgin olive oil (approx.)	15 mL
1 tbsp	Montreal steak spice	15 mL
	Mango Salsa (page 181)	

1. Trim leaves from cauliflower, being careful to leave the stem and core intact. Place cauliflower, stem side down, on a cutting board and, starting about 1 inch (2.5 cm) to the left of center, cut two 1-inch (2.5 cm) thick "steaks." Reserve extra cauliflower for another use. Place steaks on a plate and brush lightly on both sides with oil to evenly coat. Sprinkle evenly with steak spice.

2. Transfer cauliflower steaks to freezer bag, arranging them in a single layer. Remove excess air and seal bag.

3. Cook in preheated water bath, covered, for 1 hour. The cauliflower steaks should be tender; if they aren't, return bag to water bath and cook, checking for doneness every 15 minutes. Remove bag from water bath and let stand for 5 minutes.

4. Heat a heavy skillet over medium-high heat. Add cauliflower steaks, one at a time, and sear for about 2 minutes per side or until lightly browned. Serve hot or let cool to serve warm or chill. Spoon mango salsa on top or serve on the side.

Serving Suggestion

- To add protein to the meal, serve the steaks with quinoa or a rice and bean dish. Red Curry Quinoa with Squash and Black Beans (page 144) would make a nice, hearty accompaniment.

Three-Bean and Lentil Loaf

Say goodbye to dry vegetarian bean loaf. Cooking this loaf in a dish in the sous vide keeps it moist, lets it firm up and is super-easy, too. It's so hearty, no one will miss the meat. Serve a crispy green salad on the side, or go retro and simmer up a mixture of peas and carrots and a dollop of mashed potatoes.

MAKES 4 SERVINGS

Sous vide time: 2 hours

Tips

If you can't find 19-oz (540 mL) cans of beans, buy two 14- to 15-oz (398 to 425 mL) cans and measure out 2 cups (500 mL) rinsed drained beans for each of the black beans and red kidney beans; refrigerate extras in an airtight container for up to 3 days.

Leftovers can be cooled, covered and refrigerated for up to 5 days. Reheat individual portions in the microwave on Medium (50%), or in a 350°F (180°C) toaster oven, until steaming hot.

If you like sauce on your meatloaf, serve topped with Versatile Cheese Sauce (page 178) or Easy Tomato Basil Sauce (page 179).

- Preheat water bath to 180°F (82°C)
- Food processor
- 8-cup (2 L) shallow casserole dish, greased
- Extra-large resealable freezer bag
- Wire rack

1	can (19 oz/540 mL) black beans, drained and rinsed	1
1	can (19 oz/540 mL) red kidney beans, drained and rinsed	1
7 oz	drained firm tofu, broken into chunks	210 g
½ cup	coarsely chopped onion	125 mL
1 tsp	salt	5 mL
1 tsp	freshly ground black pepper	5 mL
½ tsp	dried thyme	2 mL
½ tsp	garlic powder	2 mL
1 cup	quick-cooking rolled oats	250 mL
1 cup	rinsed drained canned lentils	250 mL
1 cup	canned diced tomatoes, with juice	250 mL

1. In food processor, combine black beans, kidney beans, tofu, onion, salt, pepper, thyme and garlic powder; pulse until beans and tofu are coarsely chopped but not puréed.
2. Transfer bean mixture to a large bowl and add oats, lentils and tomatoes, mixing with your hands or a spatula until evenly blended.
3. Pack into prepared casserole dish, smoothing top. Cover dish tightly with plastic wrap and place in freezer bag. Remove excess air and seal bag.
4. Place rack in preheated water bath and place dish on rack. Cook, covered, for 2 hours. Remove bag from water bath and let stand for 5 minutes.
5. Preheat broiler with rack 8 inches (20 cm) from heat.
6. Remove dish from bag and remove plastic wrap. Broil loaf for about 8 minutes or until browned. Cut into slices or wedges to serve.

Red Curry Quinoa with Squash and Black Beans

When you make vegetable and grain dishes in a slow cooker, you often end up with a dry crust around the outside, or you have to add so much liquid the flavor gets lost. The sous vide mimics a slow cooker in that it lets flavor infuse into the dishes you make, but you don't have to add a lot of liquid and the food stays moist. This vegetarian dish is hearty, colorful and fragrant with mild curry spices and coconut.

**MAKES
4 SERVINGS**

Sous vide time: 1 hour

Tip

When using canned or Tetra Pak coconut milk, shake well before opening. If there is still thick cream visible, whisk well before measuring. Extra coconut milk can be refrigerated in an airtight container (or in the Tetra Pak) for up to 5 days or frozen for up to 3 months.

Variation

If you prefer a spicy curry, use a medium or hot yellow curry paste or a Thai red curry paste. Or stick with the tikka curry paste and add ½ tsp (2 mL) cayenne pepper or 1 minced serrano chile pepper.

- **Preheat water bath to 185°F (85°C)**
- **Large resealable freezer bag**

1 tbsp	vegetable oil	15 mL
1	small onion, chopped	1
1	clove garlic, minced	1
3 tbsp	tikka curry paste	45 mL
	Salt	
4 cups	cubed peeled butternut squash (1-inch/2.5 cm cubes)	1 L
1 cup	coconut milk (see tip)	250 mL
1 cup	ready-to-use vegetable broth	250 mL
1 cup	quinoa, rinsed	250 mL
1 cup	rinsed drained canned black beans	250 mL
2 tbsp	freshly squeezed lime juice	30 mL
	Chopped fresh cilantro	

1. In a medium saucepan, heat oil over medium heat. Add onion, reduce heat to medium-low and cook, stirring, for about 8 minutes or until soft and starting to turn golden. Add garlic, curry paste and ½ tsp (2 mL) salt; cook, stirring, for 2 minutes or until garlic is softened. Stir in squash until coated with spices. Remove from heat and pour in coconut milk and broth, stirring to scrape up any brown bits stuck to pan.

2. Transfer squash mixture to freezer bag and add quinoa and beans, stirring to combine. Remove excess air and seal bag.

3. Cook in preheated water bath, covered, for 1 hour. The squash should be tender; if it isn't, return bag to water bath and cook, checking for doneness every 15 minutes. Remove bag from water bath.

4. Open bag, stir in lime juice and season to taste with salt. Ladle into serving bowls and garnish with cilantro.

Lazy Vegetarian Cabbage Roll Stew

Cabbage rolls can be tedious, but they're oh-so-delicious. Now you can take the lazy — or should we call it smart? — way out and make a hearty stew that tastes just like cabbage rolls with none of the fiddly rolling. And the best part? The house doesn't smell like you've been cooking cabbage, as the aromas are all contained in the bag.

Tips

Set the freezer bag in a large bowl and fold over the top portion to keep the bag open and upright as you add the ingredients to the bag.

We find that rice doesn't cook evenly when mixed with other ingredients, so we've used cooked rice here. See page 36 for sous vide rice cooking instructions. The rice gets quite soft and breaks down by the time the stew is done, adding a nice thick texture. If you prefer rice with a firmer texture, leave it out before cooking the stew, then just stir in hot cooked rice at the end.

This stew tastes even better after it sits. To make it ahead, prepare through step 3, then immerse bag in ice water to chill. Refrigerate in the sealed bag for up to 3 days. Reheat in a saucepan over medium-low heat, stirring often and adding water as necessary, or heat individual portions in the microwave on Medium-High (70%) for 3 to 4 minutes, until hot.

- Preheat water bath to 190°F (88°C)
- Large resealable freezer bag

2	stalks celery, finely chopped	2
2	carrots, finely chopped	2
2	cloves garlic, minced	2
1	onion, chopped	1
4 cups	coarsely chopped green cabbage (about 14 oz/420 g)	1 L
1 cup	cooked long-grain brown or white rice	250 mL
½ cup	medium-grind bulgur	125 mL
1 tsp	sweet paprika	5 mL
1 tsp	dried marjoram or oregano	5 mL
½ tsp	dried thyme	2 mL
¼ tsp	caraway seeds (optional)	1 mL
	Salt and freshly ground black pepper	
1	can (28 oz/796 mL) diced tomatoes, with juice	1
1 cup	water	250 mL
2 tbsp	tomato paste	30 mL
	Chopped fresh dill (optional)	

1. In freezer bag, combine celery, carrots, garlic, onion, cabbage, rice, bulgur, paprika, marjoram, thyme, caraway seeds (if using), ½ tsp (2 mL) each salt and pepper, tomatoes, water and tomato paste. Stir until evenly combined.

2. Press vegetable mixture into an even layer. Remove excess air and seal bag.

3. Cook in preheated water bath, covered, for 2½ hours. The cabbage and bulgur should be tender; if they aren't, return bag to water bath and cook, checking for doneness every 15 minutes. Remove bag from water bath.

4. Open bag and season to taste with salt and pepper. Ladle into serving bowls and, if desired, garnish with dill.

Lentil and Tofu Chili

You won't miss the meat in this hearty chili. It is simple to put together, and the flavors become rich and well blended while it slowly cooks in the sous vide. It's a terrific dish to cook as a vegetarian option for parties where chili is on the menu, or to make at the beginning of the week for lunches and quick reheated dinners.

**MAKES
4 SERVINGS**

Sous vide time:
2 hours

Tip

To make ahead, prepare through step 3, then immerse bag in ice water to chill. Refrigerate in the sealed bag for up to 5 days. Reheat in a saucepan over medium heat, stirring gently, or heat individual portions in the microwave on Medium-High (70%) for 2 to 3 minutes, until steaming.

- **Preheat water bath to 180°F (82°C)**
- **Large resealable freezer bag**

2 tbsp	vegetable oil	30 mL
1	small onion, chopped	1
1	stalk celery, finely chopped	1
1 tsp	chili powder	5 mL
1/2 tsp	garlic powder	2 mL
	Salt and freshly ground black pepper	
1 cup	rinsed drained canned lentils	250 mL
1 cup	diced canned tomatoes, with juice	250 mL
7 oz	drained firm tofu, cut into cubes	210 g

1. In a medium saucepan, heat oil over medium heat. Add onion and celery; cook, stirring, for 5 minutes or until softened. Add chili powder, garlic powder, 1/2 tsp (2 mL) salt and 1/4 tsp (1 mL) pepper; cook, stirring, for 30 seconds. Stir in lentils and tomatoes.
2. Transfer onion mixture to freezer bag and add tofu, stirring gently to combine. Remove excess air and seal bag.
3. Cook in preheated water bath, covered, for 2 hours. Remove bag from water bath.
4. Open bag and season to taste with salt and pepper. Ladle into serving bowls.

Serving Suggestions

- Top the chili with your favorite toppings, such as shredded cheese, sour cream and crumbled tortilla chips.
- Serve over cooked brown rice or quinoa.

Side Dishes

Perfect Poached Asparagus

Asparagus. So simple, so good. It's great as a side dish or on its own. The sous vide produces a tender-crisp poached asparagus without any watery taste. However you prefer to serve it, make sure to snap off the bottoms and discard them, as they tend to be stringy and tough.

**MAKES
4 SERVINGS**

Sous vide time:
12 minutes

Tips

When buying asparagus, look for bright green stalks with tightly closed tips.

Rinse asparagus well, holding the tips vertically under running water to make sure all grit is washed away. The leaves at the tip tend to catch the dirt as they push through the soil.

Thicker asparagus can benefit from peeling before cooking.

We prefer a flaky sea salt, such as fleur de sel, freshly ground sea salt or kosher salt, for the pleasant, clean burst of salt flavor it contributes, but you can use any salt you have on hand.

Cooled asparagus can be refrigerated in the sealed bag for up to 3 days.

- **Preheat water bath to 180°F (82°C)**
- **Large resealable freezer bag**

1 lb	asparagus (medium thickness)	500 g
2 tbsp	butter, cut into small pieces	30 mL
	Salt	

1. Remove woody stems from asparagus by snapping lower section off each stalk. Place asparagus in freezer bag, arranging in a single layer, and add butter. Remove excess air and seal bag.

2. Cook in preheated water bath for 12 minutes. The asparagus should be tender but resilient; if they aren't, return bag to water bath and cook, checking for doneness every 2 minutes. Remove bag from water bath.

3. Serve warm or immerse bag in ice water to cool completely. Season asparagus to taste with salt before serving.

Serving Suggestions

- Chilled asparagus makes a great summer salad. Top with shaved Parmesan cheese or sharp (old) Cheddar cheese and a simple olive oil vinaigrette.
- Drizzle Hollandaise Sauce (page 177) over warm or cold asparagus, or use asparagus on Eggs Benedict (see box, page 34) for a delightful treat.

Beets with Olive Oil and Sea Salt

Beets add a splash of color and earthiness to any plate and are a versatile vegetable for side dishes and salads. This simple recipe lets their flavor shine.

MAKES 4 SERVINGS

Sous vide time: 1 hour

Tips

You can use any color of beets you prefer, but it is best to cook light and dark beets in separate bags, to prevent the colors from bleeding.

We prefer a flaky sea salt, such as fleur de sel, freshly ground sea salt or kosher salt, for the pleasant, clean burst of salt flavor it contributes, but you can use any salt you have on hand.

Cooled beets can be refrigerated in the sealed bag for up to 3 days.

Variation

For a reasonable facsimile of pickled beets, add 1 tbsp (15 mL) balsamic vinegar with the oil before cooking.

- **Preheat water bath to 190°F (88°C)**
- **Large resealable freezer bag**

1 lb	beets	500 g
1 tbsp	extra virgin olive oil	15 mL
¼ tsp	sea salt	1 mL

1. Peel beets, cut in half lengthwise and slice thinly into half-moons. Place in a medium bowl and add oil and salt, stirring to evenly coat beets.

2. Transfer beets to freezer bag, arranging in a single layer, and add any remaining oil mixture. Remove excess air and seal bag.

3. Cook in preheated water bath, covered, for 1 hour. The beets should be tender; if they aren't, return bag to water bath and cook, checking for doneness every 15 minutes. Remove bag from water bath.

4. Serve warm or immerse bag in ice water to cool completely.

Serving Suggestions

- These beets make a nice side dish for roasts and savory meat pies.
- Chilled beets make a lovely salad. Arrange them on top of baby greens and dress with a simple vinaigrette.

Easy Beet Soup

For an excellent summer soup, cook an extra 2 cups (500 mL) sliced peeled beets (all one color) in a third bag, then combine the extra cooked beets with their liquid, 2 cups (500 mL) ready-to-use chicken or vegetable broth and ¼ cup (60 mL) plain yogurt in a blender or food processor and purée until smooth. Refrigerate until chilled, for up to 2 days, then season to taste with salt and pepper.

Brussels Sprouts with Bacon and Pecans

As a child, I was most unfond of Brussels sprouts. Many a long night was spent sitting at the dinner table until I finished the overcooked lump on my plate. But now I've grown to love them, especially when they're cooked nicely, with a little crunch and some flavor, as these are. And, of course, bacon makes everything better. ~ *Jay*

Sous vide time: 1 hour

Tips

Choose Brussels sprouts that are all about the same size, for even cooking. Trim off the base and remove any tough or discolored outer leaves. Rinse well and cut the sprouts in half lengthwise. If they are very large (around 2 inches/5 cm), you can cut them into quarters lengthwise to make sure they cook through (but those large ones are usually better shredded for a raw slaw).

To make ahead, prepare sprouts through step 2, then immerse bag in ice water to cool completely. Refrigerate in the sealed bag for up to 3 days. Proceed with step 3, increasing the cooking time in step 4 to about 5 minutes.

- **Preheat water bath to 185°F (85°C)**
- **Large resealable freezer bag**

3 cups	Brussels sprouts, trimmed and halved	750 mL
1 tbsp	olive oil	15 mL
¼ tsp	salt	1 mL
¼ tsp	freshly ground black pepper	1 mL
3	slices bacon, chopped	3
⅓ cup	pecan halves	75 mL

1. In freezer bag, combine Brussels sprouts, oil, salt and pepper; shake to combine, then arrange sprouts in a single layer. Remove excess air and seal bag.

2. Cook in preheated water bath, covered, for 1 hour. The sprouts should be tender; if they aren't, return bag to water bath and cook, checking for doneness every 15 minutes. Remove bag from water bath.

3. In a skillet, cook bacon over medium heat until brown and crisp. Add pecans and cook, stirring, for 3 to 4 minutes or until toasted.

4. Drain off cooking liquid from Brussels sprouts and add sprouts to skillet. Cook, stirring, for 1 to 2 minutes or until combined and hot.

Brussels Sprout Waldorf Salad

Leftover Brussels sprouts can be used for a new, healthy twist on a Waldorf salad. For each cup (250 mL) of sprouts, add ½ chopped apple, ¼ cup (60 mL) raisins and ¼ cup (60 mL) yogurt.

Braised Red Cabbage with Apple and Cranberries

Sweet, tangy and still a little crunchy, this braised cabbage goes great with pork, chicken or fish. In a pinch, you could even use it cold as coleslaw or a topping for tacos or pulled pork sandwiches.

MAKES 8 SERVINGS

Sous vide time: 2½ hours

Tips

It's tricky to arrange the cabbage in a single layer in the freezer bag when it's raw, so we found the best way to make sure it cooks evenly is to let it cook for an hour, until it's slightly softened, then knead it in the bag to distribute it. Use waterproof silicone oven mitts to protect your hands from the hot water. If you prefer a more hands-off method, divide the cabbage mixture between 2 medium freezer bags to start and press it into an even layer before removing the air.

Cooled cabbage can be refrigerated in the sealed bag for up to 3 days.

- **Preheat water bath to 190°F (88°C)**
- **Large resealable freezer bag**

1	apple (peeled or unpeeled), diced	1
4 cups	thickly shredded red cabbage	1 L
½ cup	dried cranberries	125 mL
3 tbsp	olive oil	45 mL
3 tbsp	red wine vinegar	45 mL
¼ tsp	ground cinnamon	1 mL
	Salt and freshly ground black pepper	

1. In a large bowl, combine apple, cabbage, cranberries, oil, vinegar, cinnamon and ¾ tsp (3 mL) each salt and pepper, tossing to evenly coat cabbage.
2. Transfer cabbage mixture to freezer bag and add any remaining liquid. Remove excess air and seal bag.
3. Cook in preheated water bath, covered, for 1 hour. Remove bag from water bath and gently knead the cabbage to make sure it is spread out evenly. Return bag to water bath and cook for 1½ hours. The cabbage should be tender; if it isn't, return bag to water bath and cook, checking for doneness every 15 minutes. Remove bag from water bath.
4. Serve immediately or immerse in ice water to cool completely. Season to taste with salt and pepper before serving.

Variations

To change the flavor, you can substitute balsamic or apple cider vinegar for the red wine vinegar.

You can substitute raisins or chopped dried cherries for the dried cranberries, or leave out the dried fruit.

For a classic European flavor, add ½ tsp (2 mL) caraway, mustard or celery seeds with the cinnamon.

Honey Butter Glazed Heirloom Carrots

Heirloom carrots have a brighter, fresher flavor than regular orange carrots and come in a variety of colors, often available in mixed bags or at farmers' markets. This dish is inspired by a classic from my childhood: carrots in brown sugar and butter. It's a perfect side dish for almost any entrée. If you get blue or purple carrots in your mix, I'd suggest cooking them in their own bag, so the colors don't bleed. ~ *Jay*

MAKES 4 SERVINGS

Sous vide time: 1 hour

Tips

When slicing the carrots, cut them into uniformly thick coins for the most even cooking.

This recipe can be doubled, tripled or quadrupled, using 1 large freezer bag for each double batch. Just be sure there is enough room in the sous vide container to allow the water to circulate around the bags.

Cooled carrots can be refrigerated in the sealed bag for up to 3 days.

- **Preheat water bath to 185°F (85°C)**
- **Medium resealable freezer bag**

2 cups	sliced carrots (about 3)	500 mL
2 tbsp	butter, cut into small pieces	30 mL
1 tbsp	liquid honey	15 mL
¼ tsp	salt	1 mL

1. In freezer bag, combine carrots, butter, honey and salt; shake to combine, then arrange carrot slices in an even layer, overlapping just slightly, as necessary. Remove excess air and seal bag.

2. Cook in preheated water bath, covered, for 1 hour. The carrots should be tender; if they aren't, return bag to water bath and cook, checking for doneness every 15 minutes. Remove bag from water bath.

3. Serve warm or immerse bag in ice water to cool completely.

Serving Suggestion

- Leftover cooked carrots make a great addition to soup. Chop them small and add as a garnish, or add into any soup that you plan to purée.

Corn on the Cob

Cooking this summer favorite sous vide enables you to relax while you prepare the rest of your dinner and enjoy time with your guests. You can finish it on the grill for that fresh barbecue flavor.

<table>
<tr><td>MAKES 4 SERVINGS</td></tr>
</table>

Sous vide time: 35 minutes

Tips

If you have very long cobs of corn that won't fit in the freezer bag, cut them in half crosswise and use 2 or more bags as necessary to keep the cob pieces in a single layer with a little space in between each.

It's very handy to use sous vide when cooking corn for a big party. Use a very large container, such as a cooler (see box, page 10) and line up cobs of corn in extra-large freezer bags. Just be sure the water can flow around each bag.

Leftover cooked corn is a great addition to soups, salads and salsas. Stand the corn in a bowl with the stem end down and use a serrated knife to carve the kernels off the cob directly into the bowl.

To use corn cold for salads, at the end of step 2, immerse bag in ice water to cool completely. Cooled corn can be refrigerated in the sealed bag for up to 3 days.

- **Preheat water bath to 185°F (85°C)**
- **Large resealable freezer bag**

4	ears corn, shucked	4
¼ cup	butter, cut into small pieces	60 mL
½ tsp	salt (approx.)	2 mL

1. Place corn in freezer bag, leaving space between each cob, if possible, and sprinkle with butter and salt. Remove excess air and seal bag.

2. Cook in preheated water bath, covered, for 35 minutes. The corn should be tender; if it isn't, return bag to water bath and cook, checking for doneness every 5 minutes. Remove bag from water bath.

3. Serve warm, brushing corn with butter from bag and sprinkling with more salt, if desired.

Variations

Add 2 tbsp (30 mL) chopped fresh basil with the butter and salt in step 1.

Substitute 2 tbsp (30 mL) mayonnaise for the butter, brushing it over the cobs before placing them in the bag, and add a pinch of hot pepper flakes with the salt. Sprinkle cooked corn with 1 tbsp (15 mL) freshly squeezed lime juice and pinch of freshly ground black pepper.

Add ¼ cup (60 mL) puréed roasted red bell pepper and ¼ tsp (1 mL) dried rosemary with the butter and salt in step 1.

To grill the cooked corn, preheat barbecue grill to high. Lightly brush cobs all over with olive or vegetable oil. Grill, turning often, for 1 to 2 minutes per side or just until sizzling and marked.

Fingerling Potatoes with Olive Oil and Herbs

With sous vide cooking, you get the creamy, buttery texture of boiled potatoes without risking the mushy texture from a few too many minutes in the boiling water. Whether you're enjoying these potatoes as a simple side dish or incorporating them into another recipe, you'll be impressed with the ease of making them and the perfect texture every time.

**MAKES
4 SERVINGS**

**Sous vide time:
1½ hours**

Tips

When cooking at higher temperatures, covering the sous vide cooking container helps to improve heat efficiency and reduces water loss (for more information, see page 16).

Cooled potatoes can be refrigerated in the sealed bag for up to 3 days.

Variation

Poached Baby Red Potatoes with Sea Salt and Cracked Pepper: In place of the fingerling potatoes, use baby red potatoes, cut in half. Increase the oil to 2 tbsp (30 mL), add ¼ tsp (1 mL) freshly cracked black pepper and omit the rosemary and oregano. Cook as directed, then season with more salt and cracked black pepper before serving.

- **Preheat water bath to 190°F (88°C)**
- **Medium resealable freezer bag**

1 lb	yellow-fleshed fingerling potatoes or other small potatoes	500 g
1 tbsp	extra virgin olive oil	15 mL
¼ tsp	salt (preferably sea salt)	1 mL
¼ tsp	dried rosemary	1 mL
¼ tsp	dried oregano	1 mL

1. Cut potatoes into quarters lengthwise (or in half, if small). Place in a medium bowl and add oil, salt, rosemary and oregano, stirring to evenly coat potatoes.

2. Transfer potatoes to freezer bag, arranging in a single layer, and add any remaining oil mixture. Remove excess air and seal bag.

3. Cook in preheated water bath, covered, for 1½ hours. The potatoes should be tender when pierced with a fork; if they aren't, return bag to water bath and cook, checking for doneness every 15 minutes. Remove bag from water bath.

4. Serve immediately or immerse bag in ice water to cool completely.

Serving Suggestions

- These potatoes are excellent on their own, straight from the bag, or you can transfer them to a hot, well-oiled skillet and cook, stirring, over medium-high heat for 5 to 7 minutes or until golden brown. Alternatively, spread the potatoes on a foil-lined baking sheet and bake in a 450°F (230°C) oven for about 10 minutes, until browned, for oven-baked goodness.
- Fingerling potatoes make excellent potato salad because they hold their shape and absorb the flavors of the salad dressing. Toss the potatoes in a vinaigrette while still warm, or let cool and mix with a tangy yogurt-mayonnaise dressing with chopped egg and fresh chives.

Rosemary and Garlic Sour Cream Potatoes

This side dish brings back memories of baked potatoes and scalloped potatoes. Comfort food is both familiar and reassuring. Serve these potatoes with steak or chicken.

Sous vide time: 1½ hours

Tips

Use medium- or low-starch potatoes, such as basic round white potatoes or yellow-fleshed potatoes (like Yukon Golds). They hold their shape best when cooked.

This recipe can be doubled, tripled or quadrupled, using 1 large freezer bag for each double batch. Just be sure there is enough room in the sous vide container to allow the water to circulate around the bags.

Cooled potatoes can be refrigerated in the sealed bag for up to 3 days.

- **Preheat water bath to 190°F (88°C)**
- **Medium resealable freezer bag**

1	clove garlic, minced	1
2 cups	thinly sliced white potatoes (about 2 medium)	500 mL
¼ tsp	salt	1 mL
¼ tsp	freshly ground black pepper	1 mL
Pinch	dried rosemary, crumbled	Pinch
¼ cup	full-fat sour cream	60 mL

1. In a medium bowl, combine garlic, potatoes, salt, pepper, rosemary and sour cream, stirring to evenly coat potatoes.
2. Transfer potato mixture to freezer bag, arranging in a single layer. Remove excess air and seal bag.
3. Cook in preheated water bath, covered, for 1½ hours. The potatoes should be tender when pierced with a fork; if they aren't, return bag to water bath and cook, checking for doneness every 15 minutes. Remove bag from water bath.
4. Serve warm or immerse bag in ice water to cool completely.

Creamy Potato Salad

These potatoes make a good base for potato salad. Chill, then add ¼ cup (60 mL) chopped celery, 2 chopped radishes, a chopped hard-cooked egg and 1 tbsp (15 mL) chopped fresh chives. Top with a sprinkle of paprika for a true retro feeling.

Cinnamon-Spiced Sweet Potatoes

Whether you serve them warm at holiday dinners or chill them for salads in the summer, these easy sweet potatoes give you a side dish alternative that everyone is sure to love.

Tips

We like to leave the skin on the sweet potato for extra texture, to preserve more nutrients and for the extra dietary fiber, but you can peel it if you prefer. If you're not peeling it, scrub it well with a firm brush under running water before chopping.

This recipe can be doubled, tripled or quadrupled, using 1 large freezer bag for each double batch. Just be sure there is enough room in the sous vide container to allow the water to circulate around the bags.

Cooled potatoes can be refrigerated in the sealed bag for up to 3 days.

Variation

Mashed Sweet Potatoes: Peel the sweet potato before cutting it into pieces. After step 3, let cool for 5 minutes, then transfer sweet potato to a bowl or pot. Mash, adding 1 tbsp (15 mL) additional olive oil, 1 tbsp (15 mL) butter and/or ¼ cup (60 mL) cream (any type). Season to taste with more salt and pepper.

- **Preheat water bath to 185°F (85°C)**
- **Medium resealable freezer bag**

1	large sweet potato (about 1 lb/500 g), cut into ½-inch (1 cm) pieces	1
1 tbsp	extra virgin olive oil	15 mL
1 tsp	pure maple syrup	5 mL
¼ tsp	salt	1 mL
¼ tsp	freshly ground black pepper	1 mL
¼ tsp	ground cinnamon	1 mL

1. In a medium bowl, combine sweet potato, oil, maple syrup, salt, pepper and cinnamon, stirring to evenly coat sweet potato.
2. Transfer sweet potato to freezer bag, arranging in a single layer, and add any remaining oil mixture, pressing to spread the sweet potato pieces out as much as possible. Remove excess air and seal bag.
3. Cook in preheated water bath, covered, for 45 minutes. The sweet potato should be tender; if it isn't, return bag to water bath and cook, checking for doneness every 15 minutes. Remove bag from water bath.
4. Serve warm or immerse bag in ice water to cool completely.

Sweet Potato Chickpea Salad

Add one 14-oz (396 mL) can of chickpeas, drained and rinsed, 1 cup (250 mL) chopped cucumber and 1 tbsp (15 mL) balsamic vinegar to chilled potatoes for a nice summer salad.

Provençal White Beans

I love the combination of flavors found in herbes de Provence — typically rosemary, thyme, savory, marjoram and a hint of lavender — and the way it makes something simple, like white beans, seem special. This sous vide cooking method does take some time, but you don't have to remember to presoak the beans, and it is even easier than boiling water. ~ *Jennifer*

MAKES 4 TO 6 SERVINGS

Sous vide time: 6 hours

Tips

If you don't have a shallot on hand, use ¼ cup (60 mL) coarsely chopped onion instead.

In place of the herbes de Provence, you can substitute ⅛ tsp (0.5 mL) each dried thyme and rosemary.

This is a perfect way to cook beans for a cold salad. After step 3, immerse the bag in ice water to chill the beans quickly, or let cool and refrigerate in the sealed bag for up to 5 days, then drain and add to salads.

- **Preheat water bath to 190°F (88°C)**
- **Medium resealable freezer bag**

1 cup	dried white pea (navy) beans	250 mL
1	shallot, coarsely chopped	1
1	clove garlic, cut in half	1
¼ tsp	dried herbes de Provence	1 mL
	Salt and freshly ground black pepper	
3 cups	water	750 mL
1 to 2 tbsp	extra virgin olive oil	15 to 30 mL

1. Place beans in a sieve and pick out any stones or discolored beans. Rinse well and drain.
2. In freezer bag, combine beans, shallot, garlic, herbes de Provence, ½ tsp (2 mL) salt, pepper to taste and water. Remove excess air and seal bag.
3. Cook in preheated water bath, covered, for 6 hours. The beans should be tender; if they aren't, return bag to water bath and cook, checking for doneness every 30 minutes. Remove bag from water bath.
4. Transfer bean mixture to a sieve or colander to drain. Transfer to a warmed serving dish or bowl. Toss with oil to taste and season with salt. Serve warm.

Chili Lime Pinto Beans

These beans require no presoaking and no babysitting once you put them in the water bath, making them super-easy. The flavors infuse as they cook, and the cooked texture is a nice firm yet tender bean. Whether you serve them as a side dish or a component of burritos or a salad, these are sure to become a new standby recipe.

Tip

To use the beans cold, after step 3, immerse the bag in ice water to chill them quickly, or let cool and refrigerate in the sealed bag for up to 5 days, then drain, add lime zest, lime juice and salt to taste, and add to salads.

Variation

For spicier beans, add ¼ tsp (1 mL) chipotle chile powder with the chili powder.

- **Preheat water bath to 190°F (88°C)**
- **Medium resealable freezer bag**

1 cup	dried pinto beans	250 mL
1	clove garlic, cut in half	1
½ cup	chopped onion	125 mL
1 tsp	chili powder	5 mL
½ tsp	dried oregano	2 mL
	Salt and freshly ground black pepper	
3 cups	water	750 mL
½ tsp	grated lime zest	2 mL
2 tbsp	freshly squeezed lime juice	30 mL

1. Place beans in a sieve and pick out any stones or discolored beans. Rinse well and drain.
2. In freezer bag, combine beans, garlic, onion, chili powder, oregano, ½ tsp (2 mL) salt, pepper to taste and water. Remove excess air and seal bag.
3. Cook in preheated water bath, covered, for 6 hours. The beans should be tender; if they aren't, return bag to water bath and cook, checking for doneness every 30 minutes. Remove bag from water bath.
4. Transfer bean mixture to a sieve or colander to drain. Transfer to a warmed serving dish or bowl. Toss with lime zest and lime juice, and season with salt. Serve warm.

Serving Suggestion

- Add the beans to burritos or on top of a taco salad, or mash and spread them on a taco or tostada (or anywhere you'd use refried beans).

Desserts

Crème Caramel

Crème caramel is one of the first "fancy" desserts I learned to love in restaurants as a child, and one of the first I learned to make (my mom was a brave and willing teacher!), and I still love to make and eat it. The classic recipe uses a water bath in the oven, making it perfect (and logical) to adapt it for sous vide cooking, with the canning jars replacing the traditional ramekins. I may never go back to the oven method now that I've made it this way. ~ *Jennifer*

MAKES 4 SERVINGS

Sous vide time: 45 minutes

Tip

Avoid stirring the caramel as it boils. Stirring can cause crystals to form, which can make the sugar seize. If the caramel is browning unevenly, you can gently swirl the pan and rotate the pan on your burner to avoid hot spots. You'll know it's getting close to being ready (and time to dump the water out of the jars) when the bubbles slow down and get louder, and the color turns from golden to a deep caramel brown. Be sure not to leave the caramel unattended once the color starts to change — it can burn quickly.

- **Preheat water bath to 179°F (81.5°C)**
- **4 wide-mouth 8-oz (250 mL) canning jars, with two-piece lids**
- **2 wire racks**

³/₄ cup	granulated sugar, divided	175 mL
¹/₄ cup	water	60 mL
1¹/₄ cups	milk	300 mL
¹/₂ cup	half-and-half (10%) cream	125 mL
4	large eggs	4
1¹/₂ tsp	vanilla extract	7 mL

1. In a small, heavy-bottomed saucepan, combine ¹/₂ cup (125 mL) sugar and water. Bring to a boil over medium heat, stirring to dissolve sugar. Boil, without stirring, for about 10 minutes or until syrup is a deep caramel color.

2. Meanwhile, pour hot tap water into the canning jars to warm the glass; set aside.

3. Just before caramel is ready, empty water from jars. Remove caramel from heat and, as soon as bubbles subside, pour into jars, dividing equally (it's okay if the caramel doesn't cover the bottoms of the jars evenly; it will melt in the water bath). Let cool.

4. In another small saucepan, combine milk and cream. Heat over medium heat, stirring occasionally, just until steaming. Remove from heat.

5. In a heatproof bowl, whisk together the remaining sugar and eggs until slightly thickened and foamy. Gradually pour milk mixture into egg mixture in a thin, steady stream, whisking constantly. Whisk in vanilla.

Tip

These jars will float, so you'll need to weigh them down. Working carefully so as not to clink the jars together, place a heatproof plate, pot lid or other flat object on top of the jars and place a jar full of hot water on top of the plate. To cover the sous vide bath, stretch plastic wrap or foil over the weighting objects.

6. Set a fine-mesh sieve over a large liquid measuring cup or a bowl with a spout. Pour egg mixture through sieve. Pour strained custard into jars over caramel, dividing equally. Wipe rims of jars and place lid discs on jars, then screw on bands just until fingertip-tight.

7. Place a wire rack in preheated water bath and place jars on rack, then weigh jars down (see tip). Cook, covered, for 45 minutes. To check for doneness, remove the lid from one jar; the custard should be set around the edges and slightly jiggly. If it isn't, replace lid, return jar to water bath and cook, checking for doneness every 10 minutes.

8. Remove jars from water bath and transfer to a wire rack. Let cool, covered, for about 15 minutes. Refrigerate for at least 2 hours, until chilled and set, or for up to 2 days.

9. To serve, remove lids and pat surface of custard dry with a paper towel. Run a knife around the edge of the custard and invert onto serving plate.

Personal Pumpkin Pie in a Jar

We love pumpkin pie in our family. It's definitely not just for holidays, and when one of us makes it (my mom's is the reigning best), we have to make extra because we tend to dig in for breakfast before it even gets to dessert time. The slow, constant temperature of the sous vide creates a super-smooth and creamy filling. ~ *Jennifer*

Tips

To prevent temperature shock and jar breakage, it's important to use room-temperature ingredients in this recipe. Let the refrigerated ingredients stand at room temperature for about 30 minutes before preparing the pumpkin filling.

Fill these jars and add them to the water bath one at a time, rather than all at once, to make sure they don't cool off, as that can cause cracking.

This recipe can easily be doubled if your sous vide container is large enough to arrange 8 jars in a single layer.

Variations

For an extra-gingery zip, add 1 to 2 tbsp (15 to 30 mL) minced crystallized ginger with the spices, or julienne crystallized ginger and sprinkle it on top for garnish just before serving.

For pumpkin custard, omit the crumb crust.

- Preheat water bath to 179°F (81.5°C)
- 4 wide-mouth 8-oz (250 mL) canning jars, with two-piece lids
- 2 wire racks

½ cup	gingersnap cookie or graham cracker crumbs	125 mL
1 tbsp	butter, melted	15 mL
⅓ cup	packed brown sugar	75 mL
¾ tsp	ground cinnamon	3 mL
½ tsp	ground nutmeg	2 mL
½ tsp	ground ginger	2 mL
Pinch	salt	Pinch
2	large eggs, at room temperature	2
1¼ cups	pumpkin purée (not pie filling), at room temperature	300 mL
1 cup	evaporated milk or half-and-half (10%) cream, at room temperature	250 mL

1. Pour hot tap water into the canning jars to warm the glass; set aside. Place a wire rack in preheated water bath.

2. In a small bowl, combine cookie crumbs and butter until evenly moistened; set aside.

3. In a large liquid measuring cup or a medium bowl, whisk together brown sugar, cinnamon, nutmeg, ginger, salt and eggs until blended. Whisk in pumpkin and evaporated milk until incorporated.

4. Working with one jar at a time, empty water and, working quickly, sprinkle one-quarter of the crumb mixture in the jar, pressing it down lightly. Add about one-quarter of the pumpkin mixture (about ⅔ cup/150 mL). Wipe rim of jar and place lid disc on jar, then screw on band until fingertip-tight. Place jars on the rack in the bath as they are filled.

5. Cook, covered, for 1 hour. To check for doneness, remove the lid from one jar; the pumpkin filling should be set around the edges and just slightly jiggly in the center. If it isn't, replace lid, return jar to water bath and cook, checking for doneness every 10 minutes.

6. Remove jars from water bath and transfer to a wire rack. Remove lids and let cool. Serve warm or at room temperature, or replace lids and refrigerate for about 2 hours, until chilled, or for up to 3 days.

Plain but Good Cheesecakes

A go-to staple for entertaining, perfectly cooked individual cheesecakes can now be made using your sous vide. It produces a smooth, creamy texture every time, the individual portions are the ideal size, and there are no messy attempts at cutting neat slices. Serve with fresh berries, a fruit coulis or chocolate or caramel sauce on top, or serve unadorned for the cheesecake purists.

**MAKES
4 SERVINGS**

Sous vide time: 1 hour

Tips

To prevent temperature shock and jar breakage, it's important to use room-temperature ingredients in this recipe. Let the refrigerated ingredients stand at room temperature for about 30 minutes before preparing the cheesecake batter.

These jars may float, so you'll need to weigh them down. Working carefully so as not to clink the jars together, place a heatproof plate, pot lid or other flat object on top of the jars and place a jar full of hot water on top of the plate. To cover the sous vide bath, stretch plastic wrap or foil over the weighting objects.

Variations

Coffee Cheesecakes: Add 2 tsp (10 mL) instant espresso powder or 1 tbsp (15 mL) instant coffee granules with the yogurt.

Citrus Cheesecakes: Add 1 tbsp (15 mL) grated lemon, orange or lime zest (or a mixture) with the yogurt.

- Preheat water bath to 170°F (77°C)
- 4 wide-mouth 8-oz (250 mL) canning jars, with two-piece lids
- Electric mixer
- 2 wire racks

4	graham crackers, each about 2½ inches (6 cm) square	4
8 oz	brick-style cream cheese, softened	250 g
¼ cup	granulated sugar	60 mL
1	large egg, at room temperature	1
¼ cup	plain Greek yogurt (not fat-free), at room temperature	60 mL
2 tsp	vanilla extract (or ¼ tsp/1 mL vanilla bean powder)	10 mL

1. Pour hot tap water into the canning jars to warm the glass; set aside.

2. Using a serrated knife, cut corners off graham crackers to shape them to fit in bottom of jars; set aside.

3. In a large bowl, using the electric mixer, beat cream cheese and sugar until smooth. Beat in egg until well blended. Beat in yogurt and vanilla just until incorporated.

4. Empty jars and, working quickly, place graham cracker in the bottom and fill with cream cheese mixture, dividing equally (about ½ cup/125 mL per jar). Wipe rims of jars and place lid discs on jars, then screw on bands just until fingertip-tight.

5. Place a wire rack in preheated water bath and place jars on rack; if the jars float, weigh them down (see tip). Cook, covered, for 1 hour. To check for doneness, remove the lid from one jar; the cheesecake should be set around the edges and just slightly jiggly in the center. If it isn't, replace lid, return jar to water bath and cook, checking for doneness every 10 minutes.

6. Remove jars from water bath and transfer to a wire rack. Remove lids and let cool. Replace lids and refrigerate for about 2 hours, until chilled, or for up to 3 days.

Individual Flourless Chocolate Cakes

Warm chocolate air is the best description I can think of for these little flourless cakes. They are different from their oven-baked counterparts in that they don't get a crust on the outside and collapse, but you get that same ethereal, rich chocolate taste, and they are definitely decadent — everything I want in a chocolate dessert! You can put them in the sous vide to cook while you enjoy your dinner, and they'll be perfectly cooked and warm in time for dessert. ~ *Jennifer*

**MAKES
4 SERVINGS**

Sous vide time:
45 minutes

Tips

If you don't have the small 4-oz (125 mL) jars, use wide-mouth 8-oz (250 mL) jars and cook for 40 minutes.

For the best flavor and texture in these cakes, use the best-quality dark chocolate (check the label to make sure cocoa liquor or chocolate is the first ingredient and there are as few ingredients as possible) and good-quality cocoa powder (a higher fat content is better).

These jars will float, so you'll need to weigh them down. Working carefully so as not to clink the jars together, place a heatproof plate, pot lid or other flat object on top of the jars and place a jar full of hot water on top of the plate. To cover the sous vide bath, stretch plastic wrap or foil over the weighting objects.

- Preheat water bath to 175°F (79°C)
- Four 4-oz (125 mL) canning jars, with two-piece lids (see tip)
- Electric mixer
- 2 wire racks

2 oz	dark chocolate, chopped	60 g
2 tbsp	butter	30 mL
2	large eggs, separated	2
Pinch	salt	Pinch
¼ cup	granulated sugar, divided	60 mL
2 tbsp	unsweetened cocoa powder	30 mL
1 tsp	instant espresso powder (optional)	5 mL
½ tsp	vanilla extract	2 mL
	Confectioners' (icing) sugar	

1. Pour hot tap water into the canning jars to warm the glass; set aside.

2. In a small saucepan, melt chocolate and butter over medium-low heat, stirring until smooth. Remove from heat and let cool.

3. In a medium bowl, using the electric mixer, beat egg whites and salt until frothy. Gradually beat in 2 tbsp (30 mL) sugar, then beat until stiff, glossy peaks form. Set aside.

4. In a large bowl, beat the remaining sugar, cocoa powder, espresso powder (if using), egg yolks and vanilla until blended. Beat in cooled chocolate mixture. Fold in one-third of the egg whites until blended, then fold in the remaining egg whites just until no streaks of white remain.

Tip

Cooled cakes can be covered and refrigerated for up to 3 days to serve cold (but they really are best freshly cooked and warm).

Variations

Flourless Coconut Chocolate Cakes: Toast 2 tbsp (30 mL) sweetened flaked or shredded coconut in a small, dry skillet over medium heat, stirring constantly, for 2 to 3 minutes or until lightly browned and fragrant; immediately transfer to a bowl and let cool. Sprinkle toasted coconut over top of batter, dividing equally, after filling the jars in step 5.

Flourless Mint Chocolate Cakes: Omit the espresso powder. Add 1 tbsp (15 mL) chopped fresh mint when folding in the egg whites in step 4. Sprinkle 2 tbsp (30 mL) miniature semisweet chocolate chips over top of batter, dividing equally, after filling jars in step 5.

5. Empty jars and, working quickly, fill with cake batter, dividing equally (about $1/3$ cup/75 mL per jar). Wipe rims of jars and place lid discs on jars, then screw on bands just until fingertip-tight.

6. Place a wire rack in preheated water bath and place jars on rack, then weigh jars down (see tip, page 164). Cook, covered, for 45 minutes. To check for doneness, remove the lid from one jar; the cake should be puffed and look dry on top, and a toothpick inserted in the center should come out with a few moist crumbs clinging to it. If the cakes aren't done, replace lid, return jar to water bath and cook, checking for doneness every 10 minutes.

7. Remove jars from water bath and transfer to a wire rack. Remove lids and let cool for 15 minutes (or longer, but they're best served warm). Serve dusted with confectioners' sugar.

Serving Suggestions

- Top with lightly sweetened whipped cream and fresh raspberries or sliced bananas.
- Make these in the larger jars (see tip, page 164) and serve with a scoop of salted caramel, vanilla or raspberry ripple ice cream on top.

Mason Jar Lemon Pudding Cakes

These have a thin sauce in the bottom, rather than a thick pudding, but they are as tasty and comforting as old-fashioned pudding cakes. This version does hold much better than traditional pudding cakes, so they can be made ahead and enjoyed cold. We even got an "OMG" text from our friend Joanne when she ate her sample, so we declared these a sous vide win.

MAKES 4 SERVINGS

Sous vide time: 45 minutes

Tips

You'll need 1 to 2 lemons for the grated zest for these cakes. Extra grated zest can be wrapped and refrigerated for up to 3 days or frozen for up to 3 months. Squeeze out extra juice from the lemons and refrigerate it in an airtight container for up to 3 days or freeze it — those zested lemons go bad quickly in the crisper.

We find that 2% or whole milk are best for cakes and sauces (or combination desserts, like this one); lower-fat milk doesn't give cakes the desired tenderness, or sauces the desired body.

- Preheat water bath to 175°F (79°C)
- 4 wide-mouth 8-oz (250 mL) canning jars, with two-piece lids
- 2 wire racks

Sauce

¼ cup	granulated sugar	60 mL
1 tsp	grated lemon zest	5 mL
1¼ cups	milk	300 mL
½ tsp	vanilla extract	2 mL

Cakes

¾ cup	all-purpose flour	175 mL
1½ tsp	baking powder	7 mL
¼ tsp	salt	1 mL
1	large egg	1
2 tsp	grated lemon zest	10 mL
2 tbsp	freshly squeezed lemon juice	30 mL
1 tsp	vanilla extract	5 mL
⅓ cup	granulated sugar	75 mL
3 tbsp	butter	45 mL
½ cup	milk	125 mL

1. Pour hot tap water into the canning jars to warm the glass; set aside.

2. Sauce: In a small saucepan, combine sugar, lemon zest and milk. Bring just to a gentle simmer over medium heat, stirring until sugar is dissolved (do not let boil). Pour into a liquid measuring cup or a bowl with a spout, stir in vanilla and cover to keep warm. Set aside (reserve saucepan).

3. Cakes: In a medium bowl, whisk together flour, baking powder and salt.

4. In a heatproof medium bowl, whisk together egg, lemon zest, lemon juice and vanilla.

Serve cakes with a dusting of confectioners' (icing) sugar or a sprinkle of flavored granulated sugar (try vanilla sugar, lavender sugar or citrus sugar) for garnish.

Cooled cakes can be covered and refrigerated for up to 3 days to serve cold. The sauce will thicken when chilled.

5. In saucepan (no need to clean it), combine sugar, butter and milk. Warm over medium-low heat, stirring just until butter is melted and sugar is dissolved (do not let boil). Gradually pour into egg mixture in a thin, steady stream, whisking constantly until blended.

6. Pour egg mixture into flour mixture and stir just until evenly moistened.

7. Empty jars and, working quickly, fill with cake batter, dividing equally (about $1/2$ cup/125 mL per jar). Gently pour sauce over cake batter, dividing equally. Do not stir. Wipe rims of jars and place lid discs on jars, then screw on bands just until fingertip-tight.

8. Place a wire rack in preheated water bath and place jars on rack. Cook, covered, for 45 minutes. To check for doneness, remove the lid from one jar and insert a toothpick into the cake layer; it should come out clean. If it doesn't, replace lid, return jar to water bath and cook, checking for doneness every 10 minutes.

9. Remove jars from water bath and transfer to a wire rack. Remove lids and let cool for at least 15 minutes. Serve warm or let cool completely.

Variations

Lime Pudding Cakes: Substitute grated lime zest and lime juice for the lemon (use Key limes, if they're available).

Orange Pudding Cakes: Substitute grated orange zest for the lemon zest in the sauce and cakes, and use $2^1/2$ tbsp (37 mL) orange juice in place of the lemon juice in the cakes.

Fudgy Vegan Chocolate Avocado Cake

Creamy avocado and flax seeds replace butter and eggs in this vegan cake. Don't be alarmed: the rich chocolate enhanced by coffee hides the green color and the taste of the avocado, so your family and friends won't wonder what kind of science experiments you've been up to! It's fudgy and moist, and definitely a treat.

MAKES 4 SERVINGS

Sous vide time: 2 hours

Tips

We used a 6-cup (1.5 L) casserole dish about 6 inches (15 cm) square to test this cake. You can use a 6-inch (15 cm) square or round cake pan, or another dish or pan approximately the same size, as long as it holds at least 4 cups (1 L) volume.

For the best texture, make sure the avocado is ripe and soft for this recipe. If you have a glut of ripe avocados, you can peel, pit and cut them into chunks and freeze in airtight containers for up to 3 months. Let thaw before adding to recipes.

To brew the coffee for the cake, use twice as much coffee as you would for a typical cup. If you want to avoid caffeine, use a good-quality brewed decaffeinated coffee, making sure to brew it double strength to add a good, deep flavor to the cake.

- Preheat water bath to 180°F (82°C)
- Immersion blender or blender
- 4- to 6-cup (1 to 1.5 L) baking dish (see tip), bottom lined with parchment paper
- Extra-large resealable freezer bag
- 2 wire racks

1 tbsp	ground flax seeds (flaxseed meal)	15 mL
½ cup	strong brewed coffee	125 mL
1¼ cups	all-purpose flour	300 mL
⅓ cup	unsweetened cocoa powder	75 mL
1 tsp	baking powder	5 mL
½ tsp	salt	2 mL
1	soft ripe avocado, cut into chunks (about 4½ oz/140 g peeled and pitted)	1
¾ cup	coconut sugar	175 mL
¼ cup	plain nondairy milk	60 mL
3 tbsp	vegetable or melted coconut oil	45 mL
1 tsp	vanilla extract	5 mL
1 tsp	balsamic or cider vinegar	5 mL

1. In a large liquid measuring cup, using the immersion blender (or in blender), combine flax seeds and coffee; let stand for 5 minutes to soften seeds.

2. Meanwhile, in a large bowl, whisk together flour, cocoa powder, baking powder and salt.

3. Add avocado, coconut sugar, milk, oil, vanilla and vinegar to flax seed mixture and purée until smooth. Pour over flour mixture and stir until moistened.

Tips

To weigh the baking dish down in the water bath, place a heatproof plate, pot lid or other flat object on top of the dish and place a jar full of hot water on top of the plate. To cover the sous vide bath, stretch plastic wrap or foil over the weighting objects.

After it sits, this cake improves even more in taste and in the way it cuts. Cover the cooled cake and refrigerate until chilled, for at least 8 hours or for up to 1 day.

4. Spread in prepared baking dish, smoothing top. Cover dish with plastic wrap or foil, sealing tightly over the top. Place dish in freezer bag, remove excess air and seal bag.

5. Place a wire rack in preheated water bath and place dish on rack; weigh down, if necessary (see tip). Cook, covered, for 2 hours. To check for doneness, uncover dish and insert a toothpick into the center of the cake; it should come out with just a few moist crumbs clinging to it. If it doesn't, cover dish and return to bag. Return bag to water bath and cook, checking for doneness every 15 minutes.

6. Remove dish from bag, uncover and let cool completely in dish on a wire rack. Cut into squares or wedges to serve.

Variations

For a gluten-free version, use a gluten-free all-purpose flour blend in place of the all-purpose flour.

If you don't need to make a vegan cake, you can use regular dairy milk in place of the nondairy milk and granulated or packed brown sugar instead of the coconut sugar.

Classic Christmas Figgy Pudding

When you're cooking for the holidays, the stovetop and oven are going at full steam and there never seems to be enough room for everything. Here's sous vide to the rescue for the figgy pudding! Set it up out of the way, and the pudding will cook to perfection while you orchestrate the rest of the meal on the stove.

**MAKES
8 SERVINGS**

Sous vide time:
4 hours

Tip

If you don't have a proper pudding mold, you can use any heavy, heatproof bowl or baking dish that holds 3 to 4 cups (750 mL to 1 L) volume. We found that a nice rounded bowl created a pretty shape for the pudding, but you can really use any shape of container with the right volume. Be sure not to use too large a dish, which would prevent the pudding from steaming properly.

- **Preheat water bath to 195°F (91°C)**
- **Electric mixer**
- **3- to 4-cup (750 mL to 1 L) pudding mold (see tip), well buttered**
- **Large resealable freezer bag**
- **Wire rack**

½ cup	finely chopped trimmed dried figs	125 mL
½ cup	milk	125 mL
¼ cup	dried cranberries, chopped	60 mL
½ tsp	grated orange zest	2 mL
¼ cup	freshly squeezed orange juice	60 mL
½ cup	all-purpose flour	125 mL
½ tsp	baking powder	2 mL
½ tsp	ground cinnamon	2 mL
½ tsp	ground nutmeg	2 mL
¼ tsp	salt	1 mL
½ cup	butter, softened	125 mL
⅓ cup	packed brown sugar	75 mL
1	large egg	1
½ cup	coarse fresh bread crumbs	125 mL
	Orange Brandy Hard Sauce (page 184)	

1. In a small saucepan, combine figs and milk. Bring to a simmer over medium heat. Reduce heat to low, cover and simmer (do not let boil) for about 5 minutes or until figs are soft. Remove from heat and stir in cranberries. Let cool, uncovered, to room temperature. Stir in orange zest and orange juice.

2. In a small bowl, combine flour, baking powder, cinnamon, nutmeg and salt.

3. In a medium bowl, using the electric mixer, beat butter until smooth and fluffy. Beat in brown sugar until well blended. Beat in egg until fluffy.

4. Using a spatula or wooden spoon, stir flour mixture into butter mixture alternately with fruit mixture, making three additions of flour and two of fruit. Stir in bread crumbs.

5. Pack pudding into prepared mold. Cut a piece of parchment paper to fit just inside top of mold and place directly on the surface. Cover mold with foil, sealing tightly over the top. Place mold in freezer bag, remove excess air and seal bag.

6. Place wire rack in preheated water bath and place mold on rack. Cook, covered, for 4 hours. To check for doneness, remove foil and parchment and insert the tip of a knife into the center of the pudding; it should come out clean. If it doesn't, replace covers, return bag to water bath and cook, checking for doneness every 15 minutes. Remove from water bath.

7. Remove dish from bag, uncover and run a knife around the edge of the mold to loosen. Invert pudding onto a serving platter and let cool slightly. Cut into wedges and serve with warm sauce.

Raisin and Honey Rice Pudding

This is an easy, hands-off technique for making creamy rice pudding. It doesn't look creamy when it first comes out of the water bath, but a little stir and some standing time, and it thickens up quite amazingly. It's the perfect dessert to pop in the water bath alongside another sous vide recipe you're cooking at the same temperature.

MAKES 3 TO 4 SERVINGS

Sous vide time: 3 hours

Tips

It's easy to make more jars of this rice pudding for more servings. Just be sure there is enough space in your sous vide container for the water to circulate around the jars, and make sure the jars don't touch each other.

When stirring food in canning jars, use a silicone spatula or a wooden utensil to avoid stressing the glass and causing cracks or fractures.

When handling jars, a canning jar lifter or good-quality silicone oven mitts are handy, as they are heat-resistant even when wet and allow you to handle the hot jar without slipping.

Store pudding in the sealed jar in the refrigerator for up to 3 days. Transfer to serving bowls and serve cold or warm gently in the microwave on Medium-High (70%) for 1 to 2 minutes per serving (or warm in a saucepan over medium heat, stirring often).

- **Preheat water bath to 180°F (82°C)**
- **8-oz (250 mL) canning jar, with two-piece lid**
- **Wire rack**

1¼ cups	milk	300 mL
¼ cup	half-and-half (10%) cream	60 mL
¼ cup	Arborio rice	60 mL
¼ tsp	ground cinnamon	1 mL
Pinch	salt	Pinch
1 tbsp	liquid honey or pure maple syrup (approx.)	15 mL
2 tbsp	raisins	30 mL
½ tsp	vanilla extract	2 mL
	Additional ground cinnamon	

1. Pour hot tap water into the canning jar to warm the glass; set aside.

2. In a large glass measuring cup, combine milk and cream. Microwave on Medium (50%) for 2 to 3 minutes or until lukewarm. (Or warm in a saucepan over medium-low heat.) Stir in rice, cinnamon, salt and honey.

3. Empty water from jar and pour in rice mixture. Wipe rim of jar and place lid disc on jar, then screw on band just until fingertip-tight.

4. Place wire rack in preheated water bath and place jar on rack. Cook, covered, for 3 hours. The rice should be tender (the pudding will thicken considerably upon cooling); if it isn't, reseal jar and cook, checking for doneness every 15 minutes. Remove jar from water bath.

5. Remove lid and, using a spatula, stir in raisins and vanilla, stirring all the way to the bottom and breaking up any clumps of rice. Replace lid and let cool for about 20 minutes to enjoy hot, or let cool further to serve warm. Once cool, pudding can be refrigerated until chilled.

6. Taste before serving and stir in more honey, if desired. Top with a sprinkle of cinnamon.

Variation

Orange Cranberry Rice Pudding: Replace the raisins with dried cranberries and add ½ tsp (2 mL) grated orange zest with the vanilla.

Chocolate Almond Bread Pudding

When I ran our gourmet food shop, In a Nuttshell, we would use bread and croissants left at the end of the day to make bread pudding, and the customers loved it (and we loved not throwing good bread away). Chocolate and almond was one of the most popular flavor combinations, so I've reworked the method for the sous vide and am really pleased with the results. You may find yourself making sure you have leftover bread so you can make this comforting dessert. ~ Jay

Tips

To toast almonds, spread them on a baking sheet and toast in a 350°F (180°C) oven for 5 to 8 minutes or until fragrant and skins split. Transfer to a bowl and let cool.

To weigh the baking dish down in the water bath, place a heatproof plate, pot lid or other flat object on top of the dish and place a jar full of hot water on top of the plate. To cover the sous vide bath, stretch plastic wrap or foil over the weighting objects.

Variation

For a dairy-free version, use vegetable oil or nondairy butter alternative to grease the dish. Replace the cream with unsweetened almond milk, and make sure to use dairy-free bread, cocoa and chocolate.

- **Immersion blender or blender**
- **8-cup (2 L) shallow baking dish, buttered**
- **Extra-large resealable freezer bag**
- **Wire rack**

$^3/_4$ cup	chopped toasted almonds (see tip), divided	175 mL
$^1/_2$ cup	granulated sugar	125 mL
$^1/_3$ cup	unsweetened cocoa powder	75 mL
Pinch	salt	Pinch
4	large eggs	4
$1^1/_2$ cups	heavy or whipping (35%) cream	375 mL
2 tsp	vanilla extract	10 mL
5 cups	cubed baguette ($^3/_4$-inch/2 cm cubes)	1.25 L
$^1/_3$ cup	chopped dark chocolate (optional)	75 mL

1. In a large liquid measuring cup, using the immersion blender (or in blender), combine $^1/_2$ cup (125 mL) almonds, sugar, cocoa, salt, eggs, cream and vanilla; purée until blended.

2. In a large bowl, combine bread cubes and egg mixture, tossing to coat. Cover and refrigerate for at least 30 minutes or overnight to soak.

3. Meanwhile, preheat water bath to 175°F (79°C).

4. Coarsely chop the remaining almonds and set half aside for garnish.

5. Stir chocolate (if using) and the remaining chopped almonds into bread mixture. Transfer to prepared baking dish. Cover dish with foil, sealing tightly over the top. Place dish in freezer bag, remove excess air and seal bag.

6. Place wire rack in preheated water bath and place dish on rack; weigh down, if necessary (see tip). Cook, covered, for 2 hours. To check for doneness, uncover dish and insert the tip of a knife into the center of the pudding; it should come out clean. If it doesn't, cover dish and return to bag. Return bag to water bath and cook, checking for doneness every 15 minutes.

7. Remove dish from bag, uncover and sprinkle with the reserved almonds. Cut into squares or wedges to serve.

Super-Easy Applesauce

Making homemade applesauce is fairly simple anyway, but with sous vide, it's even easier. You don't need to stir or babysit while the apples soften to saucy goodness, and because no added water or sugar are required, you get a pure apple flavor. Leaving the skin on the apples adds a lovely rosy hue to the sauce (if you use red apples, that is), and you get the bonus of extra fiber and vitamins, but you can peel them if you prefer.

**MAKES ABOUT
2¹⁄₂ CUPS
(625 ML)**

Sous vide time: 1 hour

Tips

Choose tart or sweet apples (or a mixture) that hold their flavor and soften when cooked. Some good choices are Empire, McIntosh, Jonathan, Jonagold, Gala, Gravenstein and Idared.

If you prefer a smooth, lighter-colored sauce, peel the apples before cooking. If you want to cook them with the skins but want a smooth sauce, pass the cooked apples through a food mill fitted with a fine plate, instead of puréeing, to remove the skins.

As this cooks, air will be released from the apples and may make the bag puff up; if this happens, open a small section of the seal and squeeze out the air (be careful: the bag and air will be hot), then reseal the bag.

The applesauce can be cooled and refrigerated in a jar or other airtight container for up to 2 weeks. Serve cold, or warm individual servings in the microwave on Medium-High (70%) for about 1 minute.

- **Preheat water bath to 180°F (82°C)**
- **Large resealable freezer bag**
- **Blender, food processor or immersion blender**

4	medium apples (about 1¹⁄₂ lbs/750 g total), cut into quarters	4
Pinch	ground cinnamon (optional)	Pinch
1 tbsp	freshly squeezed lemon juice	15 mL

1. In freezer bag, combine apples, cinnamon (if using) and lemon juice; shake bag gently to evenly coat apples with lemon juice. Remove excess air and seal bag.

2. Cook in preheated water bath, covered, for 1 hour. Remove bag from water bath.

3. Empty apple mixture into blender (or a tall cup if using an immersion blender) and pulse for a chunky sauce or purée until smooth. Serve warm or, to serve cold, let cool and refrigerate for at least 2 hours.

Variations

Apple-Pear Sauce: Use 1 pear and 3 apples.

Rhubarb Applesauce: Use 3 apples and add ¾ cup (175 mL) finely chopped rhubarb. If desired, add 2 tbsp (30 mL) granulated sugar, packed brown sugar or honey (or to taste).

Savory Applesauce: Add 1 tbsp (15 mL) chopped fresh sage and 1 tsp (5 mL) chopped fresh thyme after puréeing.

Sauces and Accompaniments

Compound Butters

At Mount Julian Restaurant at Viamede Resort, I serve tasting menus that include fresh bread and compound butters, which is a fancy name for flavored butter. These are an easy way to add bold tastes to simple cooked sous vide steak, lamb and vegetables. Make the butter ahead, then add it to hot food and the heat will soften the butter, releasing its flavor. Here are a few of my favorite combinations; hopefully, they will inspire you to create your own. ~ Jay

MAKES ABOUT ½ CUP (125 ML)

Tip

We've used salted butter, as that's what most people have on hand. If you use unsalted butter, add small pinches of salt, tasting the butter as you add them, to enhance the flavoring ingredients.

Variation

Porcini Butter: Instead of step 1, in a mini chopper or small food processor, combine 1 tbsp (15 mL) dried porcini mushroom pieces, ¼ tsp (1 mL) dried rosemary, 2 tbsp (30 mL) olive oil and the butter; process until fairly smooth. Proceed with step 2.

½ cup	salted butter, softened	125 mL

Honey Sage Butter

1 tsp	chopped fresh sage	5 mL
1 tbsp	liquid honey	15 mL

Lemon Tarragon Butter

½ tsp	dried tarragon (or 1½ tsp/7 mL chopped fresh)	2 mL
½ tsp	grated lemon zest	2 mL
1 tbsp	freshly squeezed lemon juice	15 mL

Blue Cheese Butter

2 tbsp	crumbled blue cheese	30 mL
1 tsp	chopped fresh parsley	5 mL

Sriracha Honey Butter

2 tsp	Sriracha	10 mL
2 tsp	liquid honey	10 mL

Duck Fat Butter

Pinch	ground cinnamon	Pinch
Pinch	ground cardamom	Pinch
2 tbsp	chilled rendered duck fat	30 mL

1. In a bowl, mash butter with a wooden spoon until smooth and slightly fluffy. Add desired flavoring ingredients, stirring until evenly blended (if making blue cheese butter, fold in cheese gently so the butter doesn't turn gray).

2. Spoon into a rough log shape, about 1 inch (2.5 cm) thick, on a piece of plastic wrap. Roll up into a neat log, twisting ends of plastic to seal. (Alternatively, pack butter into a ramekin or serving dish and cover.) Refrigerate for at least 4 hours, to allow flavors to blend, or for up to 1 week.

3. To serve, unwrap and slice log into medallions. Place on hot food or serve slices on a plate or in the ramekin.

Hollandaise Sauce

This classic sauce is used for everything from eggs Benedict to fish, steak and vegetables. It typically presents a challenge to cooks because of the need to whisk nonstop and maintain a constant temperature. This recipe eliminates the whisking by using a blender and keeps the temperature as precise as possible in the sous vide bath.

MAKES ABOUT 1½ CUPS (375 ML)

Sous vide time: 23 minutes

Tips

We used salted butter for this recipe. If you have unsalted butter, increase the added salt to ¼ tsp (1 mL) and add more to taste after cooking the sauce.

This recipe makes a thick, rich sauce. You can thin it out after cooking by stirring in hot water, 1 tbsp (15 mL) at a time, until you reach the desired consistency.

Leftover hollandaise can be cooled, covered and refrigerated for up to 5 days. Reheat in a 164°F (73°C) water bath for 12 minutes, until warmed through. Remove from water bath, remove lid and stir until smooth.

Use an inverted plate to weigh down the jar in the water bath, adding a jar full of water on top of the plate, if necessary, to keep the jar submerged.

- **Preheat water bath to 164°F (73°C)**
- **1 wide-mouth pint (500 mL) canning jar, with two-piece lid**
- **Blender or immersion blender**
- **Wire rack**

4	large egg yolks	4
1 tbsp	white wine vinegar	15 mL
1 tbsp	freshly squeezed lemon juice	15 mL
Pinch	salt	Pinch
Dash	hot pepper sauce	Dash
1 cup	butter, melted	250 mL

1. Pour hot tap water into the canning jar to warm the glass; set aside.

2. In blender (or in a tall cup, using an immersion blender), combine eggs, vinegar, lemon juice, salt and hot pepper sauce; purée until smooth. With the motor running, gradually drizzle in melted butter through hole in blender lid (or alongside the immersion blender), blending until butter is fully incorporated and mixture is the consistency of whipping cream.

3. Empty canning jar and pour in egg mixture. Wipe rim of jar and place lid disc on jar, then screw on band until fingertip-tight.

4. Place wire rack in preheated water bath and place jar on rack; if the jar floats, weigh it down (see tip). Cook for 23 minutes. Remove jar from water bath and let stand for 5 minutes.

5. Remove lid and stir hollandaise in the jar (a chopstick or narrow silicone spatula works well) until smooth and creamy. Serve warm.

Variations

To flavor your hollandaise, blend in ¼ tsp (1 mL) chipotle chile powder or 1 tsp (5 mL) tomato paste before adding the butter.

To make a béarnaise-style sauce, add 1 tbsp (15 mL) chopped fresh tarragon as you stir the hollandaise after cooking.

Versatile Cheese Sauce

I love cheese sauce. Maybe it's the fond memory of broccoli and cauliflower smothered in cheese sauce that my mom made for holiday meals when we were growing up, or maybe it's just because I love cheese in any shape or form, and a cheese sauce draped over anything makes it taste better. Regardless, this is my go-to recipe, and it works well on vegetables, meats, meatloaf and (of course) macaroni. ~ *Jennifer*

MAKES ABOUT 3 CUPS (750 ML)

Tips

Use the good cheese. Not the flavorless, mild rubbery cheese, but the good, sharp-tasting, aged stuff. Trust me. You'll be glad you did. Mix in other types of pungent cheese with the Cheddar (I like a mix of half-and-half, or three-quarters Cheddar), such as Swiss, Emmental, Gruyère, Jarlsberg, washed-rind semisoft cheeses like Oka and even softer cheeses like Brie (just cube those into small pieces).

You can make this cheese sauce ahead, let it cool and refrigerate in an airtight container for up to 5 days. To reheat, transfer it to a medium resealable freezer bag and warm in a 165°F (74°C) water bath (alongside other foods you're cooking), or reheat in a microwave-safe bowl or measuring cup on Medium (50%), in 1-minute intervals, stirring in between each, until warmed. To avoid curdling the cheese, do not let boil.

2 tbsp	butter	30 mL
2 tbsp	all-purpose flour	30 mL
2 cups	milk, heated	500 mL
2 tsp	Dijon mustard	10 mL
Pinch	freshly grated or ground nutmeg	Pinch
2 cups	shredded sharp (old) Cheddar cheese (8 oz/250 g)	500 mL
1/3 cup	freshly grated Parmesan cheese	75 mL
	Salt and freshly ground black pepper	

1. In a heavy-bottomed medium saucepan, melt butter over medium heat. Sprinkle in flour and cook, stirring, for 2 minutes or until bubbling but not browned.

2. Gradually pour in heated milk while whisking, adding a little at first to make a paste, then pouring more steadily as the paste thins out. Whisk in mustard and nutmeg until blended. Cook, whisking constantly, for about 8 minutes or until bubbling and thickened and the flour taste has been cooked out (be careful when you taste; it will be hot).

3. Remove from heat and stir in Cheddar and Parmesan, a handful at a time, stirring until each addition is melted and smooth before adding the next. Season to taste with salt, if necessary, and pepper. Serve hot.

Serving Suggestions

- Serve this on Perfect Poached Asparagus (page 148), Montreal Steak–Spiced Cauliflower Steaks (page 142; omit the salsa), Three-Bean and Lentil Loaf (page 143), on steak or as a dip for the Fingerling Potatoes with Olive Oil and Herbs (page 154).

- This makes enough sauce to coat 1 lb (500 g) short pasta, cooked and drained, for mac 'n' cheese.

Easy Tomato Basil Sauce

If you're cooking a plain piece of meat or poultry, a little marinara sauce can perk it up. Of course, this sauce is ideal to toss with pasta or a grain for a side dish, too. It's a quick and easy stovetop recipe you can make while the rest of the meal cooks in the sous vide.

MAKES ABOUT 4 CUPS (1 L)

Tips

The San Marzano tomatoes (or San Marzano–type, if they're not grown in Italy) in cans have a deep, true tomato flavor and are packed in a thicker juice than regular canned plum tomatoes. They're worth seeking out, especially for simple sauces like this one. If you don't have them, regular canned plum tomatoes will do; you'll need to simmer for the upper end of the time range to thicken the sauce.

This sauce can be cooled, transferred to airtight containers and refrigerated for up to 5 days or frozen for up to 3 months. If frozen, thaw overnight in the refrigerator or defrost in the microwave. Reheat in a saucepan over medium heat, stirring often, until steaming.

2 tbsp	olive oil	30 mL
1	onion, finely chopped	1
3	cloves garlic, minced	3
1	red bell pepper, chopped	1
1 tsp	dried oregano	5 mL
	Salt and freshly ground black pepper	
1	can (28 oz/796 mL) tomatoes (preferably San Marzano), with juice	1
2 tbsp	tomato paste	30 mL
¼ cup	chopped fresh basil	60 mL
	Granulated sugar (optional)	

1. In a deep medium saucepan, heat oil over medium heat. Add onion and cook, stirring, for about 5 minutes or until softened but not browned. Add garlic, red pepper, oregano and ½ tsp (2 mL) each salt and pepper; cook, stirring, for 3 minutes or until red pepper is softened.

2. Add tomatoes and tomato paste; bring to a boil, breaking up tomatoes with a spoon. Reduce heat and simmer, stirring occasionally, for 20 to 30 minutes or until sauce is thickened and flavors are blended. Stir in basil and simmer, stirring often, for 5 minutes to blend the flavors. Season to taste with salt, pepper and sugar (if desired). Serve hot.

Serving Suggestions

- Cook plain chicken sous vide (page 28), top with a spoonful of this sauce and sprinkle with grated Parmesan or shredded mozzarella cheese. Or build a hot chicken marinara sandwich.
- Serve the hot sauce over Three-Bean and Lentil Loaf (page 143), over slices of sous vide beef steak or roast (pages 20 or 22) or even over pork chops (page 24).

Sweet Peppers and Onions

Dress up a plain piece of sous vide meat or poultry with a colorful sauté of peppers and onions. We've kept the seasoning simple, so it works with any of the seasoned meats, or add your favorite spice blend or herbs to accent your meal.

**MAKES
4 SERVINGS**

Tip

You can cook the vegetables ahead and serve them at room temperature or transfer the cooled vegetables to an airtight container and refrigerate for up to 3 days. Reheat in a skillet over medium heat until sizzling.

2 tbsp	olive oil, vegetable oil or butter	30 mL
1	onion, cut in half and thinly sliced lengthwise	1
	Salt and freshly ground black pepper	
2	bell peppers (any color), cut lengthwise into thin strips	2
1 tbsp	balsamic or wine vinegar	15 mL

1. In a large skillet, heat oil or melt butter over medium-high heat. Add onion, 1/4 tsp (1 mL) salt and pepper to taste; cook, stirring, for 3 minutes or until starting to soften.

2. Add bell peppers and cook, stirring, for about 5 minutes or until vegetables are tender.

3. Add vinegar and cook, stirring, for about 1 minute to coat vegetables and let vinegar evaporate. Season to taste with salt and pepper.

Variations

Use 1/2 sweet onion in place of the regular onion.

Add 2 cloves garlic, minced, with the bell peppers.

Mango Salsa

Bright, fresh and with a blend of sweetness, tang and a touch of heat, this salsa will perk up sous vide fish, poultry or pork and is a colorful condiment for the Montreal Steak–Spiced Cauliflower Steaks (page 142). It's best made within a few hours of serving, for the freshest taste.

MAKES ABOUT 2 CUPS (500 ML)

Tip

A ripe mango should smell fragrant at the stem end and yield slightly when pressed. To speed up ripening, place the mango in a paper bag with an apple and let stand on the counter, checking daily for ripeness.

1	firm but ripe mango, cut into small cubes	1
$1/2$	red bell pepper, diced	$1/2$
$1/2$	jalapeño pepper, seeded and minced	$1/2$
2 tbsp	chopped fresh cilantro	30 mL
$1/2$ tsp	grated lime zest	2 mL
2 tbsp	freshly squeezed lime juice	30 mL
	Salt and freshly ground black pepper	

1. In a medium bowl, combine mango, red pepper, jalapeño, cilantro, lime zest and lime juice, tossing gently to combine. Season to taste with salt and pepper. Serve immediately or cover and let stand at room temperature for up to 2 hours.

Variation

When fresh peaches or nectarines are in season, substitute 3 medium, chopped, for the mango.

Cranberry Chutney

This jewel-colored chutney highlights tangy cranberries, savory onion and sweet spices. When it's first cooked, it has a slightly loose texture — partway between a sauce and a chutney — but it thickens considerably when chilled. Serve with pork, chicken, turkey or duck, with cheese or as a sandwich spread.

Tips

Fresh and frozen cranberries work equally well in this recipe. Just add an extra 15 minutes of cooking time if using frozen.

If you prefer a smooth chutney, purée the cooled chutney using an immersion blender or food processor.

You can double this recipe, using a large freezer bag.

The chutney can be refrigerated in a jar or airtight container for up to 1 month.

- **Preheat water bath to 180°F (82°C)**
- **Medium resealable freezer bag**

2 cups	cranberries (8 oz/250 g)	500 mL
¼ cup	finely chopped onion	60 mL
½ cup	granulated sugar	125 mL
¼ tsp	salt	1 mL
⅛ tsp	freshly ground black pepper	0.5 mL
Pinch	ground cinnamon	Pinch
Pinch	ground ginger	Pinch
⅓ cup	apple cider vinegar	75 mL

1. In freezer bag, combine cranberries, onion, sugar, salt, pepper, cinnamon, ginger and vinegar; shake bag gently to combine. Remove excess air and seal bag.

2. Cook in preheated water bath, covered, for 2 hours. The cranberries should be very soft and the onions translucent; if they aren't, return bag to water bath and cook, checking for doneness every 15 minutes. Remove bag from water bath and let cool for 15 minutes.

3. Empty cranberry mixture into a container or bowl and mash with a fork to break up berries to desired consistency. Let cool. Serve at room temperature or cover and refrigerate for at least 2 hours to serve cold.

Variations

Spicy Cranberry Chutney: Add ½ jalapeño pepper, seeded and minced, with the cranberries.

Apple Cranberry Chutney: Reduce the cranberries to 1½ cups (375 mL), add ½ cup (125 mL) finely chopped peeled apple and substitute packed brown sugar for the granulated sugar.

Homemade Yogurt

We eat a lot of yogurt: on cereal, on curries and stews, in place of sour cream and mixed into salads in place of or combined with mayo. We do tend to buy it at the store, but every time I make yogurt, I wonder why I don't do so more often. (I even have an electric yogurt maker, though it lives in the garage.) With sous vide, it's easy to get into the habit of making your own, so you can have fresh homemade yogurt on hand all the time. ~*Jennifer*

MAKES 2 CUPS (500 ML)

**Sous vide time:
7½ to 13½ hours**

Tips

To ensure a safe product, sterilize your jar, thermometer and stirring utensil with boiling water and/or a mild bleach solution before making yogurt.

You can use low-fat or whole milk for this yogurt; nonfat (skim) milk will work, but produces a thin yogurt.

The milk powder is optional, but it does help make a thicker yogurt.

If this is your first batch of yogurt, buy a small container of plain yogurt to use as your starter. Make sure it lists active, or live, bacteria cultures on the label, and choose a yogurt without any thickeners or stabilizers. Full-fat yogurt is best for a starter. If you've already made yogurt, save 2 tbsp (30 mL) from your previous batch (as long as it was made within 2 weeks) and use that for your starter.

- **Preheat water bath to 185°F (85°C)**
- **Pint (500 mL) canning jar, with two-piece lid**
- **Wire rack**
- **Instant-read thermometer (preferably digital)**

1¾ cups + 2 tbsp	milk	405 mL
2 tbsp	instant nonfat (skim) milk powder (optional)	30 mL
2 tbsp	plain yogurt with active bacterial cultures	30 mL

1. Fill jar with hot tap water and let the glass warm for 10 minutes. Let milk stand at room temperature for the same time.

2. Empty water from jar and add milk and milk powder (if using), stirring well with a chopstick or narrow silicone spatula. Wipe rim of jar and place lid disc on jar, then screw on band just until fingertip-tight.

3. Place wire rack in preheated water bath and place jar on rack. Cook, covered, for 1½ hours. Remove jar from water bath and check the temperature of the milk; it should be 180°F to 185°F (82°C to 85°C). If it isn't, replace lid, return jar to water bath and cook, checking the temperature every 15 minutes. Remove jar from water bath.

4. Remove lid and let milk cool for at least 15 minutes, stirring occasionally, then place jar in a bowl of cold water to speed up cooling. Insert thermometer and let milk cool to between 105°F and 115°F (40.5°C and 46°C), stirring occasionally.

5. Meanwhile, reduce water bath temperature to 115°F (46°C).

6. In a small bowl, whisk about ⅓ cup (75 mL) of the cooled milk with yogurt, then stir into jar of milk. Wipe rim of jar and place lid disc on jar, then screw on band just until fingertip-tight.

7. Return jar to water bath and cook, covered, for at least 6 to 12 hours, replenishing water as necessary to keep jar immersed. Taste the yogurt after 6 hours to determine if it is to your taste (it gets tangier the longer it incubates in the water bath); if it isn't, replace lid, return jar to water bath and cook, tasting every 2 hours, until your desired taste is achieved.

8. Remove jar from water bath and immerse in a bowl of cool water, refreshing water as necessary, to cool yogurt. Refrigerate for at least 2 hours, until chilled, or for up to 2 weeks.

Orange Brandy Hard Sauce

There are some who say you can't have a steamed pudding without hard sauce. If you're in that camp, here's one that complements the Classic Christmas Figgy Pudding (page 170). It starts with caramel and adds orange, butter and brandy to finish — a holiday treat, indeed. It's also good drizzled on other steamed puddings or on ice cream, waffles, pancakes or even fruit salad.

MAKES ABOUT ³/₄ CUP (175 ML)

Tips

Avoid stirring the caramel as it boils. Stirring can cause crystals to form, which can make the sugar seize. If the caramel is browning unevenly, you can gently swirl the pan and rotate the pan on your burner to avoid hot spots. You'll know it's getting close to being ready when the bubbles slow down and get louder, and the color turns from golden to a deep caramel brown. Be sure not to leave the caramel unattended once the color starts to change — it can burn quickly.

To make ahead, transfer the cooled sauce to a canning jar or other airtight container, cover and refrigerate for up to 1 week. To reheat in a sous vide bath, fit jar with a two-piece metal lid and place in bath alongside the figgy pudding, or on its own in a 195°F (91°C) water bath, for about 15 minutes or until warmed. Or pour sauce into a small saucepan and warm over low heat, stirring often, until warm (do not let boil).

½ cup	granulated sugar	125 mL
3 tbsp	water	45 mL
¼ cup	freshly squeezed orange juice	60 mL
2 tbsp	butter, cut into cubes	30 mL
2 tbsp	brandy	30 mL
¼ tsp	vanilla extract	1 mL

1. In a small saucepan, combine sugar and water. Bring to a boil over medium heat, stirring to dissolve sugar. Boil, without stirring but swirling saucepan gently as necessary, until syrup is a deep caramel color. Remove from heat.

2. Carefully pour in orange juice and stir until bubbles subside. Stir in butter, brandy and vanilla until butter is melted and sauce is smooth. Let cool slightly, until warm.

Appendix: Food Safety

WITH ANY COOKING method, food safety must always be of utmost importance. Wash your hands. Use clean cutting boards. Clean your knives and utensils. Make sure that food is properly refrigerated and that your fridge and freezer are operating at the correct temperature. Keep hot foods hot and cold foods cold.

The main goal of food safety is to eliminate food-borne microorganisms through proper food storage and cooking techniques, including when chilling and reheating cooked foods.

To achieve the goal of food safety, we apply heat to food over a specified period of time to pasteurize it. The British Columbia Centre for Disease Control (BCCDC) "Guidelines for Restaurant Sous Vide Cooking Safety in British Columbia" define the terms "log reduction," "thermalization" and "pasteurization" to help us understand how pasteurization is achieved in sous vide cooking:

Log reduction: a log is a mathematical term that is short for logarithm, an exponent of 10. A one-log reduction of bacteria means to eliminate microorganisms by a factor of ten (10). If there were one thousand (1000) microorganisms, they would be reduced to one hundred (100). Sous vide pasteurization of all foods (except poultry) must achieve a 6.5-$\log_{10}$ reduction; in poultry a 7-$\log_{10}$ reduction is required. This is equivalent to a 99.9999% (6-log) to 99.99999% (7-log) reduction of bacteria in foods.

Thermalization: cooking of foods to a prescribed log reduction of bacteria, 6.5-log reduction for all foods except for poultry, where a 7-log reduction is required. Thermalization can take many forms, frying in a pan, boiling, microwave, etc., including sous vide pasteurization.

Pasteurization: the thermal process of heating up food for a predetermined time and temperature to reduce the number of microorganisms and pathogens by a required amount in the food. To achieve a full sous vide pasteurization, the total time food must be held at a specific temperature will be the sum of the CUT ["come up time," the time it takes for food to reach a specific internal core temperature] *plus* the time held at that temperature to reach the log reduction standard. Here is an example for a chicken breast sous vide pasteurized to an internal temperature of 65°C [149°F]. The chilled sous vide pouch of chicken is added to an immersion circulator set to 67°C [153°F], and it takes 25 minutes before the internal temperature of the chicken breast "comes up" to 65°C. The calculation for a 7-log reduction at 65°C is an additional 3.2 min. Therefore the chicken breast should be held for a minimum period of 25 min + 3.2 min = 28.2 minutes to achieve proper pasteurization.

Source: BC Centre for Disease Control, Environmental Health Services and the BC Sous Vide Working Group. January 2016. "Guidelines for restaurant sous vide cooking safety in British Columbia," pages 2–3.

Once you get past the science in the above text, you can sum it up by describing pasteurization as the process of cooking at a sufficient temperature for a long enough time to effectively kill more than 99.99% of microorganisms such as bacteria, viruses and parasites.

According to the BCCDC, the minimum sous vide temperature and time for safe pasteurization of meats is 131°F (55°C) for 89 minutes after the meat comes up to temperature. For safe pasteurization of poultry, the minimum sous vide temperature and time is 140°F (60°C) for at least 17 minutes after the poultry comes up to temperature. The BCCDC recommends against sous vide cooking poultry at temperatures lower than this.

Some of our recipes for fish and seafood suggest a cooking temperature of 120°F (49°C). Fish and seafood cooked at this temperature should be purchased as either commercially frozen product or raw sushi-grade quality. Thaw frozen fish in the refrigerator — never at room temperature — and use it as soon after purchase or thawing as possible. Pregnant women, children, the elderly and people with compromised immune systems should refrain from eating sous vide fish and seafood.

To prevent further bacterial growth, once it's removed from the water bath, food must be finished as directed in the recipe and then consumed or quickly chilled in ice water (50% ice to 50% water) to bring the food down to less than 40°F (4°C). When chilling foods in an ice water bath, check the water frequently to make sure it stays cold and add more ice or refresh with additional cold water and ice as necessary until the food feels cold. Promptly refrigerate or freeze the food for the recommended storage time.

For more information about the safety standards required for sous vide cooking in restaurants — and, by extension, in our kitchens at home — you can read the full guidelines on the BCCDC website: http://www.bccdc.ca/resource-gallery/Documents/Guidelines%20and%20Forms/Guidelines%20and%20Manuals/EH/FPS/Food/SVGuidelines_FinalforWeb.pdf.

Library and Archives Canada Cataloguing in Publication

Nutt, Jay, 1966-, author
   Sous vide basics : 100+ recipes for perfect results / Jay Nutt & Jennifer MacKenzie.

Includes index.
ISBN 978-0-7788-0582-3 (softcover)

   1. Sous-vide cooking. 2. Cookbooks. I. MacKenzie, Jennifer, author II. Title.

TX690.7.N88 2017   641.5'87   C2017-903748-X

Index

S

Sage and Butter Turkey Breast, 132
salads, 51, 70–80, 127, 131, 150, 155
salmon. *See also* fish and seafood
    Chilled Salmon Fillet with Chili Lime Mayonnaise and Onion Marmalade, 48
    Salmon Fillet with Lemon Dill Butter, 136
    Smoked Salmon Strata, 44
    Spinach and Swiss Crustless Quiche (variation), 40
salt, 17
sandwiches and wraps, 50, 58–68
sausage
    Gumbo-Style Fish Stew (variation), 139
    Maple Mustard Breakfast Sausage, 38
    Warm Potato Salad with Red Wine Vinaigrette (variation), 79
scallops. *See* fish and seafood
Seafood Chowder, 140
shrimp. *See* fish and seafood
Smoked Salmon Strata, 44
Smoky Turkey Drumsticks, 52
sous vide cooking
    advantages, 7
    air pocket removal, 14
    basic techniques, 11–12, 19–36
    in casserole dish, 15–16
    covering container, 16–17
    doneness checking, 17–18
    efficiency tips, 12
    equipment for, 9–11
    food safety with, 8, 185–86
    health benefits, 18
    ingredients, 17
    in mason jars, 14–15
    searing food, 11
Spiced Boneless Blade Steak with Roasted Garlic Caesar Salad, 70
Spinach and Swiss Crustless Quiche, 40
Squash and Black Beans, Red Curry Quinoa with, 144
Super-Easy Applesauce, 174
Super-Slow Whiskey, Garlic and Brown Sugar Beef Brisket, 87
Sweet-and-Sour Spareribs, Retro, 110
Sweet and Tangy Barbecue Sauce Chicken, 123
Sweet Peppers and Onions, 180
Sweet Potatoes, Cinnamon-Spiced, 156
Sweet Shrimp Po'boy Sandwiches with Spicy Mayo, 62
Swiss Steaks in Sweet Tomato Sauce, 89

T

Tandoori Flattened Chicken, 121
Tender Beef Steaks, 20
Tender Pork Cuts, 24
Thai Coconut Red Curry Ribs, 108
Thai Shrimp Peanut Salad (variation), 51
thermometers, 11, 17–18
Three-Bean and Lentil Loaf, 143
Three-Chile Chunky Beef and Bean Chili, 92
tofu
    Lentil and Tofu Chili, 146
    Three-Bean and Lentil Loaf, 143
tomatoes. *See also* vegetables
    Basil Chicken and Mediterranean Tomato Salad, 74
    Berbere Spice–Rubbed Chicken Thighs (variation), 126
    Butter Chicken, 128
    Caribbean-Style Catfish, 134
    Cherry Chipotle Barbecue Back Ribs, 106
    Chili Lime Fish Soft Tacos with Tomato Corn Salsa, 68
    Easy Tomato Basil Sauce, 179
    Fresh Fajitas with Carne Asada and Avocado Pineapple Salsa, 66
    Grilled Lamb Chops with White Bean and Arugula Salad, 72
    Lamb Meatballs with Yogurt Greek Salad in Pitas, 64
    Lazy Vegetarian Cabbage Roll Stew, 145
    Lentil and Tofu Chili, 146
    Mediterranean Lamb Shoulder Chops with Tomatoes, Olives and Capers, 112
    Spiced Boneless Blade Steak with Roasted Garlic Caesar Salad (variation), 70
    Swiss Steaks in Sweet Tomato Sauce, 89
    Three-Bean and Lentil Loaf, 143
    Three-Chile Chunky Beef and Bean Chili, 92
    Tomato and White Wine Braised Osso Buco, 90
    Tomato Cheddar Crustless Quiche, 39
    Warm Potato Salad with Red Wine Vinaigrette (variation), 79
tongs, 10, 11
tortillas
    Chili Lime Fish Soft Tacos with Tomato Corn Salsa, 68
    Fresh Fajitas with Carne Asada and Avocado Pineapple Salsa, 66
Tough Beef Steaks and Roasts, 22
turkey
    Sage and Butter Turkey Breast, 132
    Smoky Turkey Drumsticks, 52

V

vacuum sealing, 11, 13–14
Vegan Chocolate Avocado Cake, Fudgy, 168
vegetables (mixed). *See also* greens; *specific vegetables*
    Beef and Ale Ragoût, 94
    Beer-Braised Lamb Shanks, 114
    Gumbo-Style Fish Stew, 139
    Vegetarian Cabbage Roll Stew, Lazy, 145
    Versatile Cheese Sauce, 178

W

Warm Potato Salad with Red Wine Vinaigrette, 79
water baths, 9
water displacement method, 13–14
whiskey and bourbon
    Maple Whiskey Glazed Chicken Wings, 55
    Super-Slow Whiskey, Garlic and Brown Sugar Beef Brisket, 87
    Sweet Shrimp Po'boy Sandwiches with Spicy Mayo, 62
wine
    Beef and Ale Ragoût (variation), 94
    Coq au Vin, 118
    Tomato and White Wine Braised Osso Buco, 90

Y

yogurt and sour cream
    Brussels Sprouts with Bacon and Pecans (variation), 150
    Butter Chicken, 128
    Homemade Yogurt, 183
    Lamb Meatballs with Yogurt Greek Salad in Pitas, 64
    Plain but Good Cheesecakes, 163
    Rosemary and Garlic Sour Cream Potatoes, 155
    Tandoori Flattened Chicken, 121